Understanding
Mutual
Funds

Your No-Nonsense
Everyday Guide

STEVEN KELMAN

Penguin Books

PENGUIN BOOKS
Published by the Penguin Group
Penguin Books Canada Ltd., 10 Alcorn Avenue, Suite 300, Toronto, Canada, M4V 3B2
Penguin Books Ltd., 27 Wrights Lane, London W8 5TZ, England
Viking Penguin Inc., 40 West 23rd Street, New York, New York 10010, USA
Penguin Books Australia Ltd., Ringwood, Victoria, Australia
Penguin Books (NZ) Ltd., 182-190 Wairau Road, Auckland 10, New Zealand
Penguin Books Ltd., Registered Offices: Harmondsworth, Middlesex, England

Published in Penguin Books, 1994

10 9 8 7 6 5 4 3 2 1

Canadian Cataloguing in Publication Data
The National Library of Canada has catalogued this publication as follows:
Kelman, Steven G. (Steven Gershon), 1945 –
  Understanding mutual funds
(Financial times personal finance library)
Annual.
At head of title: Financial times.
Description based on: 1993
ISSN 1193-8994
ISBN 0-14-024381-X (8th ed.)
1. Mutual funds – Canada – Periodicals. I. Title.   II. Title: Financial times.
III. Kelman, Steven G. (Steven Gershon), 1945 –   . Mutual fund advisor.
IV. Series.

HG5154.5.K45   332.63'27   C93-030705-4

Cover design by: Creative Network
Cover illustration by: Peter Yundt

CONTENTS

Tables and Illustrations

Introduction

MUTUAL FUNDS ARE BIG business in Canada. In little more than a decade the value of funds held by Canadians has jumped from $5 billion to close to $150 billion and the number of Canadians investing in funds has climbed from a few hundred thousand to several million. The industry itself is going through a period of consolidation. Although several small fund groups have been taken over by larger companies, the number of funds offered to Canadians has climbed from only a few hundred a decade ago to about 950 by mid-1994.

More financial service companies, including banks and trust companies, have entered the fund business. People who have never considered anything other than bank or trust company guaranteed investments are looking at funds.

The reasons are simple. Mutual funds offer professional investment management at an affordable price. They offer safety through diversified portfolios. There is a broad choice of funds to meet virtually every investment objective. Finally, funds have given investors excellent returns, better than most individuals would have been able to achieve on their own.

But choosing the right fund or funds from the hundreds offered by fund dealers, stockbrokers, banks, trust companies, insurance companies or fund managers directly can be confusing. First, buyers must consider the objectives of a fund and whether those objectives are compatible with their own investment goals. Second, they must determine how a fund has performed in recent years and the reasons behind that performance.

Understanding Mutual Funds explains in detail the aspects of the fund business that you need to understand to make a wise buying decision. *Understanding Mutual Funds*, for instance, shows you how fund managers manage their funds, how you can match funds to your specific investment objectives and your age, even how to evaluate a fund salesperson.

It also contains essential information on the largest 200 mutual funds in Canada to help you determine exactly which funds might best meet your personal investment objectives. A lot has happened in the world of Canadian mutual funds since *Mutual Fund Advisor*, the predecessor to *Understanding Mutual Funds*, was published in September 1986.

Indeed much has happened in the past 24 months. As interest rates declined, falling to their lowest levels in three decades, many investors who had never considered any investments other than guaranteed certificates moved into money market, bond, mortgage, balanced and equity funds. Industry assets doubled in less than 24 months, helped by rising bond prices and a soaring stock market which in turn provided rates of return far in excess to what guaranteed investments were paying. There was some decline in the industry's assets in the first half of 1994 when bond and stock markets pulled back and GIC rates started to move higher. In fact, it appeared that some investors cashed in bond and mortgage fund holdings to return to guaranteed investments.

Nevertheless, it seems likely that funds will continue to grow due to appreciation in the value of the assets being held and influx of new money. Several industry projections predict that assets will grow to well in excess of $200 billion by the end of the decade but there are many who believe this figure will be exceeded by a wide margin. And for good reason: As the baby boomers hit their late 40s and early 50s their savings rates will rise. Moreover, the entry of banks into the fund business has brought the concept of funds to a much larger segment of the population. At the same time, industry efforts to educate the public about funds have been succeeding. The end result is that the fund industry's assets will continue to grow.

Even if interest rates surge higher, many investors who would previously have moved into GICs are now familiar with income mutual funds with their competitive returns and superior flexibility. In addition, over the past two years, many people who are concerned about the Canadian dollar have turned to funds which invest all or a portion of their assets in foreign equities and foreign currency bonds.

However, the percentage of people who own mutual funds in Canada has become quite high; in fact, it is much higher than many people in the industry thought until recently. The Investment Funds Institute of Canada, the umbrella industry body, commissioned several questions in a Gallup survey last November. The results showed 44 percent of households with incomes of $70,000 or more owned mutual funds and almost 30 percent of households with incomes of $50,000 to $70,000 owned funds. It is probable that mutual funds will continue to attract and hold a larger portion of consumer savings, but the growth rate will almost certainly slow over the next several years.

About the author

Steven G. Kelman is an investment counsellor and one of Canada's foremost experts on registered retirement savings plans and other aspects of personal financial planning. He has acted as a financial planner for individuals and as a consultant in the mutual fund industry. Mr. Kelman is a vice-president of Dynamic Mutual Funds, one of the Dundee Bancorp Inc. group of companies. He is consulting editor with the *Mutual Fund Sourcebook*, the mutual fund information guide used by fund professionals in Canada, and is an advisor on the *Mutual Fund Sourcedisk*.

Mr. Kelman is the author of *RRSPs 1995,* co-author of *Investment Strategies* (both produced by the *Financial Times of Canada*), and co-author of *Investing in Gold*. His articles have appeared in the *Financial Times*, in magazines and on the business pages of daily newspapers from coast to coast. He has lectured on financial planning, RRSPs and mutual funds across the country. For several years, Mr. Kelman taught a course on applied investments to MBA students at the Faculty of Administrative Studies at Toronto's York University.

Mr. Kelman is a chartered financial analyst and a member of the Toronto Society of Financial Analysts. After graduating in 1969 from York University with his MBA, Mr. Kelman worked as an analyst, then portfolio manager, for a major insurance company before becoming a senior analyst with an investment dealer. In 1975 he joined the *Financial Times* as a staff writer; he became investment editor in 1977. In April 1985 he joined the Dundee Group of Companies.

Acknowledgements

As I noted in previous editions, there are literally dozens of people whose views and advice are reflected in *Understanding Mutual Funds*. I would like to thank my colleagues at Dynamic Mutual Funds, Goodman & Company and Dundee Bancorp Inc. for their support and advice.

I would like to thank Elaine Wyatt at the *Financial Times of Canada* who is responsible for producing this book and the others in the series.

Steven Kelman
September, 1994

CHAPTER 1

How It Started

NINETEEN-THIRTY-TWO WAS an unlikely time to establish Canada's first open-end mutual fund. Unemployment in the depression-ravaged economy was running at about 40 percent. Canadian share prices, as measured by the *Financial Times of Canada,* were off about 80 percent from their 1929 highs. Yet it was in 1932 that thirty-one-year-old Alan Chippindale of the New York-based Calvin Bullock organization travelled to Montreal. His assignment: to start and manage Canada's first open-end mutual fund, the Canadian Investment Fund (CIF).

It was not an easy task. First, tax regulations had to be changed to accommodate the mutual fund corporation concept. Second, he faced the problem of selling a new investment concept to a public that was gun-shy, to say the least.

The only experience most people had with funds of any type involved investment trust shares. These were closed-end funds whose shares were bought and sold on stock exchanges. Most had leveraged, unpublished portfolios and there were few restrictions on what they could buy and hold in their portfolios. Chippindale's open-end fund was different in that the fund issued and redeemed shares on an ongoing basis at a price reflecting the full value of the assets the fund held.

The closed-end investment pools had performed exceedingly well during the Roaring Twenties. But when the market crashed, the value of their underlying assets plunged as well. Those investors who wanted to sell couldn't as the market for the shares had dried up.

CIF offered shares through dealers and brokers in the United States and Britain as well as in Canada. Chippindale spent $50,000 on newspaper advertising in Canada in the three months after launching the fund in December 1932. Gross sales during that period were disappointing – only about $50,000. It was years before the fund turned a profit. But Chippindale had pioneered the concepts that mutual fund investors today take for granted: regular reports to investors, redemptions at net asset value, diversification, no borrowing, and no conflicts of interest.

The concept of open-end funds caught on slowly. In 1934, Commonwealth International (now Viking Commonwealth Fund Ltd.) changed to an open-end fund from a closed-end fund. In the same year, a new fund, United Gold Equities, was established. (It later was wound up as investor interest in gold declined.) In 1938, Corporate Investors Ltd. converted to an open-end fund from a closed-end fund.

But funds really didn't take off until the 1950s. It was at this time that Investors Syndicate of Canada formed Investors Mutual of Canada. This group, with an expanding sales force, increased investor awareness in funds by selling through installment accumulation plans.

Statistics on mutual funds covering that period are sketchy. The Investment Funds Institute of Canada (IFIC) – the umbrella organization of the Canadian mutual fund industry – estimates that the market value of funds offered by its members in 1951 was about $57 million held in 22,000 accounts. But through the 1950s the industry grew quickly. By 1960 IFIC members had assets of about $540 million in 179,000 accounts. In 1963 the figure broke $1 billion in 324,000 accounts.

It was during 1962 that IFIC's predecessor organization, the Canadian Mutual Fund Association, was founded, with the objective of becoming a self-governing and self-disciplining association of mutual fund companies. The name was changed to the Investment Funds Institute of Canada in 1976.

IFIC membership includes funds representing about three-quarters of fund assets held by Canadians. Its Canadian Investment Funds Course is recognized by provincial regulators as a requirement for registration of mutual fund salespeople. Its views are sought by provincial securities commissions. Its various committees – which consider everything from advertising ethics to education – have a major influence on the funds business in Canada.

As the stock market soared in the 1960s, the industry expanded. A number of "private" funds were established during this period. Tradex Investment Fund Ltd. was set up for federal government employees posted overseas. MD Growth Investments was established by the Canadian Medical Association for its members.

At the end of 1968, IFIC-member funds controlled $2.8 billion in assets in 702,000 shareholder accounts. Sales continued at a hefty pace until 1969. But the stock market peaked in May and prices began to fall. By year-end total assets for the industry were down marginally. More importantly, redemptions began to exceed sales.

For the next nine years, the industry's shareholder base shrunk as redemptions outpaced sales. Several U.S.-based fund companies left Canada because of declining sales as well as new regulations that required Canadian ownership of investment companies. Many fund salespeople who jumped in during the boom years also left the industry, leaving their clients to fend for themselves.

Most importantly, it was in the early 1970s that the mutual fund business suffered through a scandal that shattered investor confidence. In the late 1950s, Bernard Cornfeld, an American, established Investors Overseas Services (IOS) to manage and distribute mutual funds. By the late 1960s he was the undisputed king of the fund business with more than one million investors and more than $2 billion in assets under management. His organization, which was registered in Panama, operated primarily in Europe, Central and South America and the Middle East. It was not registered with the U.S. Securities and Exchange Commission (SEC) so it could not operate in the U.S. Similarly, these offshore funds were not cleared in Canada. IOS, however, did purchase a Canadian group of funds. These were operated under Canadian law and were not involved in the subsequent IOS offshore funds scandal and the collapse of IOS.

Cornfeld and his colleagues, as controlling shareholders of IOS, were paper multi-millionaires. To convert some of this paper wealth to cash they decided to go public. Their first step was to change IOS from a Panamanian company to a Canadian one, registering the head office in Saint John, N.B. Its base of operations, however, was Switzerland. The share issue in 1969 was a roaring success, with the opening price more than double the $10 issue price.

But when IOS released its annual report in April 1970, its financial results were dismal. Moreover, its auditors questioned the value of some of the company's assets, including 22 million acres of Arctic oil leases. By the summer, IOS shares were trading at $2.

Concerns about IOS caused massive redemptions of its fund shares and, as a result, bailout proposals were made by a number of parties. In the summer of 1970 control of IOS passed to Robert Vesco, an American financier. Vesco obtained control as part of a deal that included a $5 million rescue loan to IOS. He then allegedly diverted assets of the offshore IOS funds into investments which provided indirect benefits to him. In November 1972, the SEC and other regulators in Canada, Luxembourg, the Netherlands Antilles and the United Kingdom forced IOS and its related funds into liquidation.

When the Canadian operations of IOS were liquidated by a trustee, the Eaton group of funds bought the contracts to manage the Canadian IOS funds and integrated them into the Eaton group – now the Viking group.

It took a long time for the industry to recover. By 1978 fund sales began to exceed redemptions once again and the industry began its major growth from a base of about 150 funds and an asset base of about $2 billion. By 1985 there were about 200 funds with assets exceeding $10 billion. Two years later there were more than 350 funds with assets exceeding $35 billion.

The surge reflected the growing recognition by both investors and the investment industry that funds are the best way for many people to participate in the stock and bond markets. Billions of dollars of RRSP money flows into mutual funds each year from people seeking better long-term returns than are available from guaranteed plans. And many stockbrokers who previously ignored funds or discouraged their clients from investing in funds now see them as an important source of business. Indeed, a number of investment dealers offer their own families of funds or funds managed by their chartered bank parents. Similarly, many insurance companies are offering mutual funds to their clients. Banks and trust companies have also expanded their fund operations. These newcomers have increased general investor awareness about mutual funds.

As well, the industry has expanded its product line to include a wider range of funds. Besides the traditional stock and bond funds, investors have a choice of ethical funds, precious metals funds, and funds that specialize in foreign government bonds, health-care product companies and investments in the food industry.

The October 1987 crash had a short-term negative impact on fund sales, which plunged in the months following the crash. However, sales growth returned, reflecting the variety of funds available to meet investor needs and expectations of high returns. The slide in interest rates over the past few years brought the investment of billions of dollars into mutual funds by people who had never previously invested in anything other than guaranteed investments.

Companies continue to introduce new funds to meet investor needs, real or perceived. The banking and trust industries have trained individuals to sell funds through their branch networks. Fund companies are offering more funds that have a declining redemption fee instead of a commission – funds that are designed to compete with bank and trust company funds that are sold without commissions.

The fund industry will continue to grow as more and more Canadians discover how funds can be used to meet virtually any type of investment objective and bring returns that are superior to the guaranteed investments that they traditionally have chosen.

CHAPTER 2

What Is a Mutual Fund?

A MUTUAL FUND IS A POOL of savings that belongs to many investors. This pool is invested by a professional manager or a team of managers in a broad portfolio of investments. Depending on the objectives of the fund, these can be Canadian common stocks, foreign common stocks, bonds, mortgages, preferred shares, precious metals, specialty investments, treasury bills or combinations of several groups. Some funds are designed for specific purposes, such as RRSPs, others are multi-purpose.

Funds that issue and redeem shares or units on a continuous basis are called open-end funds. There are more than 600 open-end funds offered in Canada. The value of their shares or units changes with the underlying value of the securities in the fund. But each share or unit represents a portion of the underlying portfolio. Most funds are valued daily, although some are valued weekly and a few monthly or quarterly. The fund company determines the value of the underlying portfolio at the close of the stock and bond markets, then divides that value by the number of shares or units outstanding to determine the net asset value of each share or unit. The number of shares or units outstanding varies on a day-to-day basis, depending on sales and redemptions.

AGF Canadian Equity Fund is a typical open-end fund that invests primarily in Canadian common stocks. Its portfolio, as of June 30, 1994, was valued at $466 million. At that date it had about 44.5 million units outstanding. So the value per unit was $10.47. That is the amount you would pay for a share on June 30. It is also the price you would have received for your shares if you redeemed them on that date. (Both purchase and sale prices would be adjusted by any transaction fees you might pay.)

In addition to open-end funds, there are a handful of closed-end funds. Unlike open-end funds, closed-end funds have a fixed number of shares. These are traded on stock exchanges. The market value of their shares may be greater or less than the underlying value of their securities. For example, BGR Precious Metals shares trade on the Toronto Stock Exchange. On August 5, 1994, BGR shares closed at $15.75. But the underlying value was $17.30 a share. Closed-end funds can be useful for some investors and will be discussed in detail in chapter six.

The majority of investors in funds hold open-end funds. With the exception of the chapter on closed-end funds, all examples and comments in this book refer to open-end funds.

The advantages of funds

A mutual fund offers several important advantages to you as an investor which you might have difficulty achieving on your own:

1. Diversification

Funds generally hold a large number of securities. It is common for a fund invested in Canadian common stocks to hold shares of forty or more companies. By holding such a large number of securities your risk is spread – if one company flounders, it will have little impact on the performance of the overall portfolio. Few individuals have enough assets to build a diversified portfolio on their own. With a mutual fund you can get diversification with a small amount of money.

How small? The minimum contribution allowed to most funds is between $500 and $1,000. However, most funds also have monthly contribution plans that allow you to start with as little as $100 a month. According to the Investment Funds Institute of Canada, the average investment by individuals in a fund in mid-1994 was about $12,500. But many investors hold several funds and the holdings of mutual fund investors range from a few hundred dollars to $1 million or more.

2. Liquidity

A key benefit of mutual funds is that they are liquid. You can purchase or redeem shares and units on short notice, generally locking in a purchase or sale price on the day you make your decision to buy or redeem (in the case of funds valued daily). This is an advantage to individuals who want to be able to cash in their investments at any time. In this way, holding a mutual fund can be more advantageous than holding stocks, particularly if the stocks held rarely trade in large volumes and may be harder to sell at any one time at a good price.

Orders to buy mutual fund shares or units received by the fund before the close of business on a day when shares are valued will be purchased at that price, less any sales fee if applicable. Orders received to redeem shares will be redeemed at that price, less any redemption fee if applicable, and your money will be available within a few days, generally in five. The trend in the industry is toward daily pricing and virtually all major fund groups now price daily. (In the U.S., some funds are priced hourly.)

A handful of funds, mainly real estate funds, are valued monthly and as a result are somewhat less liquid.

3. Professional management

Mutual fund investors benefit from having investment professionals decide what securities should be held and at what prices they should be bought or sold. Most fund managers have substantial experience in the investment field and have taken specialized investment courses leading to the designation of chartered financial analyst. The cost of professional management is low to mutual fund holders because the cost is spread so widely. Generally, you can expect to pay about 2 to 3 percent a year for portfolio management and other fund expenses, excluding the costs of trading the underlying securities. This management fee is generally charged to the fund rather than to your account.

Mutual funds are the only cost-effective way for individuals with limited funds to get a diversified, professionally managed portfolio. No stockbroker or other investment professional can afford to service a small account, except through mutual funds. Unless you are able to generate several thousands of dollars of trading commissions a year, you are unlikely to get timely advice and top-quality service on a stock portfolio from a stockbroker.

But small investors aren't the only investors who use mutual funds. Many wealthy individuals who don't want to be bothered making decisions about the stock market also use funds. Similarly, some people use funds for specific purposes in their investment portfolios. For instance, if you decide you want to invest part of your assets in Japanese securities, the easiest way is through a fund that specializes in this market.

The funds in Canada can be divided into two broad categories: those that invest in growth securities such as common stocks and whose objective is to provide long-term growth, and those that invest in income securities and whose objective is to provide current income or stable growth. Balanced, or asset-allocation, funds combine growth and income securities to provide growth, income and, in theory at least, superior long-term returns.

Types of funds

Growth funds historically give the highest rates of return measured over a long period of time, say ten years. While the returns of all mutual funds are a combination of capital gain and income, the major portion of return from growth funds is from capital apprecia- tion. It is impossible to predict what a growth fund's future rate of return will be. The assumption is that it will be higher than the rate of return of a fund that invests for income. That has been the case historically. But annual rates of return for growth funds vary widely. In some years, the returns will be large; in other years, the returns will be mediocre. There will be years when fund values drop.

Fixed income funds give somewhat lower long-term rates of return than growth funds. However, their annual returns are more stable because the major portion is income. This income comes in the form of interest in the case of bond and mortgage funds, and dividends in the case of preferred-dividend income funds.

Growth funds

Growth funds include common stock and real estate funds as well as balanced funds whose portfolios may include both stocks and bonds to provide more stable growth than pure growth funds.

The largest group of growth funds – about 190 funds – is Canadian common stock funds. Because they concentrate in the Canadian market, holding no more than 20 percent of their assets in foreign securities, they can be registered as RRSPs.

Most Canadian common stock funds invest across the spectrum of the market, generally sticking to issues traded on the Toronto Stock Exchange and the Montreal Exchange. A few funds, however, specialize in specific segments of the market. For example Altamira Resource Fund invests in Canadian resource issues; Dynamic

Precious Metals Fund invests in shares of precious metals producers and precious metals.

There are about eighty growth funds that invest in American stock markets. While most of these funds stick to senior blue-chip issues, others such as Royal Trust Zweig Strategic Growth Fund concentrate on specific areas, in this case, small company stocks.

If international diversification interests you, there are about 150 funds that invest outside North America. Some, such as AGF Japan Fund or Dynamic Europe Fund, concentrate on specific markets. Others, such as BPI International Equity Fund, invest in a variety of overseas markets. A few funds, such as Trimark Fund, will invest in whatever markets, including Canada and the U.S., are perceived to offer the best values. There are also about a dozen international bond funds which may provide growth through changes in currency values as well as shifts in interest rates.

Mutual funds that invest primarily outside Canada are considered "foreign property" by the federal government for purposes of the Income Tax Act and cannot be registered as RRSPs. However, they can be held in self-directed RRSPs as part of the foreign property component, provided the total foreign property holding does not exceed 20 percent of the plan.

Balanced funds

More than 140 funds call themselves balanced or asset-allocation funds. Historically, a balanced fund was one that invested a portion of its assets in bonds and a portion in stocks. Such funds aimed to have long-term rates of return that were larger than those offered by pure bond funds and more stable than pure stock funds.

The term "balanced" has been used by a number of funds which have the traditional balanced fund objectives but whose portfolios are primarily equities. Depending on their holdings, some balanced funds are eligible for RRSPs, while others are not. As a group balanced funds are significantly less volatile than pure equity funds.

Real estate funds

There are a handful of funds that invest in real estate. These differ from other mutual funds in several major respects. First, they use borrowed capital in addition to shareholder capital; virtually all other funds use just shareholder capital.

Second, their unit or share values are based on appraisals rather than actual market transactions. The net asset value per unit or share in an equity fund is determined by the value of the portfolio as measured by the closing trades in each stock divided by the number of shares outstanding. With a real estate fund, the value of the fund is based on annual appraisals of each property the fund owns. An appraisal is simply the opinion of a real estate expert of the market value of a particular property.

Third, real estate funds are less liquid than other funds and, in fact, over the years several funds have suspended redemptions because of liquidity problems. During the first quarter of 1993, four of the seven real estate funds suspended redemptions.

Income funds

The second major category of funds is income funds which aim to produce a predictable and relatively stable flow of income. Also, the rates of return on income funds are less uncertain than the rates of return from growth funds, albeit slightly lower.

Income funds can be divided into two broad categories: those that invest in bonds, mortgages or both and those that invest primarily in preferred shares of Canadian corporations. At the end of June, 1994 there were about 130 funds which invested in Canadian bonds, twenty-seven mortgage funds, six funds which invested in both bonds and mortgages and twenty-four funds which invested primarily in preferred shares of Canadian companies. In addition there were about 100 money market funds which invested primarily in treasury bills, top quality commercial paper and bank deposits, and about twenty U.S. and international money market funds.

To understand the differences between the two broad categories you have to consider how the federal government taxes individuals on the interest and dividends they receive from Canadian corporations. Interest is taxable at the marginal tax rate – the rate of tax paid on an individual's last dollar of income earned. A person with taxable income of $40,000 could have a marginal tax rate of about 41 percent, depending on the province and ignoring surtaxes. So, on $1,000 in interest income, this person would have to pay $410 in taxes.

To encourage Canadians to invest in dividend-producing shares, the government devised the federal dividend tax credit. It works like this: instead of simply adding dividend income to other sources of income, dividends are grossed up by 125 percent. Then, after you have determined how much tax you owe, you can subtract a tax credit equal to 13.33 percent of 125 percent of your dividends. In the end, you pay less tax than if you'd simply added the dividends to income in the normal way.

For example, let's say you have $1,000 of dividend income. For tax-calculation purposes this would be grossed up to $1,250. Assuming your federal tax rate is 26 percent, the federal tax payable on the dividend would be $325. From this, subtract the dividend tax credit of 13.33 percent of $1,250, or $167. The net federal tax payable on the dividend would be $158. Add the provincial tax at 54 percent of federal tax ($85) and the total tax bill on $1,000 in dividends ends up being $243, or about 24 percent of the actual dividend received. That would compare with $410, or 41 percent, on interest received by the same person. The rule of thumb is that on an after-tax basis, $1 of dividend income has the same after-tax value as $1.26 of interest income. So a 6 percent dividend yield is about equal to a 7.5 percent interest yield.

Now, back to the two categories of income funds. Funds that invest primarily in preferred shares are usually called preferred-dividend income funds. Their purpose is to maximize after-tax income. They are popular with people who want current income and the highest after-tax return possible without taking significant risk.

Bond and mortgage funds may have slightly lower after-tax rates of return than preferred-dividend income funds. But many people prefer the security of having debt instruments and are willing to give up some income as a trade-off for more security.

When an income fund is to be registered as an RRSP, bond and mortgage funds make more sense. All income is untaxed inside an RRSP and RRSP investors cannot take advantage of the tax break that comes with the preferred-dividend income.

There are several different types of non-dividend fixed income funds. There are funds that invest only in bonds, those that invest only in mortgages, funds that mix bonds and mortgages, and, finally, there are money market funds and savings funds.

Bond funds generally invest in government or government-guaranteed bonds and bonds and debentures issued by the strongest banks and corporations. Besides quality of underlying bonds and general interest rate levels there are other factors that can affect performance, such as the maturities of the various bonds held and whether a major portion of the fund is invested in bonds that are denominated in currencies other than the Canadian dollar.

Mortgage funds are designed to provide maximum current income to investors by investing in mortgages. Mortgage rates are generally at least a point higher than bond yields. They are less likely to provide capital appreciation than bond funds because mortgage funds rarely trade their mortgages.

Money market funds have similar objectives: to provide current income with no fluctuation in the value of an investor's capital. Money market funds invest in short-term debt securities with maturities of less than a year. In fact a fund can be called a money market fund only if the average term to maturity of its holdings is 180 days or less. Typically, a money market fund's portfolio will be concentrated in treasury bills, bank-guaranteed debt and short-term issues of strong corporations. Many invest only in treasury bills.

The unit value of most money market funds is fixed at either $10 or $1, so the unit value of the fund is always constant. Income earned on capital accrues to your account daily, weekly or monthly, depending on how often the fund is valued, and is generally used to purchase additional units of the fund. Money market funds are by far the least risky of mutual funds.

How funds can be used

Mutual funds can be used for virtually any type of savings or investment program. The fund or funds you use should be matched to your specific investment objective. You should also develop an understanding of what is called fund volatility or rate-of-return variability.

Unlike a guaranteed investment, you do not know what your rate of return will be from a mutual fund because the rate you earn will depend on the rates of return of the underlying investments. You expect to get back substantially more than you put in – that's the reason you would buy a fund rather than purchase a guaranteed investment certificate or hold money in the bank. However, the rates of return from some types of mutual funds are a lot more stable than rates of return of some other types of funds.

Since money market funds invest only in short-term securities, you can predict fairly accurately your rate of return over a relatively short period of time. In contrast, there are some funds whose rates of return over short periods are virtually impossible to predict. These funds may give very high rates of return over long periods but over the short-term their rates will vary widely.

For example, funds that invest in the Japanese stock market are very volatile. Much of this volatility is caused by the exchange rate of the Canadian dollar against the Japanese yen. Exchange rate fluctuations can be as much as several percentage points up or down in a month. Similarly, funds that invest in gold and other precious metals have historically been volatile.

Money market funds as a group are the least volatile, followed by mortgage funds, bond funds and preferred dividend funds. Common stock funds are more volatile than fixed income funds. Equity funds that invest in senior stocks and balanced funds are generally much less volatile than equity funds that concentrate on specific groups of stocks such as energy shares, junior companies or gold.

Stocks versus T-bills

TOTAL RETURNS
FOR PERIODS ENDING JUNE 30

Year	TSE Total Return	T-Bills
1974	-9.1%	6.8%
1975	10.0	7.5
1976	4.8	8.5
1977	3.1	8.2
1978	14.7	7.5
1979	50.4	10.2
1980	33.0	12.9
1981	19.0	14.8
1982	-39.2	16.5
1983	86.9	10.7
1984	-5.7	10.0
1985	26.7	10.7
1986	17.4	9.3
1987	24.6	8.0
1988	-5.2	8.7
1989	13.5	11.1
1990	-2.4	12.8
1991	1.9	10.9
1992	1.1	7.3
1993	20.8	6.5
1994	3.9	4.8

TABLE I

So if your savings objective is rather short term, like saving for a vacation or a down payment on a home, the fund that would best suit your needs is a money market fund. Your money would not be at risk and you would likely earn a rate of return that is a couple of points above what you would get in a bank account.

If you don't need your money for a couple of years, a mortgage or bond fund might suffice. Similarly, you could consider a preferred-dividend income fund. In this case you would have to consider the individual portfolios of the funds and your tax situation. Fixed income funds that have securities maturing in a few years are likely to be less volatile than fixed income funds whose portfolios have securities that mature in fifteen to twenty years. This will be discussed in more detail later in the book.

If you are saving for the long term, you would likely consider funds invested primarily in equities. You would expect to do better with these funds than you would with income funds. But on a month-to-month or year-to-year basis such growth funds would have more volatile rates of return than fixed income funds.

Historically, investors who are willing to accept some fluctuation in their rates of return have done better over the long haul than investors who want guaranteed returns.

The *Financial Times of Canada* has been publishing its comprehensive mutual fund surveys for almost two decades. On a ten-year basis to June 30, 1994, funds that invested primarily in Canadian equities had annual average returns of 9.7 percent. Bond funds had returns averaging 11.1 percent, while money market funds had returns averaging 8.4 percent.

In Table I you can see the dramatic difference between the year-by-year performance of the Toronto Stock Exchange Total Return Index and the rate of return you would have earned if you held treasury bills. The TSE index is a good representation of what you would have earned holding an "average" mutual fund investing in Canadian stocks. On average, you can expect a good return. However, the returns from year-to-year vary dramatically. The average annual returns for the one-year, three-year, five-year and ten-year periods ending June 30, 1994 are 3.9 percent, 8.3 percent, 4.8 percent and 9.7 percent. The returns for treasury bills for the same time periods are 4.8 percent, 6.5 percent, 8.9 percent and 9.4 percent. The picture is quite different if you choose a different ending date: the returns for the one, three, five and ten years ending June 30, 1989 are 13.5 percent, 10.3 percent, 14.8 percent and 13.0 percent for equities and 11.1 percent, 9.3 percent, 9.5 percent and 11.2 percent for T-bills.

This narrow spread between equity and T-bill returns for periods using a recent ending date is not an endorsement of treasury bills over equities. Rather, it means that returns from equities have been below expectations in some years in that particular time period.

CHAPTER 3

The Impact of the Changing Environment

THE MUTUAL FUND INDUSTRY has been and will ·continue to be dramatically influenced by developments in the marketplace. In the 12 months since the last edition of *Understanding Mutual Funds* industry assets grew from $100 million to $150 million. Much of the increase came from the "GIC refugees" who, faced with the lowest GIC rates in a generation, turned to mutual funds in the hope of maintaining the returns they had previously enjoyed from guaranteed investments.

Indeed, investors were attracted to bond funds during 1992 and 1993 as falling interest rates provided double digit bond returns. In 1993 equity funds had their best performance in years with some funds reporting returns in excess of 50 percent for the year. Investors eager to enjoy these returns flocked into mutual fund; then, as interest rates began to move higher, many equity and bond mutual funds fell in value and some of these novice investors redeemed their funds and rushed back to guaranteed investments.

Even so, the underlying trend suggests that mutual fund assets will continue to grow. Key is the changing demographic profile of the investing public. As more and more baby boomers enter their peak earning and savings years, the amount of money invested in mutual funds will undoubtedly rise. Already, 44 percent of households with incomes of $70,000 or more own mutual finds and almost 30 percent of households with incomes of $50,000 to $70,000 own funds. This market penetration is higher than many mutual fund professionals had expected and suggests a slower future growth rate than experienced over the past few years.

The stock market cycles

It is also important to remember that the capital markets move in cycles and it is unreasonable to expect annual returns of 20 or 30 percent to continue indefinitely – just as it was unreasonable to have feared that the poor returns of the previous few years would continue indefinitely. In the last rising, or bull market, which lasted from July 1982 to August 1987, the Toronto Stock Exchange 300 index climbed 202 percent over sixty months. That bull market was also helped by falling interest rates which made equities and equity funds attractive alternative investments.

While the bull market ended in August 1987, it was the October 1987 crash that demonstrated the obvious cyclical nature of the markets. The stock market slide in October 1987 was not a surprise to most professional investors. In fact, most fund managers had been building cash positions in the months prior to the decline because they felt that stocks were expensive or that the market was ahead of itself. As well, the markets had become exceptionally volatile, with the major indexes moving sharply up and down on a day-to-day basis as investor confidence rose and fell.

What caught virtually every manager off-guard was the magnitude of the decline. In the six sessions to October 23, the Toronto Stock Exchange 300 composite index – a widely used measure of stock market performance – fell about 16 percent.

The biggest drop was on Black Monday, October 19, when the TSE 300 fell 407 points, losing 11 percent of its value. However, the bloodbath really began on the previous Friday when the TSE 300, taking its lead from the New York market, fell 76 points, or 2 per cent. By the time the month ended, the TSE was more than 22 percent below its September closing level. Investors who bought near the top of the market in August saw the value of their investment, assuming they had a broadly based portfolio, plunge by one-quarter. If they bought the day the market peaked and sold the day the market bottomed, they would have lost about 31 per cent of their capital before commissions.

While some investors bought at the peak, hundreds of thousands of investors had been in funds for years, holding them as long-term investments. These investors saw the crash eliminate most of the gains they had made over the previous twelve months. Even then, many funds tied to the stock market showed significant gains in 1987 despite October. Several funds tied to natural resource stocks had gains of more than 25 percent. Some funds with substantial cash positions and broadly based portfolios showed small but positive returns.

Surprisingly, the industry was not hit with a flood of redemptions. While there was a substantial amount of switching from growth funds to more stable bond and money market funds, few fund companies reported a mass exodus from funds. In total, about 2 percent of mutual fund assets were redeemed the week of the crash.

There are several explanations for this. Many fund salespeople claim that most of their clients are long-term investors and decided to continue holding. Indeed, with ten-year rates of return for many funds in excess of 16 percent, long-term investors could still smile. But the lack of redemptions might also reflect the fact that many investors got busy signals when they tried to call their brokers to redeem. By the time they got through, the market had leveled and they decided to hold, particularly when they realized that the damage wasn't as great as they thought.

There was concern in the industry that some investors who bought their holdings partly with borrowed money would be forced to sell by banks and trust companies which had financed the purchases. However, this did not become a major problem because the crash only trimmed profits and did not eliminate them, at least for investors who had held funds for some time.

As to the cause of the crash, a simple explanation is that the number of people who wanted to sell exceeded the number of people who wanted to buy. There are many more complex explanations. One points to sales of stocks by major U.S. fund companies. Mutual fund investors can redeem at any time. Apparently, on Friday, October 16, fund companies were hit by an extraordinary number of redemptions when the New York Stock Exchange fell 108 points as measured by the Dow Jones industrial average. To raise cash to meet these redemptions, some funds became major sellers of stocks on October 19. This helped drive the market down further because many potential buyers were on the sidelines.

Those investors who bought stocks or funds which invest in stocks on October 19 did quite well. By the end of June 1989, they were showing gains of about 40 percent, using the Toronto index as a bench-mark.

The crash has had some major effects on fund investing. For one thing, many investors started taking a more cautious approach. Rather than putting everything in funds that invest in growth stocks, more and more investors are taking a balanced approach, spreading their money among different classes of assets such as bond funds, precious metals funds and money market funds.

However, new sales dried up and the incomes of people who sold funds plunged. The drop in sales hurt fund sales organizations, which quickly discovered that revenues were not enough to cover overheads. Several firms decided to close their doors. Salespeople at various firms jockeyed for position within their own firms or with other firms that offered them a better deal.

The drop in interest rates over the past few years has had a major influence on the funds industry, particularly on banks and trust companies. As rates declined they were faced with the prospect of losing deposits to mutual fund management companies which offered money market funds. In response they offered their own money market funds. Indeed, much of the growth in mutual funds in the past few years has been the movement of money from savings accounts and deposits into bank and trust company money market funds.

Many people also moved out of maturing GIC s into bond and mortgage funds, unaware that these fund unit values would decline if interest rates moved higher. When rates did rise during the first half of 1992 some people were shocked by the decline in value of their funds. They redeemed their units and moved back into guaranteed investments, which raises questions about their knowledge of the market. Although deposit-taking institutions had added a statement to their literature that mutual funds were not covered under deposit insurance, the quick retreat also raises doubts about the quality of advice that investors were given by the people selling the funds.

Finally, the cost of distributing funds has been rising, which is reflected in higher management fees and fund expenses charged to investors. The increased cost is a result of the shift from front-end loads, which are paid by the investor, to declining redemption fees, which are paid by the fund company out of management fees. During 1992, many fund companies raised sales commissions from 4 to 5 percent, a 20 percent increase in the income to the salesperson. However, to finance this increase some funds have had to ask their investors for permission to raise their management fees, which has led to embarrassing confrontations at annual meetings. Other fund companies have simply launched new rear-end load funds with higher management fees. A couple of fund companies simply tacked on an additional fee for clients who, when they bought a mutual fund with load options, chose the declining redemption fee rather than the front-end load. This has created confusion among clients and some administrative difficulties for the companies themselves.

Virtually all fund companies which sell their funds through dealers pay a portion of their management fee to the salesperson as a "trailer fee" for providing on-going service to the client after the initial sales commission has been paid. This trailer, or servicing fee, is generally one-quarter of the management fee for funds sold on a declining-redemption fee basis. So, if a fund has a 2 percent management fee, 0.25 percent of the value of the client's holding will be paid to the broker every year for as long as the client holds the fund and the broker remains the client's broker.

A new twist developed in early 1993 involving funds sold on an acquisition-fee basis. Acquisition fees are negotiable. To compete with banks and trust companies, some financial planners do not charge a commission on the load-funds they sell, receiving their compensation from the fee charged the client for advice instead. Many fund companies raised the trailer fee paid on funds sold with acquisition fees to one-half of the management fee. Some funds moved to a level load, which involves charging a 1 percent front-end commission to the client and the payment of half the management fee as a trailer to the dealer or broker. If a client redeems within one year, a redemption fee of 1 percent is charged.

CHAPTER 4

All About Growth Funds

IF YOUR INVESTMENT GOAL IS long-term capital growth, consider equity funds, which invest primarily in common stocks. These are the most popular type of fund. About 450 are included in the *Financial Times of Canada* monthly survey of investment funds.

There are several major groups of equity funds that are designed to meet particular objectives by investing in specific markets or certain areas of specific markets. Regardless of their type, all equity funds have the common thread of a diversified portfolio of shares, and performance that reflects individual funds' objectives and the skills of their managers.

Many people buy equity funds the same way they buy GICs. They look at rates of return and buy the one with the highest rate. This is a mistake. An equity fund's long-term rate of return indicates how that fund has performed in the past. It is not a guarantee, or even a strong indicator, of future performance. Performance is a single indicator which is best used combined with another indicator, volatility. Both must be viewed against the outlook for the market and the holdings of a specific fund.

In fact, it is very important to consider a fund's volatility, the stability of its monthly rate of return, when choosing an equity fund. The *Financial Times* monthly performance tables, as well as the tables of other newspapers and computer disk fund measurement products, provide information on a fund's volatility. While the method of showing volatility differs among products they all seek to provide information about the variation in a fund's monthly rate of return using a statistical measure called standard deviation.

Volatility is useful in comparing two funds with similar rates of return. For investors who buy and hold for the long term, a fund with a high historical return and a low volatility ranking would be preferable to a fund with the same return but a high volatility. On the other hand, if you're trying to catch the swings in a market cycle, you might want to choose a fund with a high volatility rating over one with a low rating.

For example, Royal Trust American Stock Fund, and Dynamic Income Fund have identical average annual returns of 12.5 percent over the ten years ended June 30, 1994. However, the stock fund is much more volatile than the income fund. A fund's volatility will change from time to time. But usually the changes are not significant because the fund objectives and investment philosophy are generally stable.

Certain groups of funds tend to be more volatile than others. Gold funds, for instance, are among the most volatile, reflecting the volatility of precious metals prices and gold mining stocks. Similarly, Japanese funds are fairly volatile as a result of swings in the exchange rates of the Japanese yen and Canadian dollar. Generally, funds that invest in a narrow segment of the market are more volatile than funds that draw their portfolios from a broad spectrum of industries. Equity funds that have relatively low volatility tend to invest in securities that are more stable in price than the general market. For example, a fund holding stocks with substantial dividend yields would have below-average volatility. One such fund is Corporate Investors Ltd., which invests in shares that pay, or are expected to pay, above-average dividends. Here is a summary of the major types of growth funds:

1. Canadian equity funds

The largest group of investment funds are those that invest primarily in Canadian stocks and are eligible for RRSPs. Most invest in a broad spectrum of industries and have rates of return that are similar to that of the Toronto Stock Exchange total return index. Others, however, have somewhat different objectives. For instance, several invest primarily in dividend-paying common shares of mature companies giving rates of return that are somewhat more stable than the market. Others specialize in specific areas of the market such as natural resources.

2. U.S. equity funds

Funds that invest in the U.S. are also very popular among Canadian investors. These funds appeal to individuals who expect the U.S. markets to outperform their Canadian counterparts or who want a

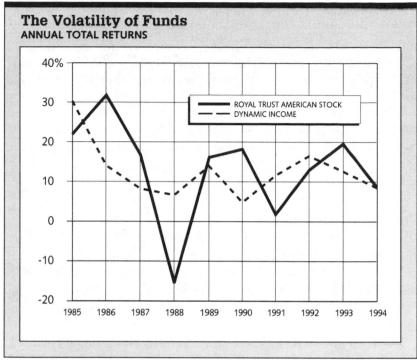

The Volatility of Funds
ANNUAL TOTAL RETURNS

ROYAL TRUST AMERICAN STOCK
DYNAMIC INCOME

CHART i

hedge against the Canadian dollar. Within this group there is a wide variety of choices. Some invest primarily in blue chips. Others base their portfolios on companies that offer above-average growth potential or in specialty areas of the marketplace.

3. International funds
International funds take advantage of investment opportunities in different countries. Some will invest in any country, including Canada. Others will exclude Canada or concentrate on overseas markets. International funds performed quite well until recently as the Canadian dollar fell against overseas currencies. In the past year or so Canadian funds had the performance edge as the Canadian dollar moved higher against most other currencies.

4. Specialty equity funds
A number of funds specialize in specific industries, specific markets or follow hedged investment strategies. For instance, Royal Trust Energy Fund invests in energy stocks. Several funds special-

ize in Japanese securities, while a number concentrate on precious metals. In addition, some funds attempt to give their investors stable rates of return through hedging strategies such as writing call options against positions. This involves buying a stock then selling a call option which gives the buyer the right to buy that stock at a set price up until a specific date.

5. Balanced or asset-allocation funds

Balanced or asset-allocation funds try to stabilize returns by combining equities with fixed income securities and varying the mix to reflect the outlook for the markets.

Canadian equity funds

Lured by promises of returns far above those available from guaranteed investments, individuals poured billions of dollars in recent years into mutual funds that invest primarily in Canadian equities. Indeed, many funds have given their holders rates of return far in excess of the rates that could be earned by holding guaranteed investments.

But it's important to realize that year-to-year rates vary widely. Over the fifteen years ended June 1994, the annual returns of the Toronto Stock Exchange total return index ranged from a low of -39.1 percent to a high of 86.6 percent.

And because stock markets move in cycles, annual rates don't tell the whole story. The returns depend on when stocks are bought and when they are sold. Over the past sixty years, the Toronto market has gone through eleven cycles consisting of declining markets followed by rising markets.

Toronto statistician Richard Anstett has compiled some of the most comprehensive statistics available on the performance of the TSE. Looking at some of the more recent cycles, Anstett notes that the Toronto market rose 193 percent in the seventy-two months ended November 1980, then proceeded to slide 44 percent over the next twenty months to June 1982. Between June 1982 and August 1987 the market rose 202 percent. Then it started its slide, which ended in late October, down 31 percent from its peak. From October 1987 to October 1989 it rose about 42 percent before pulling back 25 percent over the following twelve months. In each of these cycles, day-to-day swings varied widely. For example, the June 30, 1994

Market Cycles Since 1921
on the Toronto Stock Exchange

Bull Markets	No. of Months	% Gain	Bear Markets	No. of Months	% Loss
August 1921 to			September 1929 to		
September 1929	97	300	June 1932	33	80
June 1932 to			March 1937 to		
March 1937	57	201	April 1942	61	56
April 1942 to			May 1946 to		
May 1946	49	159	February 1948	21	25
February 1948 to			July 1956 to		
July 1956	101	273	December 1957	17	30
December 1957 to			May 1969 to		
May 1969	137	162	June 1970	13	28
June 1970 to			October 1973 to		
October 1973	40	64	December 1974	14	38
December 1974 to			November 1980 to		
November 1980	72	193	July 1982	20	44
July 1982 to			August 1987 to		
August 1987	61	202	October 1987	2	31
October 1987 to			October 1989 to		
October 1989	24	42	October 1990	12	25

Note: Changes in market sentiment reflect gains or declines of 20 percent or more. The stock market began climbing in October 1990, gaining more than 45 percent in the forty-five months to June 1993.

TABLE II

level of the TSE index was about 12 percent below its level of January 31, 1994.

The return that a broadly-based fund earns in any period or cycle depends on what happens in the market and on the skills of the fund's investment advisor. But it is difficult for a fund manager to consistently outperform the market. Superior returns do occur but usually only for short periods of time or with smaller funds. Such performance is generally due to the decisions of a single manager or a handful of individuals working together. But most managers parrot the general market or follow the crowd. As a result, on a long-term basis it is unrealistic to expect mutual funds as a whole to generate returns significantly greater than the general market.

To understand why, you have to look at the environment in which managers of broadly based Canadian equity funds have to work. You also have to consider a fund manager's objectives and management style.

Most fund managers try to outperform the market. So a manager of a broadly based Canadian equity fund would gauge his or her performance against the TSE 300 composite index, the index which includes the 300 stocks with the largest market capitalizations traded on the exchange, or against the TSE total return index, which includes dividends paid by the stocks included in the TSE 300.

There are several ways fund managers can construct portfolios. One way is to structure portfolios along the lines of the general index, overweighting or underweighting specific industry groups. In fact, there are funds such as First Canadian Equity Index Fund which invest in each industry group in the same proportion as the index.

As Table III shows, the index is divided into thirteen major industry groups: metals and minerals, gold and silver, oil and gas, paper and forest, consumer products, industrial products, real estate and construction, transportation and environmental services, pipelines, utilities, communications and media, merchandising, financial services and conglomerates. At the end of June 1994, metals and minerals were 7.71 percent of the index, while financial services were 15.64 percent. A portfolio manager who is positive on the outlook for metals and minerals but negative on banks might put a heavier weighting than 7.71 percent in metals shares and a lower weighting in financial services.

A variation of this is to adjust the cash component of the portfolio. All mutual funds hold cash. But the percentage held in cash reflects the fund manager's view on the direction of the market. A manager who expects a sharp rise in the market soon might hold only enough cash to cover normal redemptions. A manager who expects the market to pull back or who believes that prices of individual stocks are expensive might have 30 percent or more of the fund's assets in cash.Alternatively, fund managers can build portfolios choosing individual securities while ignoring what is in the general index. Many fund managers, however, end up with portfolios that are similar to the general index.

The major problem they face is finding stocks that can be bought and sold in volume. There are several thousand public companies

Toronto Stock Exchange Subindex Weights

Metals & minerals	7.71	**Real estate**	0.45
Integrated mines	5.83		
Metal mines	0.26	**Transportation & environmental**	
Non-base metal mining	1.63	services	1.49
Gold & silver	11.25	**Pipelines**	2.31
Oil & gas	12.06	**Utilities**	10.08
Integrated oils	2.07	Telephone utilities	8.03
Oil and gas producers	9.99	Gas and electric utilities	2.05
Paper & forest	4.32	**Communications**	4.14
		Broadcasting	0.43
Consumer products	9.16	Cable and entertainment	1.46
Food processing	0.52	Publishing and printing	2.25
Tobacco	0.99		
Distilleries	4.00	**Merchandising**	3.61
Breweries and beverages	1.48	Wholesale distributors	0.37
Household goods	0.33	Food stores	1.07
Autos and parts	1.40	Department stores	0.56
Packaging products	0.08	Clothing stores	0.06
Biotechnology/		Specialty stores	0.94
pharmaceuticals	0.37	Hospitality	0.61
Industrial Products	13.11	**Financial Services**	15.64
Steel	1.58	Banks	13.29
Fabricating & engineering	0.63	Trust, savings and loans	0.16
Transportation equipment	1.04	Investment companies/funds	0.83
Technology	4.32	Insurance	0.63
Cement/concrete products	0.55	Financial management	0.72
Chemicals	3.47		
Business services	1.25	**Conglomerates**	4.66

June 30 1994   SOURCE: BUNTING WARBURG

TABLE III

listed on Canadian exchanges. But only a relatively small number trade in large enough volume or have enough shares outstanding to be considered by fund managers. A fund with assets of $5 million could have a portfolio of smaller companies. But a fund of $500 million would have to have the bulk of its assets in larger companies. Otherwise its manager would be faced with a portfolio containing too many companies to be manageable.

You can figure out a stock's capitalization by multiplying its share price by the number of shares outstanding. A company with ten million shares outstanding and a stock price of $25 would have a market capitalization of $250 million.

The heaviest weighting among the 300 stocks in the TSE composite index belongs to BCE Inc., with 5.5 percent of the index on June 30, 1994. Next is Seagram Co. with 4.0 percent followed by Royal Bank with 3.3 then American Barrick with 3.0 percent. These four stocks represent about 16 percent of the total value of the TSE 300. The top ten stocks in the index represent 31 percent of the index; the top 100 represent 81 percent; the top 200 represent 95 percent. In contrast, the smallest fifty stocks in the index represent less than 2 percent of the index; the largest of that fifty is 0.05 percent of the total.

Virtually all funds have rules that limit their holdings of individual stocks. For example, concerns about liquidity would prevent a fund, along with any other funds managed by the same advisor, from holding more than 5 percent of the outstanding shares of a specific stock.

Consequently, Canadian equity funds, particularly medium and larger funds, almost always end up having larger companies as a major portion of their portfolios, and these are generally the stocks that are found in the TSE 300.

Since the federal government allows RRSP-eligible mutual funds to hold up to 20 percent of their assets in foreign stocks many Canadian equity funds have a U.S. or overseas component that may contribute to results that differ from the Canadian market.

Some managers try to beat the market by catching the swings. They build up cash when they believe the market is near the top and they spend their cash when the market is near the bottom. These managers are called market timers and they often base their decisions on technical analysis – the analysis of market cycles and graphs. Market timers face some major difficulties.

First, it is very difficult to call a market top or bottom. Second, it is even more difficult to move out of or into a stock if you have a large portfolio. The manager will simply be unable to sell as much as he or she wants at peak prices, or buy at the bottom. The third problem faced by market timers is that if they are wrong in their timing, they will drastically underperform their competitors.

The funds that do seem to outperform the market have three things in common: the decisions are made by a single person or a small group of individuals, the decisions are made quickly, and the decision-makers are not afraid to act differently from the crowd.

Moreover, their methods of choosing stocks are based on finding undervalued situations. They seek out companies whose shares trade in the market at levels below the values of the assets, less liabilities, and which offer good potential for earnings growth. Such managers will spend cash when they find plenty of stocks that meet their criteria and will build cash when shares become overvalued and they cannot find undervalued stocks to purchase.

In most cases the stocks held may not represent the largest companies. Moreover, such funds' monthly performance may differ from the general market's performance.

In contrast, many funds have their decisions made by ponderous committees that are unable to act quickly. By the time they act on the data available – which is most likely the same information available to other institutional investors – the information has been fully reflected in share prices. Consequently, such funds are unlikely to do better than the market, nor much worse.

U.S. equity funds

If you're interested in investing in U.S. markets, you can choose from among almost ninety U.S. equity funds. These are very popular among investors who believe that the U.S. market offers investment opportunities not available in Canada and who expect the U.S. economy to outperform Canada's.

Since most U.S. funds accept subscriptions in either Canadian or U.S. dollars, these funds also appeal to people who have U.S. dollar savings and want to keep this money in U.S. dollar-denominated growth securities. Similarly, individuals who plan to retire in the U.S. often invest a portion of their assets in U.S. securities.

U.S. equity funds should be considered as an alternative to U.S. stock portfolios in estate planning. If you own substantial U.S. assets, such as stocks, and you die, your estate could be subject to U.S. probate. However, holding mutual funds invested in U.S. assets avoids this potential problem because the funds are a Canadian asset.

U.S. vs. Canadian Stock Market Performance
PERCENT CHANGE OVER EACH 12 MONTH PERIOD ENDING JUNE 30

CHART II

Like Canadian equity funds, there is a wide variety of funds that invest in the U.S. Many try to parrot the major U.S. stock market indexes. For example, Jarislowsky Finsco American Equity Fund invests primarily in companies included in the Standard & Poor's 500 composite stock index and which "best represent the investment characteristics of blue-chip securities." Similarly, Green Line U.S. Index Fund tracks the performance of the S&P 500.

Other funds have investment policies that are a variation of this theme. Century DJ Fund seeks above-average rates of return by investing in major blue-chip companies with above-average earnings and dividend records.

Others attempt to beat the averages by choosing investments from a broader range of stocks. AGF Special Fund Ltd. looks for companies that are expected to grow at above-average rates of return. AGF American Growth Fund Ltd. has a similar objective but puts the greatest portion of its assets in stocks listed on the New York Stock Exchange. United American Fund seeks long-term capital growth by investing its assets in U.S. common stocks that its managers consider undervalued in relation to earnings, dividends and assets.

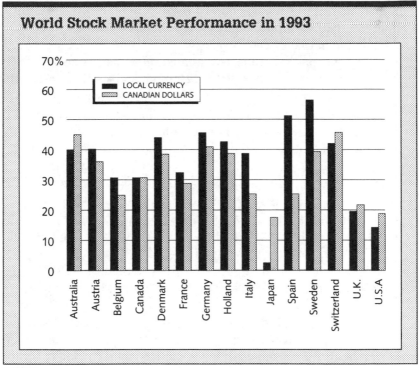

World Stock Market Performance in 1993

CHART III

The relative performance of Canadian and U.S. funds is mixed and depends on the period measured. U.S funds did much better as a group in the twelve months ended June 30, 1994, a reflection of a falling Canadian dollar and, more importantly, a stronger U.S. economy. Different measurement dates, however, will provide different results and in the twelve months ended June 30, 1994 Canadian equity funds beat their U.S. counterparts.

International equity funds
Virtually every industrialized country and many Third World nations have stock markets that trade shares of local companies. The performance of any given market reflects local and international economic conditions. And while all important markets move somewhat in concert because of the shrinking global marketplace, there can be large differences in performance. This reflects the fact that at any given time certain markets might be in an earlier or later stage of the economic cycle than North American markets. A nimble port-

folio manager can take advantage of these differences. The result is that an international fund might show gains in a year in which U.S. and Canadian markets head lower.

The performance also reflects the fact that some markets perform better than others. For example, in 1993 virtually all major world stock markets had positive returns. These ranged from Japan, with an increase of 2.6 percent, to 56.8 percent for Sweden. Canada was at the middle of the range with a 30 percent gain for the TSE 300. During 1994 the Canadian dollar fell against most overseas currencies. In fact, in Canadian dollar terms the Toronto market was among the worst performers. When adjusted for exchange rates, the Swedish market was up 47 percent and Tokyo was up 25 percent.

While there are several dozen countries with stock markets, most international funds stick with the major European, Far East and Australian markets as well as Canadian and U.S. markets. A typical fund might restrict the bulk of its portfolio to shares traded in the United Kingdom, Germany, France, Switzerland, Australia, Japan, Canada and the U.S.

Occasionally, it will invest in shares traded in other markets such as Italy, Austria, Singapore, Hong Kong or the Scandinavian countries. But equity investments in these markets usually reflect a view of the outlook for a specific company rather than an economy or currency. Trading volumes in many overseas markets are simply too light to allow a portfolio manager to invest with reasonable diversification. So while a specific overseas market may rise 57 percent, as Sweden's did in 1993, it is unrealistic to expect a fund manager to have a heavy position of Spanish stocks in a portfolio.

Managers of international funds must consider the relative values of assets in different countries, currency trends and, of course, stock market movements.

During the past few years several companies have launched funds which invest in Latin America. Others are investing in those countries which are sometimes called emerging markets – countries whose economies are moving to capitalism. Over the next several years we will likely see funds specializing in China, India, and even perhaps some of the eastern European countries and former members of the Soviet Union.

Managing an international fund can be more complicated than managing a single-market fund. Some firms have developed the expertise and have Canadian managers who base their decisions on their own research or on information supplied from abroad. Others retain overseas advisors to make recommendations. For instance, Global Strategy Fund uses N. M. Rothschild International Asset Management Ltd. of London; National Trust Global Fund uses Hill Samuel Investment Management Ltd., also of London. In contrast Dynamic Europe Fund uses the expertise of its Toronto-based manager, Goodman & Company. The rates of return of the top-performing international funds suggest that location of the manager should not be a concern for investors.

Equity funds which invest in specific markets include some of the best performers in some periods. For example, in the 12 months ended June 30, 1994, some of the top performers were funds which invested in certain areas of the Far East (month-to-month performance, however, was exceptionally volatile.) Indeed, Japanese funds and those funds which invested in Japan in the past have some of the highest 10-year returns, ranging from 15 to 20 percent.

However, the long term returns mask year-to-year volatility. In 1986, for instance, the four top-performing mutual funds in Canada were Universal Sector Pacific, formerly Universal Savings Japan (up 68 percent); Royal Trust Japanese Stock Fund (up 63.5 percent); Investors Japanese Growth Fund (up 61.2 percent); and AGF Japan Fund Ltd. (up 54.7 percent). In the twelve months ending June 30, 1992, their returns in Canadian dollars were dismal. In the subsequent twenty-four months performance was very good.

The ten-year average annual compound rates of return for Japanese funds are superior to the rates for Canadian funds over the same period. However, to understand these rates you have to look at year-by-year performance. An investment made in the Japanese market in 1976 and held until 1983 or 1984 would have performed about the same as an investment in the Canadian market, although year-by-year performance would have varied widely. But 1985 and 1986 were banner years for Japanese funds because stock prices and the yen soared.

Specialty funds

For investors who want a hefty weighting in a specific industry sector there are a number of specialty funds. These can be useful for investors who want to speculate in one industry or who want a heavier weighting in their portfolio of a specific type of investment than they can get by holding a broadly-based fund.

Specialty funds can be roughly divided into several categories: precious metals funds, energy funds, natural resource funds, technology funds, small company funds and health funds. Because these funds concentrate in specific market areas, they are often much more volatile than equity funds which invest in many industries. Precious metals funds have been among the best performers over the past two years as gold share prices rose dramatically. But the area is volatile. For example in 1979, Goldfund jumped 161.5 percent; in 1980 it added 89.7 percent. The following year it was off 38.7 percent.

Energy funds have also had their ups and downs. They rose spectacularly during the late 1970s as world energy prices soared. But the federal government's national energy program and the oil glut made them dismal performers from 1981 to 1986, underperforming the general market. In 1987 they did well because of rising energy prices and increased investor interest in energy-related stocks. Their fortunes reversed again in 1988 but during the first part of 1989 they had mixed results. In August 1990 when Iraq invaded Kuwait energy funds were indeed the market leaders.

The specialty group includes what are called "small-cap" funds. These invest in companies with smaller capitalizations. Small can mean capitalizations of less than $150 million or less than $50 million, depending on the fund.

Several studies of market performance suggest that small-cap companies outperform the general market during bull markets and don't fall as much as the general market during bear markets. The theory is that smaller companies have a better growth rate than large, mature companies. Consequently, portfolios holding small-cap companies would have, over time, superior performance. In fact, the performance of small-cap funds reflects this.

Balanced funds and asset-allocation funds

Balanced, or asset-allocation, funds have as their objective maximizing growth and income while preserving capital. They do this by changing the asset mix ratio of stocks to bonds to reflect anticipated market conditions. Some funds restrict their investments to Canadian stocks and debt securities. Others will include a wider range of instruments.

The funds that are truly balanced should be less volatile than pure equity funds because of the revenue from the fixed income portion of the portfolio or because of the types of stocks held, and indeed, the majority of balanced funds are less volatile than equity funds. Some balanced funds, however, have investment policies that allow them to hold any proportion of fixed income securities and equities so from time to time the fund could be 100 percent equities. Because they do not have to be diversified among asset classes, they may prove more volatile than funds that always have some stocks and some bonds. The vast majority, however, have both equities and fixed income securities at all times, varying the proportions according to market conditions.

While equity funds are the largest group, balanced funds have been attracting new investors at a faster pace. The toughest investment decision for many people centres upon asset mix – the percentage they should hold in Canadian stocks, bonds, short-term deposits, foreign securities and gold. For investors who don't want to get involved in this type of investment decision, a good balanced fund might make the most sense.

The latest wrinkle in this area is the asset-allocation service. These are essentially market-timing services. The fund management company (or broker) advises you when to switch from one type of fund to another – to adjust your asset mix. In theory, such a service should provide top returns. However, you should consider all the costs involved in switching. You might also question whether it is in your best interests to be in a fund that is part of an asset allocation service. If you want to remain in equities, yet the management company recommends a switch into cash, the equity fund manager might face substantial redemptions which could result in the sale of fund assets and a change in the portfolio mix. This change might not suit your objectives.

A variation of this service is the mutual fund "wrap" account in which a broker offers a portfolio of house funds. The client's money is invested in a variety of securities and managed for a flat fee based on the assets being managed. These services are relatively new and, while it's appealing to avoid the mix of commissions and fees usually charged by mutual funds, investors should make sure the annual costs will, in the end, be lower.

Real estate funds
Real estate funds invest primarily in income-producing commercial real estate properties. The return from a real estate fund includes in-

come as well as capital gains from the change in value of the under-lying properties.

Real estate funds differ in three important ways from other mutual funds. First, real estate funds use borrowed capital as well as investors' capital to purchase properties. Virtually every equity, bond, mortgage and money market fund has a prohibition against borrowing to invest. Second, real estate funds are much less liquid than other funds. Where most other funds are valued daily or weekly, real estate funds are generally valued quarterly, and in some cases monthly. Investors can only redeem on specific dates and may have to give prior notice. The problems of the commercial real estate market triggered runs on real estate funds in 1992 and 1993. As these funds lacked liquidity, most were forced to suspend redemptions and some became closed-end funds. Don't buy a real estate fund if you need liquidity.

Finally, real estate mutual funds are valued differently. Their values are based on appraisals. The net asset values per share of eq-uity, bond and mortgage funds are based on market values of under-lying assets. These reflect actual prices of trades that took place in the market at the close of trading on the day when the fund shares or units were valued.

But a real estate holding is very different from a position in BCE common shares. While BCE shares held in a mutual fund are identi-cal to shares traded on the TSE, no two pieces of real estate are ex-actly alike. They may be similar to other properties. But there are likely to be significant differences that will affect the value of one compared with the other.

The value of a real estate fund is based on appraisals of the prop-erties held by a fund. And appraisals are only educated guesses or estimates – what a qualified appraiser believes the market value of a specific property to be on a given date.

Ontario Securities Commission regulations set general invest-ment standards as well as standards for appraisals and valuation of shares. Appraisals of each property in a real estate fund are gener-ally performed annually. So in a rising real estate market the selling and buying price of a fund unit might be less than the actual value of the underlying assets.

As well, an appraisal is an estimate. There is no way of knowing whether the appraisal accurately reflects the amount that would be received if the property were sold. Moreover, if the fund were liquidated, the amount shareholders receive might be less than the net asset value of the fund. If the assets of a real estate fund were put on the block, some of its holdings might go at fire-sale prices.

While the minimum capital for an equity fund is $100,000 and for a mortgage fund $350,000, the OSC sets minimum capital requirements for a real estate mutual fund at $10 million. Any new fund must raise that amount before it can invest in real estate.

These subscriptions have to be in cash. The fund cannot issue shares in return for a property or on the condition that the seller of the property buy units of the fund. The purpose of this rule is to avoid a potential conflict of interest.

The appraiser cannot be affiliated with the fund, its manager or the property being appraised. The fee charged can't be based on the valuation or on the appraisal reaching a specified value. The OSC requires that the independent appraiser, whose name must be included in the prospectus, be a member of the Appraisal Institute of Canada and have the Accredited Appraiser Canadian Institute designation. The appraiser must also have five years' experience appraising the type of property being appraised in the province where the property is located.

Each property in the fund must be reappraised annually on the anniversary of its acquisition or last appraisal. However, the trustees of the fund are required to obtain an appraisal more frequently if, in their opinion, there is a development that may materially change the value of the property. For instance, an arm's-length bid for the property could be made at a price substantially different from the appraised value.

Equity-based mutual funds can have sharp jumps or declines in value reflecting changes in the marketplace. Values of real estate funds, however, are less volatile because their values are "managed." To prevent sharp fluctuations in a fund's unit value, no more than 50 percent of the fund's properties can be reappraised in the same calendar quarter.

Not only may values be out of date and too high or too low, but real estate funds will be shown as having relatively low volatility on the *Financial Times* monthly fund survey. As a result, comparing the volatility of real estate funds with other mutual funds is not valid.

Because real estate funds appraise their properties so infrequently, they cannot price their shares more than once every quarter. The exceptions are funds that update their annual appraisals monthly on the basis of the income stream generated by those properties.

Real estate isn't as liquid as a stock portfolio so a fund may require thirty days' notice to redeem shares. A fund must pay for the shares it redeems within fifteen days of the day on which the net asset value is calculated. If it doesn't have the cash to redeem all shares submitted, it must redeem on a pro rata, or proportional, basis.

No delay in payment can exceed six months unless approved by a two-thirds vote of investors. The suspension can't exceed twelve months unless 80 percent of investors agree. A defeat of such a motion would likely mean a fund would be forced to sell off all or part of its property portfolio to raise funds to meet redemptions.

Commodity funds

It's even possible to have a mutual fund that speculates in the futures markets. Futures are contracts calling for the delivery of a specified commodity, security or currency at a specific price on a specific date. Futures contracts cover major food commodities, precious metals, trading currencies, bonds and even the stock market. Trading in futures is very risky because investors have to put up only a fraction of the value of the underlying contract as a "down payment." Because of this enormous leverage, investors either make a lot or lose a lot.

Because of the risks involved in futures trading, anyone who wants to offer a mutual fund that invests in commodity futures must meet some stringent criteria. And while commodity funds have been brought to market from time to time in Canada, they have failed to generate lasting investor interest. Currently, it appears that none is being offered nationally, although several funds are available in British Columbia and Alberta. At least one fund is especially unique since its manager earns an incentive fee based on profits.

The lack of interest in commodity funds largely reflects the regulatory environment. First, the provincial securities regulators, whose rules must be followed by anyone who wants to sell securities to the public must be satisfied that an investor's liability is limited to the amount invested. If you speculate in commodities on your own, your liability is unlimited.

Second, the people selling such a fund generally have to be registered under the Commodity Futures Act as well as the Securities Act. This dual registration reflects the regulators' recognition that someone selling a commodities fund should have expertise both in trading commodities futures and mutual funds.

Third, to be a potential investor, you have to be wealthier and more experienced in investing than the average person. The rules demand that dealers offering such an investment must determine that the potential investor understands the nature of the investment through work experience, education, independent advice or prior experience.

As well, there are minimum suitability standards based on income and assets:

• Investors must have a minimum annual gross income of $30,000 and a net worth of $30,000. Alternatively, a net worth of $75,000 is required.

• The maximum annual management fee can't exceed 6 percent of net assets of the fund. Incentive fees can't exceed 25 percent of the profits calculated no more frequently than quarterly.

• The minimum capital for a commodity fund is $500,000.

• The prospectus must state on the front page that a participant in the fund must be able and prepared to lose his or her entire investment, that the fund is highly speculative, and that there are substantial management and advisory fees and brokerage commissions before an investor is entitled to a return on investment.

• Investors in a commodity fund must be notified within seven days of any decline in net asset value of 50 percent or more from the beginning of the year or the last valuation date.

• Potential investors must be informed in the prospectus whether the fund will wind up automatically if the fund's net asset value per share falls below a certain level. As well, the manager of the fund must disclose his or her track record in managing comparable pools.

Because of the volatile nature of commodities futures, disclosure requirements are more stringent than for other mutual funds. Investors get monthly reports on performance, commissions paid, and the like.

CHAPTER 5

All About Income Funds

FIXED INCOME MUTUAL FUNDS are primarily designed to provide maximum income rather than growth, while preserving capital. These types of funds invest in income-producing securities – bonds, mortgages, treasury bills, and in some cases common stocks and preferred shares that have high yields. By investing for income rather than growth, fixed income fund returns are more stable than equity fund returns. Some fixed income funds, specifically bond funds, can be used as growth funds in periods of falling interest rates.

Managers of fixed income funds are concerned primarily with the quality of the issuers of the securities they purchase, interest-rate trends and, depending on the fund, currency exchange rates.

Because preservation of capital is a primary objective, most fixed income funds have similar policies regarding the quality of the investments they make. All mortgage funds invest primarily in first mortgages, the most secure type of mortgage. If a borrower defaults, the holder of the first mortgage has first call on the assets. Similarly, most bond funds have a major portion of their assets in government bonds and government guaranteed obligations. Any debentures in fixed income portfolios are usually of large companies whose assets are significantly greater than their debt loads and whose earnings have historically exceeded interest expense by a broad margin.

Preferred income funds generally have the vast majority of their assets invested in preferred shares of blue-chip Canadian companies whose securities are rated highly by the widely used rating services, Canadian Bond Rating Service Ltd. and Dominion Bond Rating Service or in securities which the manager's analysis indicates are secure. In order to assign ratings, the rating services examine the income statements and balance sheets of major companies that issue preferred shares, and consider industry trends. Most preferred income funds have some common shares but the portion is generally limited to a maximum of 20 to 25 percent.

Returns from fixed income funds have two components. First, of course, there is the income which reflects interest and dividends paid by the underlying securities. Second is capital appreciation, which reflects the impact of the market on the value of the underlying securities. Although it is a secondary objective for most bond, mortgage and preferred dividend funds, capital appreciation or depreciation can be a significant portion of total return, particularly during periods of volatile interest rates.

During 1992 and 1993, interest rates declined dramatically in Canada to their lowest levels in a generation. Bond and mortgage funds produced double digit rates of return, attracting new investors to mutual funds. Many GIC investors facing renewal rates as low as 5 percent for a five-year term jumped into bond and mortgage funds unaware of the potential volatility.

In January 1994, the U.S. Federal Reserve Board decided to raise interest rates to slow economic growth and cool inflation. Other countries did so as well. Canada, faced with international concern about its deficit and the forthcoming Quebec election had to raise rates even more than other countries to attract and maintain investment capital in Canadian bonds. As a result, interest rates soared over a short period of time. Government of Canada bonds with 8 percent coupons and due June 1, 2023 fell from $1,111 at the end of Januaury 1994 to $859.50 by the end of June 1994. This was a decline of almost 23 percent. If a bond mutual fund had been completely invested in bonds of similar maturities over that period, it would have had a similar decline. However, most bond fund managers have a mix of maturities to hedge against the impact of an unexpected surge in rates.

This is an extreme example because the shift in interest rates over that time was exceptional. The volatility of a specific bond depends on the number of years to maturity – the date when the issuer will redeem the bond at face value. Bonds with only a few years to maturity are much less volatile than bonds that won't mature for decades. This is why bond funds with heavy positions in shorter term bonds perform better than funds emphasizing long-term bonds in periods of rising interest rates.

Bond fund and preferred share fund managers can control the performance of their funds through the structure of their portfolios.

Managers who expect a jump in rates sell their longer-term securities and move into shorter-term securities. Mortgage fund managers have less control because they have few, if any, opportunities to trade their portfolio to shorten or lengthen the terms of mortgages they hold. Also, the terms of the mortgages which they hold largely reflect what was available in the marketplace at the time they made their purchases. More on this later.

Some fixed income fund managers try to increase their returns by holding debt instruments issued in foreign currencies. Several provinces, some Crown corporations and many major banks and corporations borrow abroad by issuing bonds and debentures denominated in U.S. dollars, Japanese yen, Australian dollars and European currencies. Funds that hold these securities will benefit if the foreign currencies appreciate against the Canadian dollar. However, performance suffers if the Canadian dollar does better.

Preferred-dividend income funds

If your investment objective is current income, and the capital you want to invest is outside your RRSP, consider a preferred-dividend income fund. Your after-tax rate of return will generally be higher than the after-tax return from an interest-income mutual fund.

The federal government taxes various types of investment income differently. Interest income is fully taxed. In contrast, the first $100,000 of capital gains is tax free, as a lifetime exemption, subject to certain adjustments. Dividend income from Canadian corporations is treated in yet another way. To encourage Canadians to invest in shares and to help companies raise capital, the government invented the federal dividend tax credit to reduce the effective tax rate on dividend income from Canadian corporations. Your after-tax rate of return from investing for dividends should exceed the after-tax return from interest vehicles. Table IV compares the taxation of interest and dividends and shows that you would pay just under $30 tax on $100 of dividend income compared with just over $44 tax on $100 of interest income. However, pre-tax yields on dividends are generally lower than interest yields. But market spreads on an after-tax basis generally mean you get a higher return from dividends.

The impact of the dividend tax credit is to reduce the tax you pay on dividends from Canadian corporations so that on a pre-tax basis $1 of dividends is equal to about $1.26 of interest. On an after-tax

Taxation of Interest and Dividends

	Interest	Dividend
Interest received	$100.00	–
Dividend received	–	$100.00
Dividend "gross up"	–	$25.00
Taxable dividend	–	$125.00
Federal tax (29%)	$29.00	$36.25
Less dividend tax credit	–	$16.67
Net federal tax + surtax	$29.87	$20.17
Add provincial tax*	$15.66	$10.57
Total tax paid	$44.66	$30.74
NET RETURN	**$55.34**	**$69.26**

NOTE: *54% of basic federal tax. Provincial tax rates vary from province to province.

TABLE IV

basis a 6.4 percent dividend yield is equal to 8 percent interest, an 8 percent dividend yield is equal to 10 percent interest, and a 12 percent dividend yield is equal to a 15 percent interest.

Quebec sets its own tax rates independent of federal rates. A Quebec resident paying the top federal and provincial tax rates would net about $47 after tax on $100 of interest income and about $61 on $100 of dividend income.

Managing a preferred share fund is a complicated task. First, there are several different types of preferred shares. Straight preferred shares pay a fixed dividend in perpetuity. They can be very volatile in periods of rapidly changing interest rates and, as a result, many investors are reluctant to buy them. So the investment community has developed other types of preferred shares in response to changing market conditions.

Floating-rate preferred shares, for instance, offer a dividend rate that is a certain percentage of the prime rate, say 70 percent. And there are floating-rate preferreds that have a fixed-minimum dividend rate. Retractable preferreds give investors the right to return their shares to the issuer at full face value at a specific date. Sinking-fund preferreds require the issuer to purchase or redeem a specific number of shares each year so that the total issue is retired after a certain number of years. Convertible preferred shares give the holder the right to convert the shares into common stock. Investors buy convertible preferred shares because they provide more income than common shares. If the common dividend grows to a point where it exceeds the preferred they can convert the preferred share to a common.

A few companies have issued preferred shares denominated in U.S. dollars. A fund manager might also hold some common shares in a preferred fund if the yield on the shares was attractive.

Most fund managers use a similar universe of preferred shares, basing their investment decisions on quality, yield, liquidity and specific features of a preferred share, such as whether it is floating or retractable. Quality considerations don't vary much from fund to fund. All invest the majority of their assets in high-quality preferred shares. By high quality, most Canadian fund managers mean preferred shares that carry P1 and P2 ratings issued by the Canadian Bond Rating Service and Dominion Bond Rating Service. A portion of a fund may be invested in preferred shares that aren't rated or that have a lower rating if the expected returns are superior, provided the manager is satisfied with the safety of the dividend and the return is superior. Similarly, a portion of the portfolio may be invested in high-yielding common shares.

Depending on interest rate spreads, a portion of the fund might also be invested in treasury bills. Because fund expenses, such as the management fee, can be charged against interest income, a fund manager will include some interest-paying investments such as treasury bills if the interest rate is higher than the rate available from preferreds.

Interest income funds

If interest income or a stable return is your major investment objective, as it is for many investors in RRSPs or registered retirement income funds, you have your choice of four different types of mutual funds: bond funds, mortgage funds, funds that invest in both bonds and mortgages, and money market and savings funds. Savings funds, which hold wholesale bank deposits, have virtually disappeared from the marketplace.

All four are backed by assets that carry little or no risk. Bond funds, for example, include bonds and debentures that are guaranteed by governments, Crown corporations, major banks or the credit-worthiness of major corporations. Mortgage funds have as their underlying securities mortgages that are secured by specific

properties. In some cases these mortgages are insured against default, guaranteed by a government agency or guaranteed by the
manager of the fund. Money market funds generally hold treasury
bills that are guaranteed by the federal government, provincial treasury bills that are guaranteed by the issuing province, securities
issued or guaranteed by major financial institutions and sometimes
top-quality short-term notes issued by major corporations.

As a result, with an interest income mutual fund you don't have
to worry much about losing your money. On rare occasions, bond
funds suffer defaults, but the quality of the overall portfolios as well
as the various guarantees make the impact of any losses insignifi-
cant to the value of an interest income fund.

There are, however, some differences among the four different
types of income interest funds, and these affect the returns you may
receive. These differences reflect the types of securities they hold.
To understand how this works you have to look at the underlying
securities in which such funds invest.

Let's assume you have a choice of three funds. The first invests
only in Government of Canada treasury bills, the second in Government of Canada bonds and the third in mortgages guaranteed by the
federal government under the National Housing Act. In all three
cases we have Ottawa guaranteeing the underlying securities.

Even so, the returns you can earn from these funds may differ
widely. For instance, during the twelve months ended June 30,
1993, the top ten bond funds (excluding specialty bond funds) had
rates of return that ranged from 19.2 percent to 13.8 percent; the top
ten mortgage funds had returns between 10.6 percent and 8.6 percent; and money market funds had returns clustered around 5 percent. The high returns of bond and mortgage funds during the year
reflect the sharp declines in bond yields and mortgage rates during
that year.

Of course, that is only one period. Looking at the six months
ended June 30, 1994 when interest rates surged, bond fund returns
ranged from -14.9 percent to 2.8 percent; mortgage fund returns
ranged from -10.2 percent to 2.9 percent while money market fund
returns were clustered around 1.8 percent.

Money market and savings funds have the most stable rates of return. That's because the securities they hold are very short term and
will be redeemed at full face value by the issuer within one year. So
the rates of return on money market funds are almost entirely in-

come, with little that can be attributed to changing market values of the underlying securities.

A mortgage fund is more volatile than a money market fund. A mortgage fund holds securities that may mature in as little as six months or as long as five years. Its rate of return includes the interest paid on the mortgages it holds, plus or minus an adjustment to the market value of the mortgages in its portfolio. The market values change with changes in mortgage rates. If rates go up, the values of mortgages in the portfolio decline, with longer-term mortgages declining more than shorter-term mortgages.

A $50,000 five-year mortgage issued at 12.5 percent, for example, would have a higher market value if new five-year mortgages were available at 10 percent. But mortgage funds are not as volatile as this example seems to indicate because fund holdings include both short- and long-term mortgages. Also, new money coming into the fund or mortgages coming up for renewal will enter at prevailing rates. This serves to stabilize returns. In addition, when rates fall dramatically, as they did in 1992 and 1993, some borrowers would pay interest penalties to switch to lower rates.

Bond funds are generally more volatile than mortgage funds because they hold securities that may not mature for twenty years or more. A manager expecting rates to fall will increase the percentage of bonds which mature in, say, twenty years. This way the portfolio locks in a high rate of return. Conversely, a manager expecting higher rates will move into the shorter end of the market.

To sum up, money market and savings funds have the most stable rates of return. But over the long haul that stability has a cost. The cost comes in the lower rates of return that money market funds earn over the longer term compared with bond or mortgage funds. Bond funds have given higher long-term total returns than mortgage funds. But they have been more volatile and in some years have underperformed mortgage funds. For current income, however, mortgage funds often have an edge over bond funds because mortgage rates are generally higher than bond yields. Funds that invest in bonds and mortgages combine the characteristics of both types of funds.

Bond funds

The primary objective of most bond funds is to earn the maximum interest income possible without taking significant risk. But an important part of a bond fund's total return can include capital gains that stem from trading. Still, earning income is more important. The fund manager meets this objective by investing in quality bonds. Virtually all bond funds offered in Canada hold a major portion of their assets in government and government-guaranteed bonds, issues guaranteed by the major chartered banks and high-quality corporate debt. Some, such as AGF Canadian Bond Fund, restrict their holdings to Government of Canada bonds.

The investment policies of bond funds generally reflect the investment objectives of the conservative investors who use them for their RRSPs, RRIFs and for income. Even though virtually all funds invest in the same quality of issuers, performance can vary widely. These variations reflect the expertise of the fund manager as well as the fund's investment policy.

There are many ways that bond fund managers can increase returns. Most involve structuring a portfolio to reflect anticipated moves in interest rates. A fund manager who expects long-term rates to fall might increase the fund's holdings of long-term bonds. This would lock in high-yielding coupons of bonds which mature in, say, twenty years. Conversely, a manager who expects interest rates to rise will move into shorter-term bonds. A manager who expects rates to rise then decline might hold a mixture of long and short bonds with few medium-term holdings.

The actual management of the bond portfolio can be quite complicated. Not only does the manager have to consider the direction of interest rates, but also the relative yields of short-term and long-term bonds. In some periods long-term bonds yield significantly more than short-term bonds. At other times their yields will be about the same. There have been some occasions, such as 1989 and the first half of 1990, when short-term rates have actually been higher than long-term rates.

Managers will trade bonds to improve yields. Each trade may improve the yield of a small portion of the portfolio by only a fraction of a percentage point. But done often enough, this can have a significant impact on overall performance.

Bond funds can also generate significant capital gains. This can happen when a manager sells bonds at a profit. For instance, a fund manager expecting an imminent drop in rates might buy discount bonds – bonds that sell at a discount to their face value because their coupons offer lower yields than new bonds.

Fund managers can also boost yields by increasing the portion of their portfolios invested in corporate bonds. Corporate bonds generally have higher coupon rates than government bonds of the same maturity. The higher yields, of course, reflect the fact that corporate bonds don't have the backing of a government. In addition, corporate bonds aren't as liquid as government bonds so the spread between the buy and sell prices can be significantly wider. As a result, the trading costs of a fund that has a heavy corporate component may be higher.

Another way of potentially boosting return is to invest in bonds denominated in foreign currencies. Crown corporations, provinces, banks and companies sometimes raise money outside Canada by issuing bonds and debentures in foreign currencies. The U.S. dollar is the most common currency used but Canadian governments and companies also commonly raise money in French francs, Australian dollars, New Zealand dollars, Japanese yen, Swiss francs and German marks.

Even though these bonds are denominated in foreign currencies, their issuers are Canadian so they are eligible for inclusion in RRSPs and pension funds. A fund manager might hold foreign currency bonds if the interest rate paid were substantially higher than the rate paid on Canadian dollar bonds of the same issuer and same maturity and there appeared to be no foreign exchange risk. Or, the manager might want to hold foreign currency bonds because he or she expected a sharp decline in the value of the Canadian dollar.

Specialty bond funds

Most of the bond funds offered by investment counsellors, investment dealers, banks and trust and insurance companies are designed to appeal to investors seeking income rather than capital appreciation. These funds are eligible for RRSPs and pension funds.

There are several exceptions, such as AGF Global Government Bond Fund. It invests in bonds issued by central governments of countries with developed capital markets. Its objective is high income and capital appreciation. Dynamic Global Bond Fund invests primarily in foreign currency bonds issued by Canadian governments, agencies and corporations, and by organizations such as the World Bank. Consequently the fund is RRSP eligible.

Some years ago, one company launched a "junk-bond" fund that invested in lower-quality bonds of U.S. corporate issuers. The fund provided a yield much higher than other bond funds offered in Canada. The fund failed to attract investor attention and was dropped. Apparently, few investors understood how the manager selected securities for the portfolio.

Mortgage funds

Mortgage funds are designed to provide maximum interest income for investors. Because mortgage rates are generally at least a point higher than bond yields, mortgage funds pay more current income per dollar invested than bond funds. Unlike bond funds, mortgage funds rarely trade what they buy. Consequently, capital gains are unlikely to be part of a mortgage fund investor's income – unless he or she redeems fund units when interest rates are relatively low at a value in excess of average cost. And because few mortgages are available with interest rates fixed beyond five years, mortgage funds as a group are less volatile than bond funds.

A mortgage is a loan secured by property. A residential mortgage is on a home; a commercial or industrial loan is on a commercial or industrial property. Commercial and industrial loans often have longer terms than residential mortgages and higher yields. A property can have several mortgages on it representing several loans. A second mortgage is less secure than a first mortgage; a third mortgage is less secure than a second mortgage. Virtually all the major bank, trust company, investment counsellor and insurance company mortgage funds hold first mortgages only. The amount of the loan is generally no more than 75 percent of the value of the property (in some markets a lower ratio will be used). Lenders can go higher than the 75 percent ceiling but in these cases they usually insure the mortgage against default.

Some funds, such as London Life Mortgage Fund, invest in residential, commercial and industrial mortgages. But most restrict their investments to residential mortgages.

Because the funds invest in first mortgages, investors needn't worry much about losses. For example, First Canadian Mortgage Fund, offered by the Bank of Montreal, invests only in mortgages that amount to no more than 75 percent of the value of the property or are guaranteed under the National Housing Act or insured by the Mortgage Insurance Co. of Canada. If a mortgage goes into default, the bank guarantees to buy it at no penalty to the fund.

As part of its marketing strategy, the bank has had its fund reviewed by the Canadian Bond Rating Service and Dominion Bond Rating Service, the first fund to be rated by the two agencies. Both gave it an "AAA" rating, which demonstrates minimum risk and good returns. Generally, ratings are used for institutional investment products rather than investments aimed primarily at smaller investors.

Unlike bonds, mortgages – especially residential mortgages – are not traded actively. Consequently, mortgage fund managers are somewhat restricted in their ability to change the structure of their portfolios in anticipation of changes in interest rates. Mortgage fund managers, particularly of bank and trust company funds, have little choice in the terms of mortgages purchased by the funds. The mix of six-month, one-year, three-year and five-year mortgages is dependent largely on market conditions rather than on what the managers want. For instance, if most mortgage customers of the sponsoring bank or trust company choose four- and five-year terms – as happens in periods of rising interest rates – then that's where new money in the fund will be invested. Conversely, in periods of falling rates, when managers would like to increase the portion of four- and five-year mortgages, more borrowers will opt for shorter-term mortgages.

How this affects a fund depends on the portion of mortgages up for renewal in a given period and the growth rate of fund sales. Of course, if demand for longer-term mortgages drops drastically, then the spread between longer-term and shorter-term mortgages will narrow, shifting some of the demand.

The difference in the rate of return between two mortgage funds reflects the manager's ability to keep the portfolio balanced to minimize interest rate risk and keep the unit value relatively steady. Funds offered by the larger financial institutions probably have more flexibility because the funds are often a small fraction of the total mortgage portfolio offered by the institution, in some cases less than 1 percent of the total. This gives fund managers some discretion over mortgages that will be acquired by the fund.

Bond and mortgage funds

There are a number of funds that invest in both bonds and mortgages. Some have rigid asset-mix ratios. Others don't follow fixed ratios. Several may include common and preferred shares with attractive yields and the opportunity for capital appreciation. Rates of return of these funds, as a group, are more volatile than simple mortgage funds but less volatile than pure bond funds.

Money market funds

Money market funds provide interest income with virtually no risk to capital. In fact, most money market and savings funds price their units at a constant value – $1 and $10 are the most common. Yields on these funds move in concert with short-term yields such as on treasury bills. Interest earned on the fund is used to purchase additional units on investors' behalf. Income is credited to clients' accounts daily in the case of funds that price their units daily and weekly in the case of funds that price weekly. Depending on the fund, interest compounds weekly or monthly.

Money market funds invest in a portfolio of highly liquid short-term debt instruments which generally mature within one year and have an average maturity of less than 180 days. These include federal and provincial government treasury bills, chartered bank certificates of deposit and instruments guaranteed by chartered banks, such as bankers' acceptances, and short-term notes issued by the most credit-worthy major corporations. Changes in the yields on money market funds may lag or precede changes in the prime rate, depending on the holdings of the portfolio and the moves in the "short end" of the market, say T-bills maturing in less than thirty days. Therefore, in periods of volatile interest rates, the yield a buyer gets on a fund reflects the yield generated by the portfolio and may not match current yields. In fact, in July 1992 many money market funds were providing yields that exceeded T-bill rates by a percentage point.

Most fund management companies disclose two rates of return or yields for their money market funds in their advertisements. The first is the indicated yield; the second is the effective yield. The indicated yield is more accurate. Generally, it is the yield earned by the fund in the latest seven-day period and calculated on income accrued or paid during the seven days. It's shown on an annualized basis. The effective yield is based on the compounding of the indicated yield; it assumes that the fund will continue to yield this amount every week – which is not likely.

Fund companies are required to show the indicated yield in any advertising that includes yields. They have the option of showing the effective yield but do not have to do so. The effective yield, however, could mislead an investor into expecting a higher return than will actually be earned, especially if rates are declining.

It would be more accurate for a fund company to show its indicated yield and the period or average term to maturity over which investors could expect to continue to earn that yield. Both the indicated yield and average term to maturity will change as new units are sold or investors redeem.

Returns vary moderately among money market funds, with the differences reflecting the aggressiveness of the manager. Some funds will restrict their holdings to instruments that mature within ninety days and keep them until maturity. Even a sharp jump in interest rates would have only a moderate impact on such funds' performance. Other funds might hold instruments with longer maturities to pick up a slightly higher return or because they expect rates to fall. Managers of these funds would trade their holdings to increase yields, too. Rates will also reflect management fees which vary from 0.5 percent to 1 percent or more.

Income payments

Before buying an income fund, find out how often you will receive your income payments. Bond funds usually distribute income quarterly or monthly, mortgage funds distribute income quarterly, preferred share funds distribute income monthly, and money market funds usually distribute income weekly, or monthly. Realized capital gains for bond funds and preferred share funds are generally distributed at year end.

Knowing the payment dates may have a bearing on the timing of your purchase. For instance, don't buy a bond fund the day before the dividend date because you'll be responsible for paying taxes on the interest paid, if the holding is outside your RRSP, even though you held the fund for only a day before the payment date. You will receive the interest but you will have converted a portion of your capital into taxable income.

Make sure you're aware of any restrictions on interest payments. For example, you are only entitled to a specific month's interest in the AGF Canadian Bond Fund, formerly Canadian Trusteed Income Fund, if you hold the units for a full calendar month. In this case, you would buy on the last day of the month and redeem on the first.

CHAPTER 6

All About Closed-End Funds

NOT ALL FUNDS ISSUE NEW shares automatically when investors want to buy. A handful of funds called closed-end funds have a fixed number of shares or units. These are traded on a stock exchange such as the Toronto Stock Exchange. Closed-end precious metals funds even have their own TSE subindex. If you want to own shares of a closed-end fund, you have to buy them from someone who already owns them by placing an order with your stockbroker.

Closed-end funds, like other funds, invest in a portfolio of investments. Most closed-end funds are specialty funds that invest in particular areas such as precious metals, global investments or bonds. These funds are closed-end investment holding companies.

There is also a small group of funds called income trusts. These use investors' and borrowed capital to invest in a portfolio of fixed income investments that pass on the interest income to investors.

Some closed-end investment holding companies that invest in gold and in international portfolios are corporations, just like other companies listed on stock exchanges. But instead of making or selling something, they invest capital. They have the same powers and responsibilities as other corporations. In fact, they can have much more leeway in their investment policies than open-end funds.

In addition, their profits are taxable like those of other corporations. Any income earned or capital gains realized by a closed-end fund are taxable at corporate rates. This differs from open-end funds where income and gains generally flow through to the individual investor. Since corporations aren't eligible for the lifetime capital gains exemption, the rate of return to an investor holding a closed end fund might be lower than the rate of return earned on an open-end fund with a similar investment program.

Closed-end funds have been around for more than half a century, but their numbers increased in the early 1980s. The surge in popu-

A Survey of Closed-End Funds

Fund	TSE Share Price	Net Asset Value
BGR Precious Metals Inc.	$15.75	$17.30
First Australia Prime Income	11.88	12.88
First Mercantile Currency	10.25	13.80
Germany Fund of Canada	15.88	17.97
New Altamira Value Fund	9.13	10.61

August 5, 1994

TABLE V

larity of closed-end funds coincided with the push by brokerage houses to promote self-directed RRSPs. At the time, shares listed on Canadian stock exchanges could be held in self-directed RRSPs without restrictions. Closed-end funds qualified, even if their portfolios held investments, such as gold bullion, that would be ineligible if held directly in an RRSP or if their portfolios exceeded the 10 percent limit on foreign property in RRSPs.

Therefore, closed-end funds were promoted by investment dealers as a way of getting around the intent of the rules restricting RRSP investments. During this period Central Fund of Canada Ltd., one of the older closed-end funds, became a gold fund and had a share issue. Three new closed-end gold funds – Goldcorp Investments Ltd., Guardian-Morton Shulman Precious Metals Inc. and BGR Precious Metals Inc. – were also established. Shortly after, several global funds were underwritten – Guardian Pacific Rim, Guardian International Income and Worldwide Equities.

Ottawa revised its rules in 1986 so that closed-end funds that were primarily invested in foreign securities would be considered foreign property and, at that time, limited to 10 percent of an RRSP. Closed-end funds that were already primarily invested in foreign property were "grandfathered" provided they did not arrange to issue additional shares after December 4, 1985.

In the past few years several real estate open-ended mutual funds suffered from liquidity problems when the market for commercial real estate plunged in many areas of the country. To provide liquidity to their unitholders when they could not redeem their units, several converted to closed-end funds which were listed for trading on the Toronto Stock Exchange.

Altamira Investment Services Inc., a manager of very popular no-load mutual funds, launched a closed-end fund in 1993, the New Altamira Value Fund. This provided an Altamira product on which stock brokers could earn commissions.

Closed-end funds have a limited following compared with open-end funds. That's largely because closed-end funds have tended to trade at a significant discount to the value of their underlying assets. The discounts apparently reflect the relative lack of liquidity of closed-end funds. Shareholders of open-end funds can redeem their shares at full net asset value on any valuation day. But holders of closed-end funds can sell their investments only if other investors are buyers. In a falling market, potential buyers of a closed-end fund might be scarce. The discount from underlying asset value will increase accordingly, reducing the market value of the fund units.

In a rising market the discount may shrink or even disappear. If, for instance, foreign investors become heavy buyers of closed-end gold funds as a way of buying a portfolio of Canadian gold shares, their prices might rise sharply.

The discount might also shrink on speculation that a closed-end fund might convert to an open-end fund. In mid-1987, Guardian Pacific Rim announced it was asking shareholders to approve a proposal to convert the closed-end fund to an open-end fund. Its shares were trading at a 17 percent discount to asset value before the announcement. Two months later the discount had shrunk to about 12 percent. Similarly, Privatization Investment Fund became an open-end fund at the end of 1987. The fund's units traded for as little as $3 in October 1987 but at the end of the year, when redemptions were allowed, their value was just over $10 per unit.

Although there can be disadvantages to the fact that the shares of a closed-end fund cannot be redeemed on demand, there are also advantages. For instance, managers have more leeway in making investments. Because shareholders can't redeem shares on demand, the manager of a closed-end fund might decide to invest more heavily in shares with restricted marketability than would the manager of an open-end fund. About 90 percent of the portfolio of open-end funds must be in liquid investments.

Also, a closed-end fund might invest in part with borrowed funds. For investment income trusts, the Ontario Securities Commission restricts debt to a maximum of 25 percent of the assets of the fund. In contrast, open-end funds may not borrow other than temporarily to meet redemptions – even then only up to 5 percent of assets.

The minimum equity capital for an investment income trust closed-end fund is $1 million. The minimum for an equity mutual fund is $100,000. The investment policies of closed-ends funds are generally included in their annual reports.

CHAPTER 7

What to Do First

MUTUAL FUNDS CAN BE USED successfully to meet both your short-term and long-term objectives, either inside RRSPs or outside of them. The trick, of course, is to make sure the funds you choose meet your objectives and are compatible with your financial picture.

Assuming you've taken care of the basics, such as making sure you have adequate life and disability insurance, an up-to-date will and a cash cushion equivalent to several months' salary, the first thing you should do is make a list of your investments, including your home, and your debts.

Interest paid on personal debts such as outstanding credit card balances and mortgages is generally not deductible from income for tax purposes. The cardinal rule to follow is to pay off all personal debt before starting any long-term investment program outside your RRSP.

Look at it this way. Paying off your debt is like making a risk-free investment that pays premium rates of return. Bank credit card charges are around 18 percent, higher in some cases. And while some mutual funds have given moderately higher long-term rates of return, you wouldn't run out to borrow money at 18 percent in the hope of earning 20 percent, particularly if the 20 percent rate wasn't guaranteed and the 18 percent wasn't deductible from tax. Yet that is exactly what you would be doing if you invested in mutual funds while carrying unpaid balances on your credit cards.

Paying off your mortgage isn't as cut-and-dried as paying off your credit card debts because mortgage rates are generally a lot lower than the historical rates earned on equity-based mutual funds. Even so, you should still pay off your mortgage as quickly as possible. You always have the option of borrowing against the equity in your home and using the proceeds to buy mutual funds. You'll still owe money on your home. But this way the interest on the loan will be tax deductible. Whether you should borrow against your home is another story. More on this later.

Once you've got your balance sheet in order, you should develop a basic understanding of how the federal government taxes different types of investment income. Knowing this will help you structure your portfolio so that you'll pay the least amount of income tax possible on your investment income.

There are four basic types of investment income to consider: interest from Canadian sources, dividends from Canadian corporations, interest and dividends from foreign sources and capital gains.

Interest income from Canadian sources, such as interest earned on bank and trust company deposits, Canada Savings Bonds and mortgages, is fully taxable at marginal tax rates. (Remember, your marginal tax rate is the rate of tax you pay on the last dollar you earn. As income increases, so does your tax rate in most cases. So your marginal rate is the highest rate of tax you pay.)

Interest income and dividends from foreign corporations are fully taxable at your marginal tax rate. This includes interest earned on foreign bank deposits, such as a trust company account in Florida, income from a U.S.-based money market fund or from one of several Canadian money market funds which hold U.S. dollar short-term investments. It also includes dividends from U.S. corporations such as General Motors Corp. and International Business Machines Corp., even if the shares are listed on Canadian exchanges or flowed through to you through a Canadian mutual fund.

Dividends from Canadian corporations, whether paid directly or flowed to you through a mutual fund, are eligible for the dividend tax credit which effectively reduces the rate of tax paid.

Capital gains are the gains made on the sale of capital property. This includes real estate, stocks, mutual funds and precious metals. The property can be Canadian or foreign. Gains on the sale of your principal residence are tax free and excluded from capital gains, but gains on the sale of a second property, such as a cottage, are considered capital gains for tax purposes.

In its February 22, 1994 budget, the federal government ended the lifetime capital gains exemption of $100,000, except for farms and small business corporations where the $500,000 limit continues to apply. (It had already eliminated real estate gains from the capital gains exemption in February 1992.)

If you have unrealized capital gains at the close of business February 22, 1994 you can elect to claim them when you file your 1994 income tax return. This allows you to choose the February 22, 1994 price as your cost price for tax purposes in the future. You will only be able to claim these gains against the portion of your lifetime exemption that you have not used.

Even without the lifetime exemption, capital gains are still effectively taxed at a lower rate than interest income because only 75% of the gain is taxable. For example, if you have $50,000 realized capital gains, only $37,500 or 75 percent would be taxable. This $37,000 would be taxable at your marginal rate.

Although you can apply unrealized capital gains at February 22, 1994 against your lifetime exemption there is a wrinkle you must consider: You can apply capital gains to your lifetime exemption only after subtracting any cumulative net investment losses. Only those gains that exceed your cumulative net investment losses (investment losses less investment income) can be applied against the lifetime exemption.

It is important to note that inside RRSPs – the largest if not the only major savings program for many people – investment income compounds untaxed. However, when money is withdrawn from an RRSP either directly or in payments from an annuity or registered retirement income fund, the money is fully taxable whether it reflects interest income, dividends or capital gains.

Consequently, you should structure your total savings and investment package to reflect this tax treatment of investment income. In fact, many people don't do this and end up paying more tax than they should. Many people hold interest-paying investments such as CSBs and guaranteed investment certificates outside their RRSPs and growth mutual funds inside their plans. They pay tax on the interest earned outside their RRSPs. The capital gains inside their RRSPs grow untaxed but they will eventually be fully taxed when withdrawn from the RRSP.

If these people restructured their holdings so that their growth assets were outside their RRSPs and their interest-paying assets were inside their RRSPs they would reduce their taxes. They would still own the same assets, but the interest would compound untaxed inside their RRSPs while any capital gains earned would be eligible for the lifetime capital gains exemption.

If you currently hold interest-paying assets outside your RRSP and growth assets inside your RRSP you can switch them around dollar-for-dollar using a self-directed RRSP available through virtually all investment dealers and most trust companies.

CHAPTER 8

How to Meet Your Objectives

ONCE YOU HAVE STRUCTURED your savings and investments, the next step is to list your specific investment objectives. They could include saving for the down payment on a house, saving for retirement, saving for your children's education, investing for current income or simply investing for long-term growth.

Investment objectives can generally be categorized as short-term, medium-term or long-term. For our purposes, short term means up to a couple of years, medium term means three to ten years, and long term is anything longer than that.

Generally, short-term savings objectives are best met with money market funds simply because they are virtually risk-free. If you know that you will need the money fairly soon for a specific purpose, then a money market fund is for you.

If you won't need the money for three years or more, you have far more leeway. You can use fixed income funds without too much worry. Even in years with sharp increases in interest rates, most fixed income funds show positive returns. Over a three-year period, virtually all fixed income funds show positive returns.

Whether you use equity funds really depends on how much risk you are willing to take. There is nothing wrong with using equity funds for medium-term investment objectives, provided you can accept the risk. It depends largely on whether you might find yourself forced to sell your holdings in a period when prices are down.

For long-term objectives, consider equity funds, which have traditionally outperformed fixed income and money market funds over most periods of a decade or more.

Your investment objectives should be considered as flexible guidelines. There will be times when even long-term investors may want a heavy portion of assets invested in income and money market funds because of nervousness about the stock market. There will be other times when stocks seem very inexpensive and conservative investors who would normally invest for income may move into growth funds. Saving for the down payment on a home is usually considered a short-term objective; your strategy for saving for children's education will depend on the children's ages. If you start the program when your child is born it's a long-term program. If you wait until the child is in his or her teens, it's a short- to medium-term program. Similarly, a twenty-year-old's RRSP is a long-term savings program while a sixty-three-year-old's RRSP is a short-term program.

The rule of thumb is that the shorter the term of the savings program, the more conservative you should be and the less risk you should take.

Meeting short-term objectives

If you're going to need your money soon, perhaps within a year or so, it is probably best to play it safe and invest in a money market fund. You'll earn, at least in most periods, a relatively low return and pay tax on the interest earned but you'll know that you are not taking any risk and you'll get all your money back, plus interest.

Alternatively, you may want to look closely at preferred dividend funds. Many have had relatively stable returns. Depending on your income and tax bracket, the difference in rate of return between a money market fund and dividend fund can be significant. But remember: dividend funds, while relatively stable, are still more volatile than money market funds. Indeed, all dividend funds had negative rates of return in the six months ended June 30, 1994, an exceptional period for interest rates.

Generally, equity funds, and to a lesser extent bond funds, are too volatile to meet short-term savings objectives, particularly if a decline in capital will affect your lifestyle. If you're saving for the down payment on a home, don't invest in equity funds if a decline in the value of your investment will keep you out of that home. If you do invest in equity funds, particularly a specialty fund, in the hope of significant short-term performance, realize that you are a speculator – possibly even a gambler – betting that the market will perform as you expect.

Meeting medium-term objectives

If you are a conservative investor your best bet is probably a fixed income fund, either a bond or mortgage fund for an RRSP, or a preferred dividend fund if you want to maximize your after-tax return.

You can, of course, go into asset allocation or growth funds, too. It all depends on where the market is. A lot can happen in relatively short periods of time. During the first three months of 1987 the Toronto Stock Exchange 300 total return index gained 22.8 percent. But the stock market doesn't always move up, as many investors learned when the index plunged 31 percent between its August peak and October trough. Unless you've got a crystal ball, or more than enough financial assets to meet your medium-term objectives, you should look at fixed income funds rather than equities.

Meeting long-term objectives

If you won't need the money for more than a decade, go for growth using equity-based funds. Even if you measure performance using a market bottom as an ending date, such as the summer of 1982, almost all equity funds show positive returns over a ten-year period.

Of course, it makes little sense to jump into equity funds at a market top. If you are a bit nervous about the near-term direction of the market, take a conservative stance by putting only part of your money into equity funds and place the rest in money market funds.

Alternatively, look for funds that have heavy cash components, indicating that the manager has the same concerns as you. You should also consider balanced, or asset-allocation, funds because managers of these funds change asset mixes to reflect market conditions, increasing or decreasing equities according to market outlook. And remember, there are always exceptions to the rules. Many investors have had better returns from bond funds than from equity funds over the past decade. This reflects the downward trend in interest rates.

Meeting personal objectives

The following pages outline six common savings and investment objectives and how mutual funds can be used to meet them.

1. Saving for the down payment on a home

If you're saving for a home, you are probably hoping to buy within a couple of years. This makes your savings program relatively short term and you can't risk having to redeem your holdings when the market is down. Consequently, your investments should be confined to low-risk funds – funds in which the investment policies virtually guarantee your principal and interest.

Money market funds are the only funds that meet these requirements. They should be used exclusively if you expect to need your money within a year or so.

If you don't intend to buy a house for several years, you can accept more risk in the expectation of earning a higher rate of return. Look at dividend income funds or bond funds. While more volatile than money market funds, both are substantially less volatile than equity funds. Over most one-year periods, bond funds have done better than money market funds. In periods of sharply rising interest rates, a bond fund could do worse than a money market fund, as most did during the first half of 1994, even declining in value. Nevertheless, over a three-year period or longer you will almost certainly do better in dividend income or bond funds than in money market funds, if history holds true for the future.

Again, there are always exceptions and three-year returns from bond or dividend income funds for the three years ended June 30, 1990 were below rates from money market funds. Still, an investor who had started a medium-term program in the summer of 1987 using fixed income funds might have switched into a money market fund part-way during the three years locking in high rates of return.

You may be tempted to use equity funds to save for the down payment on a home. Indeed, long-term returns and some recent gains may make this a tempting option. Just remember that equity funds are volatile and that there will be some periods when prices will drop dramatically. If you can't afford to see the value of your savings drop, then don't go near equity funds.

2. Paying down your mortgage

Most banks and trust companies allow you to prepay the principal outstanding on your mortgage. The limit is generally 10 percent of the principal annually on the anniversary of the mortgage, although some institutions allow 15 percent. As well, you can pay off any or all of your mortgage at the renewal date.

Paying off your mortgage should be a priority before starting any long-term savings program other than your RRSP. You pay interest on your mortgage using after-tax dollars. This means that you have to earn about $1.72 to pay off every $1 of interest, if your taxable income is between $29,591 and $59,180 in 1994, depending on your province of residence. If it's higher, you have to earn at least $1.96 to pay $1 of interest after tax.

Therefore, if your mortgage rate is 10 percent, you would have to earn more than 19 percent on your investments before tax to break even. And remember, paying down your mortgage is a risk-free investment.

You can, of course, have your cake and eat it too by paying down your mortgage, borrowing against the equity in your home, then investing the capital. That way your mortgage interest is deductible. This strategy will be covered in detail in the next chapter.

3. Saving for your children's education

Since for most families, saving for children's education is a medium- to long-term objective, mutual funds fit the bill. What you must remember is that any interest or dividends earned on the money you invest for your children, even if it is invested in their names, is taxable in your hands. However, any capital gains earned are attributed to the child. And interest or dividends earned on interest or dividends on which you paid tax is deemed to be your child's.

You should also keep in mind that if you have invested child tax credit cheques directly in your children's names, any interest or dividends earned are taxable in their hands, not yours. Each child can earn several thousand dollars of interest and dividends tax free, so it makes sense to use child tax benefits as the cornerstone of any education savings program if you qualify.

If you prefer to be on the conservative side when it comes to investing your children's money, use a bond or a mortgage fund. Alternatively, choose a balanced fund. If university or college is a decade or more away, consider growth funds to give you a higher expected rate of return.

Many families use a combination of income and growth funds. Child tax credit cheques, inheritances and gifts from other than immediate family are invested in bond and mortgage funds while other capital is invested for growth. Just remember, when the children are a few years away from university, educational savings become a short-term objective. You may want to lock in your profits from growth funds and move into income or money market funds.

You can also consider a mutual fund registered education savings plan, a RESP. The capital contributed to a RESP (limited to $1,500 a year for each child under new rules effective after February 20, 1990) is not deductible for tax purposes. However, any income earned within the RESP grows untaxed. The income is taxable in the child's hands when withdrawn to finance post-secondary education but the capital you invested originally is withdrawn tax-free. However, the child's total income will probably be low and many of the expenses of education can be deducted by the student, so little or no tax will likely be paid. There is one potential problem; the money must be used to finance post-secondary education. However, if the child who is named as beneficiary does not continue his or her education, you can name another beneficiary.

A number of mutual fund companies, including Mackenzie Financial Corp., offer RESPs through mutual fund dealers and brokers.

4. Saving for retirement through RRSPs

By far, the largest single use of mutual funds is in RRSPs. Some estimates indicate that up to one-third of the $150 billion that Canadians have invested in mutual funds is in RRSPs. Because of the federal government's requirement that limits the foreign component of RRSP assets, RRSPs are concentrated in Canadian equity and balanced funds, bond funds and mortgage funds.

However, as noted previously, investors are allowed 20 percent foreign content in their RRSPs. To maximize foreign content, many people have mutual funds in their RRSPs that invest outside Canada. This can be done by holding your mutual funds in a self-directed RRSP. These are available from virtually every organization involved in marketing mutual funds.

An RRSP is an extremely tax-efficient way of saving for retirement. Your contribution is deductible from income for tax purposes and you are saving untaxed dollars. Also, income within an RRSP grows untaxed. It is not until you withdraw money from an RRSP, either by cashing in your plan or by using one of the retirement options, such as a registered retirement income fund (RRIF) or annuity, that the proceeds are taxed.

Your contribution limit is 18 percent of the previous year's earned income up to a maximum contribution of $13,500 for 1994, $14,500 for 1995 and $15,500 for 1996. From these contribution limits you must subtract any contributions made to a pension plan by you or by your employer on your behalf.

Contributions must be made in the taxation year or within sixty days of year end to get a deduction for the tax year. It is possible to build a hefty cache of savings in your RRSP. When investing these savings in mutual funds, there are two important questions you should ask yourself: how does your RRSP fit in with your other savings? How much risk are you willing to take?

Remember, when you withdraw money from an RRSP, it will be fully taxable whether your gains are interest, dividends or capital gains. If you are saving both inside and outside an RRSP and you have both growth and interest-paying investments, you should structure your holdings so that as much of the interest-paying portion as possible is inside your RRSP. Keeping the growth portion outside your RRSP allows you to benefit from the lower tax rate applied to capital gains.

Many people, however, use asset allocation funds in their RRSPs as well as for other savings. They should continue with this approach and ignore the tax consequences. While this route might have some impact on after-tax returns, they are likely to be minor compared with the benefits of asset allocation.

As far as risk is concerned, you have two strategies from which to choose, one that is active and one that is passive. The active strategy is to change the mix of mutual funds constantly, moving into growth funds when they offer the best values and into income funds and money market funds when the outlook for equities is cloudy. This strategy, if successful, will give you the best returns from growth and income while preserving capital.

The passive strategy reflects the view that your age dictates the type of mutual funds you hold – the younger you are the more risk you can afford to take, the closer you are to retirement the more conservative you should be. The following are some guidelines based on age for structuring your retirement savings between interest-paying and growth investments. They apply to your total retirement savings, including those outside your RRSP.

If you are in your twenties, you have at least three decades before retirement. You can accept volatility in your RRSP and should invest the bulk of your RRSP for growth. Over the years you'll experience some ups and downs. But over the long haul you will probably come out significantly ahead of what you would have by playing it safe. If you're in your thirties, you still have many years to go before retirement, so you can still put the bulk of your assets into equity funds, as much as 80 percent, and invest the remaining 20 percent for income. If you're in your forties, you should become a bit more conservative and move to around 60 percent in growth funds and 40 percent in bond funds, mortgage funds or both.

Once you're in your fifties, retirement is in sight. Consider moving to 40 percent growth and 60 percent income. When you're within a decade of retirement, your main objective should be preservation of capital rather than growth. Move to 80 percent income and 20 percent growth as a longer-term hedge against inflation.

But remember, these are only guidelines. People who are approaching retirement with substantial investment assets – more than enough to comfortably finance their retirements – may decide to keep most of their assets invested for growth. Indeed, someone who started investing in his or her twenties might well decide to remain in equities because of the wealth he or she would likely accumulate. Similarly, if you have an adequate pension plan you might opt to keep the bulk of your RRSP invested for growth.

You also have to consider market conditions. It doesn't make much sense to plunge into equity funds if it looks like the markets are due for a sharp correction, even if you won't be retiring for thirty years or more. Similarly, people approaching retirement may want to put more of their money in growth funds if the market has been declining and prices seem relatively cheap.

You should also consider the portfolio components of the funds you hold. For example, balanced funds hold a blend of growth and income investments. You may want to consider this in structuring your RRSP. A fifty-year-old man or woman might hold 50 to 60 percent of his or her RRSP in a balanced fund and the remainder in bond funds, rather than 40 percent in growth funds. Remember that the objective of retirement savings is to finance retirement. Therefore, it should be the most conservative portion of your portfolio.

5. Registered retirement income funds
You can't have an RRSP beyond December 31 of the year in which you turn seventy-one. You have to roll your RRSP into an annuity or registered retirement income fund (RRIF) or cash it in and pay tax on the proceeds.

The RRIF option meets the needs of most investors. With a RRIF you can hold the same investments as in an RRSP. Moving from an RRSP to a RRIF is a simple matter which involves filling out a form provided by your fund broker or the mutual fund company with which you have your RRSP.

You can withdraw as much from your RRIF each year as you want. The minimum amount you are allowed to withdraw is determined by your age. However, the rules changed at the beginning of 1993.

Under the rules for 1992, which continue to apply to RRIFs set up prior to 1993, minimum RRIF withdrawals were based on the amount of money in a plan at the end of the previous year, divided by the difference between ninety and the RRIF owner's age, or spouse's age if it is lower. For example, someone who was seventy-one years old at the end of 1991 and has a RRIF which had $100,000 in it at the end of 1991 would be required to withdraw a minimum of 1/19 or $5,263 in 1992, 1/18 in 1993 and 1/17 in 1994.

Under new rules effective in plans commenced after 1992, a RRIF can be structured to provide a lifetime income. The new rules require moderately higher minimum withdrawals than under the old rules for people seventy-one to seventy-seven, and lower minimum withdrawals for people seventy-nine to eighty-nine. For people younger than seventy-one, the old fractions based on age or spouse's age from age ninety will continue to apply.

You can convert your RRSP to a RRIF at any age. But because you have to withdraw some capital from a RRIF each year, you should postpone rolling your RRSP into a RRIF until you retire and need income from your plan. The first payment may be received in the year in which you open your plan, but you have the option of starting payments in the following year. In fact, you can postpone receiving your first payment, if you want annual payments, to December 31 of the year you turn seventy-two.

Your RRIF should be invested conservatively with the objective of providing income rather than growth. Consequently, it should be invested primarily in bond and mortgage funds. A portion, however, can be invested in equity or balanced funds to give you a longer-term hedge against inflation.

Overall preservation of capital is of the utmost importance because you will be withdrawing money from your plan each year. If you had a significant portion invested in growth funds and the market turned down, you could find yourself redeeming fund units after prices have fallen. You could seriously erode your financial security.

Again, this is a general guideline. If you retire with substantial assets you may decide you can afford to accept the volatility associated with growth funds and keep a major portion of your assets in growth funds.

6. Financing retirement outside a RRIF

Circumstances sometimes offer the option of a unique solution. Someone with limited assets and income would generally opt for a safe solution such as investing in bond mutual funds. However, sometimes the safe solution isn't always the best. Take, for instance, a widow with $50,000 in capital and no income other than government benefits. If she invested for interest income she would get her basic government benefit. But if she invested for growth and cashed in a portion of her units each month her income would largely be a return of her own capital and she might qualify for the guaranteed income supplement because her "income" doesn't fit the government definition. Such strategies aren't for everyone and they should be examined against an individual's circumstances.

CHAPTER 9

Strategies and Gimmicks

MAKING $1 MILLION THROUGH mutual funds isn't difficult. All it takes is the ability to set aside money each year and a long time to do it. If you can set aside $4,000 a year and earn an average annual return of 12 percent you'll have $1 million in less than thirty years. If you could earn an average of 16 percent, you would have $1 million in less than twenty-five years.

Saving can be difficult because of the temptations to spend. So virtually every mutual fund company has a program to make saving less painful. Depending on the fund company or the salesperson, such plans are called dollar-cost averaging plans, automatic-purchase plans or pre-authorized purchase plans. You decide how much you want to invest each month or every three months and in which funds, fill out a bank authorization form and supply a sample cheque marked "void." The fund company will do the rest. Each month on the same date, the amount you chose will come out of your bank or trust company account and be invested in the fund or funds you pick. The plans are available for RRSPs and non-sheltered savings.

A key advantage of such plans is that if the market declines, your purchases will buy more mutual fund units, lowering your average cost. Conversely, you'll raise your average cost in rising markets. But with these programs you're in funds for the long term and in the end you'll do well.

You can establish a savings plan with as little as $100 a month. Chart IV shows how your investment would have grown if you had contributed $100 a month to a typical equity fund invested in the Canadian market during the ten years ended June 30, 1994. It assumes you purchased the fund either on a no-load basis or with a declining deferred redemption fee so that all your money is invested. The chart is based on monthly returns of a Canadian equity

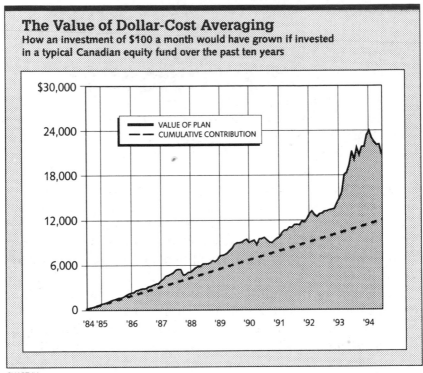

The Value of Dollar-Cost Averaging
How an investment of $100 a month would have grown if invested in a typical Canadian equity fund over the past ten years

CHART IV

fund and assumes contributions are made at the end of the month. Different funds use different dates for investing contributions.

Withdrawal plans

A second type of plan offered by mutual fund companies is the withdrawal plan. These plans allow you to invest a lump sum and withdraw a constant amount each month. For example, you might invest $100,000 in a typical equity fund with monthly withdrawals of $1,000. Only a small portion of the $1,000 is regarded as realized capital gain by the federal government in the early years of the plan – most is seen as a return of capital.

The table in appendix one simulates the results over ten years of a $1,000 monthly withdrawal plan from a Canadian equity fund started with $100,000 on June 30, 1984. Acquisition and redemption fees are ignored because many funds now allow such a plan to be set up with no acquisition fees and ignore or reduce substantially any redemption fees which might be applicable.

It is important to realize that different ten-year periods would provide different results. June 30, 1984 was at a relatively low point in the market cycle. During the subsequent 12 months the market rose and the plan would have risen in value to about $112,000, even after withdrawing $12,000. At the end of 10 years the plan would have been worth almost $132,000. In contrast, in the year following June 30, 1983 the market declined and the value of the plan would have dropped to $82,000 on June 30, 1984 and only $58,000 after 10 years, reflecting the fact that withdrawals had exceeded earnings significantly in that first year. Users of such plans should be prepared to cut their withdrawals if the value of their capital falls significantly.

It's important not to forget that a portion of your withdrawals could be taxable capital gain or dividend. This portion will vary from year to year depending on fund distributions as well as capital gains realized from selling units. In years of little or negative growth, much, if not all, of your withdrawals would simply be a return of your own capital and would not be taxable.

Leverage programs

Be very cautious about borrowing money to buy mutual funds. The use of borrowed money to invest, called leveraging, is a marginally profitable exercise in some cases and unprofitable in others. It can, however, be very profitable if used wisely. The key is to examine any proposal thoroughly and work out your projections on an after-tax basis. You must compare how you would fare with leverage and without.

Investing in growth funds with borrowed money is big business. In fact, it has been estimated in the industry that as much as a third of all mutual fund purchases made prior to the 1987 crash were made with borrowed money.

Of course, the reason for using borrowed money to invest is to make more money more quickly. If you can put $100,000 of the bank's money to work along with your own $100,000 you'll double your profit before interest expense and tax. Your interest is deductible. If the bank charges you 10 percent and your marginal tax rate is 41 per cent, your after-tax cost of borrowing is 5.9 percent or $5,900. (In fact, loan rates vary widely at different points in the economic cycle and were running at about 16 percent during the first half of 1990). If you have $5,900 a year available for investment, instead of investing the money you could use it to finance a loan of $100,000.

Leverage has been extremely popular in the fund industry as a means of building business. Several major fund groups have arrangements with banks to finance leverage programs. Many individual salespeople make their own arrangements to bring clients to banks. Several years ago, one trust company, First City Trust, even produced a video on leverage designed to encourage investors to use borrowed money to buy mutual funds.

Leverage can be profitable in some situations but in many it is unlikely you will be compensated for the risk involved. If you are approached to buy funds using borrowed money, make some projections. In these projections, use several rates of return and various different interest rates for your cost of borrowing. By doing this you will have a range of possible results and can understand your potential risks and rewards. You should also determine the cushion you must have to protect yourself against a rise in interest rates or a fall in the market. Before implementing your leverage program, ask yourself whether you could afford to continue with a leverage program if interest rates rose sharply. Similarly, determine the magnitude of a market correction your bank will tolerate before asking you to put up additional security. In fact, you might want to have a generous credit line available to provide additional security.

The following eight examples look at the results of leverage under certain circumstances and specific assumptions. In each case the amount borrowed is $100,000. The annual interest expense varies from 7.25 percent (the prime rate at time of writing) to 8.25 percent (prime plus one) and 10 percent. The rates of return used vary from 12 percent to 30 percent. A 50 percent marginal tax rate is assumed for all examples except the third which assumes a 41 percent marginal tax rate.

The key assumption in the examples is that if the investor did not use his capital to pay the interest on a loan of $100,000, he or she would invest it. For example, at a 50 percent marginal tax rate and prime rate of 7.25 percent, the after-tax cost of the loan is $3,625. Our example therefore assumes that the investor would have invested $3,625 if he or she had not used a leverage program.

Six of the eight examples cover one-year holding periods. While leverage is generally used for a longer term, a strategy that would be profitable over one year would be profitable over five years. Similarly, if it would not be profitable over a year, neither would it be profitable over five years.

The first five examples look at the results of leverage in which an investor with $100,000 borrows another $100,000, a relatively common strategy. Each example uses a rate of return of 12 percent. The interest rates used, however, range from 7.25 percent to 10 percent. We have assumed a marginal tax rate of 50 percent except for the third example (Table VIII) in which we have used a marginal tax rate of 41 percent to show the impact of tax rate on profits.

The sixth example (Table XI) uses a rate of return of 15 percent and an interest rate of 7.25 percent. The seventh example (Table XII) uses a rate of return of 30 percent, a return one might expect from a specialty fund under certain market conditions. The eighth example (Table XIII) assumes $100,000 has been borrowed against the equity of a home and that interest only is paid over the subsequent five years.

In the first example (Table VI), we have assumed a rate of return of 12 percent, an interest rate of 7.25 percent and a marginal tax rate of 50 percent. In this case, our individual has a capital gain at the end of year one of $24,000 using leverage. $6,000 is tax free and 50 percent tax on the remaining $18,000 leaves her with an after-tax gain of $15,000. Although her bank charges her interest of 7.25 percent, her after-tax interest expense is only $3,625 because interest on money borrowed for investment purposes is deductible. This cost of borrowing reduces her profit to $11,375.

Without leverage our individual would have had a capital gain of $12,000 at the end of a year — $7,500 after tax. But she would also have the $3,625 which would otherwise have been her after-tax interest expense. Adding this back gives her a total increase in equity of $11,125 over the 12 months. The leverage route would have given her $250 more. In this case the benefits of leverage are clearly marginal and the increased profit doesn't compensate for the risk she's taken.

If we take this example a step further and use a five-year holding period (Table VII), leverage seems a lot more appealing. The after-tax gain from leverage grows to $95,293 compared to $47,646 without leverage. In the leverage example we have to subtract interest of $3,625 a year for a total increase in equity of $77,168. Where leverage is not used, the $3,625 would have been available for investment. It would have produced a capital gain of $4,904 — $3,065

Borrowing to Invest — One-Year Holding Period
12% RETURN – 50% TAX RATE – 7.25% INTEREST

	Without Leverage	With Leverage
Equity	$100,000	$100,000
Loan	0	100,000
Total investment	100,000	200,000
Capital gain (12%)	12,000	24,000
Taxable gain (75%)	9,000	18,000
Tax (50% of taxable gain)	(4,500)	(9,000)
After-tax gain	7,500	15,000
Cash available for investment	3,625	0
Interest expense	0	(3,625)
Increase in equity after one year	$11,125	$11,375

TABLE VI

Borrowing to Invest — Five-Year Holding Period
12% RETURN – 50% TAX RATE – 7.25% INTEREST

	Without Leverage	With Leverage
Investment	$100,000	$100,000
Loan	0	100,000
Total investment	100,000	200,000
Capital gain (12%)	76,234	152,468
Taxable gain (75%)	57,176	114,351
Tax (50% of taxable gain)	(28,588)	(57,176)
After-tax gain	47,646	95,293
Gain from investing cash flow	3,065	0
Cash available for investment	18,125	0
Interest expense	0	(18,125)
Increase in equity after five years	$65,771	$77,168

TABLE VII

after tax. This provides the investor who has not leveraged with a total increase in equity of $65,771 — $11,397 less than with the leverage program. (We have ignored any taxes that would have been due on distributions during the five-year period. Taxes would have

Borrowing to Invest — One-Year Holding Period
12% RETURN – 41% TAX RATE – 7.25% INTEREST

	Without Leverage	With Leverage
Equity	$100,000	$100,000
Loan	0	100,000
Total investment	100,000	200,000
Capital gain (12%)	12,000	24,000
Taxable gain (75%)	9,000	18,000
Tax (50% of taxable gain)	(3,690)	(7,380)
After-tax gain	8,310	16,620
Cash available for investment	4,278	0
Interest expense	0	(4,278)
Increase in equity after one year	$12,588	$12,343

TABLE VIII

reduced the growth rate over the five years, and in this example, reduced the benefits of leverage somewhat.)

The third example (Table VIII) is similar to the first example but with one change in the assumption. We have lowered our individual's marginal tax rate to 41 percent. This means that she pays less tax on her capital gain. However, it also means that she gets to deduct less of her interest expense which means higher borrowing costs. Using leverage gives her an after-tax capital gain of $16,620 and after-tax interest expense of $4,278 for an increase in equity after one year of $12,343. If she had not used leverage she would have had an after-tax capital gain of $8,310 — plus the capital she would have had to pay her interest costs for a total increase in equity after one year of $12,588. Clearly, a lower tax bracket makes a substantial difference and our individual would have been better not to use leverage. In fact, leverage is best left for individuals who are in the top marginal tax brackets.

Examples four and five (Tables IX and X) use interest rates of 8.25 percent and 10 percent. Both examples indicate that leverage loses its lustre as the spread between the cost of funds and the expected rate of return narrows. In both examples investing without leverage would have been the wiser choice.

Borrowing to Invest — One-Year Holding Period
12% RETURN – 50% TAX RATE – 8.25% INTEREST

	Without Leverage	With Leverage
Equity	$100,000	$100,000
Loan	0	100,000
Total investment	100,000	200,000
Capital gain (12%)	12,000	24,000
Taxable gain (75%)	9,000	18,000
Tax (50% of taxable gain)	(4,500)	(9,000)
After-tax gain	7,500	15,000
Cash available for investment	4,125	0
Interest expense	0	(4,125)
Increase in equity after one year	$11,625	$10,875

TABLE IX

The best leveraging scenarios

A more rewarding use of leverage is when you expect to earn a significant above-average return over a short period of time. Indeed, this strategy would have generated huge returns over the twelve months ended June 30, 1993 with the purchase of many equity and resource funds. In the subsequent twelve months a leverage program would have given relatively poor results.

Of course, past performance isn't necessarily an indication of future performance and if you are sure you are correct in your outlook for the economy and markets you might want to use leverage. Let's say your favourite portfolio manager has suddenly reduced the cash position of his portfolio from 40 percent to 10 percent. That tells you that he expects a jump in the market. As a result you go out and borrow $100,000 to buy units of his fund, matching the $100,000 you already own. Your intention is to hold for one year. If your capital appreciation is 15 percent (Table Table XI) your increase in equity after one year will be $15,125. This exceeds the $13,000 increase in equity you would have had without using leverage.

If, however, you were able to earn a 30 percent return (Table XII), your increase in equity after one year would be $33,875 using leverage and $22,375 without using leverage.

Borrowing to Invest — One-Year Holding Period
12% RETURN – 50% TAX RATE – 10% INTEREST

	Without Leverage	With Leverage
Equity	$100,000	$100,000
Loan	0	100,000
Total investment	100,000	200,000
Capital gain (12%)	12,000	24,000
Taxable gain (75%)	9,000	18,000
Tax (50% of taxable gain)	(4,500)	(9,000)
After-tax gain	7,500	15,000
Cash available for investment	5,000	0
Interest expense	0	(5,000)
Increase in equity after one year	$12,500	$10,000

TABLE X

Borrowing to Invest — One-Year Holding Period
15% RETURN – 50% TAX RATE – 7.25% INTEREST

	Without Leverage	With Leverage
Equity	$100,000	$100,000
Loan	0	100,000
Total investment	100,000	200,000
Capital gain (15%)	15,000	30,000
Taxable gain (75%)	11,250	22,500
Tax (50% of taxable gain)	(5,625)	(11,250)
After-tax gain	9,375	18,750
Cash available for investment	3,625	0
Interest expense	0	(3,625)
Increase in equity after one year	$13,000	$15,125

TABLE XI

Borrowing against your home

Many Canadians are house-rich but cash-poor. They have a substantial net worth, but it's tied up in a single asset. Some mutual fund salespeople see this as an opportunity, both for the homeowner and for themselves. They might recommend that a homeowner borrow

Borrowing to Invest — One-Year Holding Period
30% RETURN – 50% TAX RATE – 7.25% INTEREST

	Without Leverage	With Leverage
Equity	$100,000	$100,000
Loan	0	100,000
Total investment	100,000	200,000
Capital gain (12%)	30,000	60,000
Taxable gain (75%)	22,500	45,000
Tax (50% of taxable gain)	(11,250)	(22,500)
After-tax gain	18,750	37,500
Cash available for investment	3,625	0
Interest expense	0	(3,625)
Increase in equity after one year	$22,375	$33,875

TABLE XII

thousands of dollars using the home as collateral to invest in funds. A withdrawal plan would be used to finance the interest costs.

This type of program can be profitable, but what happens if interest rates skyrocket and the stock market plunges? This happened in 1981 when the prime lending rate reached a record 22.75 percent and the stock market fell by 43 percent over about eighteen months. The hapless homeowner would find his equity dissipating if he has to sell his mutual fund investment after the market has dropped in order to pay the higher interest charges.

Unless you can handle the interest payments out of your personal income, not the cash flow from the mutual fund, you shouldn't be in a leverage program that uses your home as security. The risks are simply too great.

You can see in Table XIII how you would fare after five years if you borrow $100,000 and finance the borrowing costs with the cash flow from the fund. We've assumed a return of 12 percent and interest costs of 7.25 percent. At the end of five years your gain would be $76,234; only 75 percent of this, or $57,176, would be taxable. A tax bill of $28,588 would leave give you an after-tax gain of $47,646. At $3,625 a year, your total after-tax interest expense would be $18,125. Your profit would be $29,521.

Borrowing Against Your Home — Five-Year Period
12% RETURN – 50% TAX RATE – 7.25% INTEREST

	Without Leverage	With Leverage
Loan against home	0	100,000
Total investment	0	100,000
Capital gain (12%)	4,904	76,234
Taxable gain (75%)	3,678	57,176
Tax (50% of taxable gain)	(1,839)	(28,588)
After-tax gain	3,065	47,646
Cash available for investment	18,125	0
Interest expense	0	(18,125)
Increase in equity after five year	$21,190	$29,521

TABLE XIII

Your alternative to borrowing to invest is simply investing the cash you would have had to use to pay the interest on your loan. In this case, $3,625 invested every year would grow to $23,029 at the end of five years ($18,125 capital and $4,904 capital gain). This would result in an increase in equity after five years of $21,190. Borrowing to invest gives you the higher return — but you've exposed yourself to much greater risk.

Leverage is sometimes used even by very conservative investors. For example, an individual with a locked-in investment, such as a GIC, might decide to borrow against it to buy equity funds with the intention of paying off the loan when the GIC matures.

Many people started leverage programs while the lifetime capital gains exemption was in place, often tying their leverage program to interest-generating investments. This allowed them to reduce their cumulative net investment loss to take full advantage of their lifetime exemption. With the end of the lifetime exemption in February such programs should be re-examined.

No "tax-free" withdrawals
A gimmick promoted by some fund salespeople – and one you should avoid – is the so-called "tax-free" withdrawal from RRSPs. It is a misnomer. Any money withdrawn from an RRSP is taxable.

What these salespeople really propose is a loan to purchase mutual funds. This loan is often secured by a mortgage although demand loans are also common with the interest payments financed by withdrawals from the client's RRSP. Because interest for investment purposes is deductible, the interest deduction offsets the increase in taxable income that stems from pulling money out of the RRSP. In the end, the client's tax bill remains the same – but the RRSP withdrawal is definitely taxable.

The idea behind the "tax-free" withdrawal, other than boosting sales commissions, is to convert a portfolio that will be fully taxed on withdrawal to one that will be taxed at capital gains rates.

This strategy is far too risky for most people, especially those approaching retirement and whose major investment assets are their RRSPs. It converts a conservative investment program which is designed to finance retirement to one that leaves the investor exposed to unpredictable results if interest rates move higher.

When to use leverage

Leverage can be used successfully in some circumstances to meet specific objectives. For example, you might decide that you want to use part of your investment assets for speculation, perhaps 10 percent of the total. You could earmark these for specialty funds, such as gold funds, which you expect to do much better than broad-based funds in the short term. Alternatively, you might decide to borrow an amount equal to 10 percent of your investment assets and use the loan to buy a specialty fund in the hope of making a substantial gain of 50 percent or more within a year.

Just remember that the funds that are top performers in one period may turn out to be among the worst performers in a later period. As a result, be prepared to be nimble. And don't invest with borrowed funds for speculation unless you can afford to take a loss.

Also, don't second guess your fund manager. It makes little sense to borrow money to buy a fund that is heavily invested in cash because its manager believes the market is vulnerable. The time to use leverage is when your fund manager is bullish.

Trading mutual funds

You can make a lot of money by simply buying funds and holding them for a long time. A single investment of $10,000 earning 12 percent a year and held for thirty years would be worth almost

$300,000. Investing $2,000 a year for thirty years at an average return of 12 percent would build to $540,000. In fact, most fund management companies recommend a buy-and-hold strategy.

Their argument is that the fund manager makes the decisions necessary to maximize gains and preserve capital, moving into those industry groups that offer the most potential at any given time and building cash when the market looks like it is going to move lower.

Some investors take a different tack. Rather than buying and holding, they trade funds. They try to buy in at the beginning of a trend and to sell at the top to lock in profits. People who invest this way are called market timers. They may trade their whole fund portfolio. Or they may trade only the specialty funds such as gold funds, energy funds or Japanese funds – groups that tend to have wide swings in rates of return over relatively short periods. The success of market timers depends on their own skills or those of their advisors. If you are going to trade funds, however, investigate trading costs before you start your program.

As a general rule, there is no charge to switch within a no-load group of funds. Among the groups selling load funds, the commission varies from group to group. Some do not charge for switching. Several have a maximum charge of 2 percent. Some other fund management companies state that the maximum commission applies when switching. However, most commissions are negotiable and most switching within groups can be done for commissions of 2 percent or less. Switching costs also vary among fund families with declining redemption fees. In some cases there is a service charge for switching. In others exchanges are not looked at as redemptions. It is all a matter of understanding the rules before you commit your funds.

If your fund portfolio includes funds of a number of management groups, your trading costs could be higher. Even so, you are unlikely to pay full commissions. Again, commissions are negotiable and you should be able to establish a rate with your dealer that reflects the volume of turnover in your portfolio. Some salespeople offer funds at zero commission but charge a transaction fee.

A bit of advice: If you are going to trade funds, become familiar with the portfolios of the funds you plan to trade. You wouldn't want to cash in a specific fund because of worries about market direction, only to find out later that the manager had similar concerns and had moved to a heavy cash position to preserve capital. In the same vein, you wouldn't want to sell 20 percent of a Canadian equity fund to buy a gold fund, only to find out later that your manager had taken a 20 percent position in gold stocks. You can get the portfolio information from the latest fund quarterlies or your fund sales representative.

Diversification

Diversification is a very important investment concept. By diversifying your investments, you spread your risk. If one investment goes sour, it is more than offset by the other investments you hold. Mutual funds are diversified portfolios – a mutual fund that invests in stocks would generally have a minimum of twenty different stocks.

Even so, you may want to diversify your fund holdings because you're concerned about tying your fortunes to a single manager, one market or one class of assets.

You can diversify a portfolio of mutual funds in two ways. The first is by asset mix, using different types of funds such as Canadian equity, American equity, fixed income and global investments. The second is by using two or more funds of the same type but different investment strategies – if one manager does poorly the others will carry the day.

Diversification by asset mix is fairly common and makes sense. Many people will hold a Canadian equity fund and a fixed income fund in their RRSP and hold a global fund and an American fund outside their RRSP. The actual mix depends largely on their age, the capital available and how much exposure they want in a given class of assets or a specific market.

Diversification within a specific type of fund also makes sense. However, many investors who diversify within a specific type of fund fail to meet their objective. They or their advisors neglect to look at the portfolios or the managers of the funds they buy. Consequently, they end up with two or more funds with similar portfolios and management styles. An extreme irony would be purchasing two Canadian equity funds offered by competing fund organizations but which, in fact, have the same fund manager.

CHAPTER 10

Fees, Loads and Commissions

IT'S IMPORTANT TO DEVELOP an understanding of all the fees and costs connected with mutual fund investment. First, they vary widely. Second, they can have a significant impact on the rate of return earned.

Fees and charges can be broken down into two broad categories: sales commissions and administrative and management fees. In some cases they overlap so that part of the administrative fee is, in reality, on-going compensation to a salesperson for either selling you a fund or for giving you continuing service. Until recently, many major fund groups withheld a portion of the commission paid when you purchased a fund with an acquisition fee. This was used to finance incentive programs and advertising. But whether costs are included as sales commissions or administrative fees, they affect your net returns from holding mutual funds.

Sales fees have become more complex in recent years. In addition to the traditional no-load funds, which don't charge any commission, and the front-end load funds, which can be bought only on payment of an acquisition fee, there are funds that have flat redemption fees, funds that have declining sales charges and funds that have ongoing sales charges. Some funds even combine two types of sales fees so you'll pay a fee when you buy and when you redeem. A number of groups give you the option of buying either with an acquisition fee or a declining deferred redemption fee. Others have cloned their front-end load funds and offer a group with declining sales charges but with higher management fees. A few funds have registration fees or administration fees.

Rates of return published in the *Financial Times of Canada* and similar tables do not take sales fees into consideration but do account for all administrative and management fees charged to the fund. If the published rate of return for a fund is 15 percent and its management fee is 2 percent, the fund actually returned 17 percent. The return that investors realize is 15 percent.

Management fees range from about 0.75 percent to more than 3 percent. They include the fees paid to the portfolio manager and they may also include the expenses of operating the fund. In some cases they reflect compensation paid to the salesperson. Funds must disclose all compensation and incentive arrangements in their prospectuses, a requirement introduced by the Ontario Securities Commission in 1987. Over the past decade many mutual fund companies have offered various types of incentives to boost sales, a practice that is common in many industries. These incentives have ranged from giving salespeople small appliances for opening new accounts to providing fur coats or educational conferences on luxury ocean liners or in exotic foreign resorts. These incentives have disappeared for the most part. Instead, fund companies now tend to compete on commissions.

No-load funds

Some funds do not carry any up-front sales fee or back-end redemption fee. Funds offered or sponsored by banks and trust companies generally, but not always, fall into this category. A few fund management companies offer these no-load funds through investment dealers as well as directly to investors. The fund companies compensate the dealer by paying them part of the management fee for as long as the client holds the fund. This payment, which ranges from 0.25 percent to 1 percent of the value of the client's holding, is called a "trailer." Most load funds also pay trailers.

Rear-end load funds

During late 1989 and early 1990 many fund companies modified their commission schedules and dealer compensation programs. Competition from banks and trust companies which do not charge acquisition fees forced many fund companies to introduce declining deferred redemption fees as an option for purchasers. With these, you don't pay a commission when you buy into a mutual fund; all your money is invested for you. But, even though you don't pay an acquisition fee, the fund company pays your broker a commission of about 4 to 5 percent. You will have to pay a redemption charge only if you redeem within a specific period. The fee is highest in the first year and tapers down to zero, usually after seven years. The fee differs between fund groups but usually ranges from about 5 per cent if you redeem within one year of purchase down to 1 percent if you redeem in the seventh year. If you redeem after the seventh year, you won't have to pay any redemption fee. These fees vary widely and are not negotiable. The redemption fee on Maritime Life Growth Fund, for instance, is 10 percent on first-year redemptions and declines by 1 percent a year until it reaches zero after the tenth year.

Typical Back-End Charges	
Year of Redemption	Charge
During first year	4.5%
During second year	4.0%
During third year	3.5%
During fourth year	3.0%
During fifth year	2.5%
During sixth year	2.0%
During seventh year	1.0%
After that	nil

TABLE XIV

Some brokers and dealers were initially reluctant to introduce their clients to funds with deferred declining sales charges because they were used to charging up to 9 percent. This reluctance has disappeared for the most part because of competitive pressures from banks and trust companies and their no-load funds. In fact, most funds sold in the past year have been rear-end load.

Different fund groups have different bells and whistles. For instance, in some cases the redemption fee applies to the value of units at the time the investment was made, rather than the market value at the time of the redemption. Dividends reinvested may be exempt from the redemption fee and shares purchased with reinvested dividends are considered the first shares redeemed. You may also get exchange privileges within a fund group without triggering redemption fees. Also you may get the privilege of redeeming up to say, 10 percent of your holdings a year without triggering a redemption fee. This is an important privilege for someone who has an automatic withdrawal plan or who holds fund units inside a registered retirement income fund.

Load funds

No-load funds are a minority in Canada, but their numbers are growing as more banks and trust companies jump into the fund business. As well, declining deferred redemption fee sales have become increasingly important to funds which are sold by brokers and

Typical Equity Fund Commission Schedule

Amount Paid	Maximum sales charge
Up to $14,999	9%
$15,000 to $24,999	8%
$25,000 to $49,999	7%
$50,000 to $99,999	5%
$100,000 to $249,999	4%
$250,000 to $499,999	3%
$500,000 to $999,999	2%
$1 million and over	1%

TABLE XV

dealers. Still, a substantial portion of fund business written each year is in load funds — funds that pay a commission to the dealer or broker who places the order.

The most common form of load funds is the front-end load fund, which requires payment of a commission of up to a maximum 9 percent. Virtually all front-end load funds have tapered commission schedules, with the commission charged declining according to the size of the purchase.

There is no standard commission schedule and each mutual fund company can taper its commission rates in a different way. There can even be differences between the funds managed by one company. Typically, a fund would charge a maximum commission of 9 percent on purchases of up to $24,999 and 7 percent on purchases of $25,000 to $50,000; 5 percent on purchases from $50,000 to $100,000; 3 percent on $100,000 to $250,000; 2 percent on $250,000 to $500,000 and 1 percent on anything greater. Several preferred dividend funds have maximum commission rates of 5 percent. Some dealers will add up the purchases made within a year for commission-calculating purposes to give clients the commission rate that would be paid if all the purchases had been made at once. Mutual Investco Inc. calculates sales charges on lifetime purchases of all funds in the Mutual group of funds.

Negotiating commissions

Commissions charged on front-end load funds are generally negotiable. The phrase in the prospectus is "maximum sales charge" or "not to exceed." This phraseology allows a salesperson to discount commission to reflect a client's purchase of several funds so that the commission charged would be the same as if the client put all of his or her money in one fund. As well, it creates a competitive environment in which some brokers and salespeople are more willing to cut commissions than others. They might, for instance, accept a

3 percent commission on a $5,000 order rather than the maximum 9 percent. Of course, a broker who accepts 3 percent on a small order is unlikely to provide any service other than filling the forms and accepting your cheque.

Most people choose a deferred declining redemption fee fund. However, some people will choose front-end load funds for one of a variety of reasons. They might be active traders and a reduced front-end load is cheaper than redeeming a deferred-load fund after several months. Or, they might just want the flexibility of being able to move without concern about hefty penalties.

Discount stockbrokers will generally place an order for half the maximum commission noted in a fund prospectus. But most dealers will cut commissions drastically if they aren't expected to provide any advice or service. As a group, stockbrokers are more likely to cut commissions than independent salespeople. But there are no hard rules. Many salespeople won't cut commissions other than to reflect the dollar value of a client's purchases. These salespeople usually provide detailed financial planning and feel they are compensated for their efforts only if they charge full commissions. Some financial planners do not charge any commission, receiving their compensation on a fee-for-service basis by the client and a trailer from the fund company.

The sale of load funds without the load is becoming very popular among sophisticated investors. These investors are well aware that they can buy no-load funds from banks and some fund companies and they believe that the size of their accounts justifies a substantial discount. Some dealers have been advertising the sale of load funds without a commission. In some cases they'll charge a one-time registration fee, perhaps $45, and provide little if any advice. Their compensation comes from the fund company through the payment of a trailer. The latest twist involves level-load funds for which the client pays a small acquisition fee, perhaps 1 percent, when they buy and a small redemption fee if they sell within a year. In this case, the broker would receive an extra 1 percent trailer each year.

Redemption fees

A handful of funds charge a flat fee when you redeem units. It can be a small amount, as is the case with Associate Investors Ltd., which charges a 1 percent redemption fee. Most funds can charge a redemption fee of up to 2 percent if an investor who paid less than

2 percent commission then redeems within a short time, usually within one year of purchase. In some cases management has the option of waiving this fee. This is often done as a good-will measure and depends on the circumstances.

Paying at both ends

A few fund groups such as the Viking Group of Funds charge a commission both when you buy and when you sell. Viking Group of Funds has a 3.5 per cent commission on purchases of all Viking Funds up to $25,000, and a redemption fee using the same scale. The total sales and redemption fee cannot exceed 9 percent of the amount invested.

Many fund groups apply a charge if you want to transfer your money to another fund within the group. Others allow transfers free of charge. While the fee can be as much as full commission rates, many groups charge a 2 percent fee for a transfer.

Management expense ratio

All fees, other than direct and some indirect sales fees and specific fees such as RRSP trustee fees, are almost always reflected in the management expense ratio. This ratio, expressed as a percentage of total assets, includes the management fee and the expenses paid by the fund. Some funds pay all expenses out of the management fee. Others charge the expenses directly to the fund. However, the management expense ratio is all-inclusive and allows comparisons among funds.

There is one company that charges some fees, such as management fees, directly to the client rather than to the fund. (This is an exception to the rule.) However, its published rates of return are net of fees. Consequently, investors can make valid comparisons. Management expense ratios vary widely. For some equity funds they are as low as 0.75 percent; others exceed 3 percent. Most range from 1.5 percent to 2.75 percent. Indeed, management expense ratios have been rising in recent years. Management expense ratios for income funds are marginally lower. Many fund groups have raised their management fees in recent years to reflect rising costs, including sales costs such as trailer fees (see next section). Consequently, management expense ratios have been rising for some but not all funds. While management expense ratios are reflected in fund rates of return, it is important for investors to make any necessary adjustments to historical rates of return to keep them in perspective. Funds disclose their latest five years' management expense ratios in their annual reports.

The management expense ratio is important because it is often the only part of a performance number that is predictable. For instance, few investors are going to worry about whether a management expense ratio is 1.5 percent or 2.5 percent if a fund's long-term rate of return is 15 or 16 percent. But, in years when the markets are lacklustre or show negative returns, a one percentage point difference in management expense ratio becomes significant.

Trailer fees

Another shift in the mutual fund industry is toward trailer fees. Trailer fees are paid by management on an ongoing basis to the selling broker to encourage the broker to continue to service the client and to discourage switching. Trailer fees are usually one-quarter of the management fee but can be as much as one-half.

If you've purchased your mutual fund units from one dealer and later switch your account to another firm, your trailer will move to the new firm provided your account shows you are dealing with the second firm. Therefore, a fund salesperson may insist you have all your dealings under one roof.

If you've purchased funds and aren't happy with the advice you're getting, find a salesperson with whom you feel comfortable. Even if you don't purchase additional funds, the salesperson may be happy to give you advice, provided the funds in question pay a trailer and he or she becomes involved with your account.

Trailers are a point of contention in the industry. Some want them banned entirely as a hidden charge, while others argue they are a payment made by the fund company, not the client, to encourage ongoing service. Provincial securities commissions are likely to require the fund industry to provide more detailed disclosure about trailers and the investors' rights, if any, to direct them.

Distribution fees

The move to funds sold with deferred declining redemption fees, or rear-end loads, has caused a profit squeeze on fund companies that sell through intermediaries. To cover the cost of paying sales commissions, some fund groups have raised management fees. Others have launched funds sold only with redemption fees and charge a heftier management fee than their comparable funds sold with acquisition fees. A few are trying a different approach. They continue to offer funds with either an acquisition fee or redemption fee; however, clients who choose to buy on the redemption fee basis are charged a distribution fee of about 0.5 percent. This fee is taken from their accounts when the fund makes a dividend distribution. If the dividend is not high enough to cover the fee, units are redeemed from the client's account.

Additional fees

Depending on the funds you hold, you may face additional charges. A few funds have nominal charges for pre-authorized purchases or cheques issued on redemption. Trustee fees for RRSPs are an additional charge for virtually all funds and are charged against your account or billed separately. The point is, fees vary widely, so you should know what they are before you commit to buy.

All fees are fully disclosed in a fund's prospectus and should be considered by an investor. If you examine a fund with a distribution fee, remember that it is not reflected in rates of return published in the business press. When comparing two funds sold with redemption fees – where one charges a distribution fee and the other does not – the rate of return for the fund with a distribution fee should be reduced by 0.5 percent in order for the comparison to be valid.

Load versus no-load

Every fee you pay will affect your final return. Table XIII compares the growth of an investment of $10,000 over thirty years in three funds which have different types of sales charges. Each fund earns the same rate of return of 14 percent before sales charges and management fees. The figures show what investors would receive if they redeemed at the beginning of any year.

The first fund is a front-end load fund with a management expense ratio of 2.3 percent, so its compound rate of return is 11.7 percent. The management expense ratio is the average for Canadian equity funds sold with front-end loads. We will assume the investor paid a 5 percent front-end load.

The second fund has a deferred declining sales charge of 4.5 percent in the first year decreasing by 0.5 percent each year to zero in the ninth year. This fund has a management expense ratio of 2.6

Comparing Load and No-Load Funds

Yr.	Front- End Load	Back- End Load	No Load	Yr.	Front- End Load	Back- End Load	No Load
1	$ 9,500	$ 9,550	$10,000	16	$ 49,948	$ 50,498	$ 58,518
2	10,612	10,694	11,250	17	55,792	56,255	65,833
3	11,853	11,976	12,656	18	62,320	62,668	74,062
4	13,240	13,410	14,238	19	69,611	69,812	83,319
5	14,789	15,016	16,018	20	77,756	77,771	93,734
6	16,519	16,813	18,020	21	86,853	86,637	105,451
7	18,452	18,826	20,273	22	97,015	96,513	118,632
8	20,611	21,078	22,807	23	108,366	107,516	133,461
9	23,022	23,600	25,658	24	121,045	119,773	150,144
10	25,716	26,422	28,865	25	135,207	133,427	168,912
11	28,725	29,434	32,473	26	151,026	148,638	190,026
12	32,085	32,790	36,532	27	168,697	165,582	213,779
13	35,839	36,528	41,099	28	188,434	184,459	240,502
14	40,033	40,692	46,236	29	210,481	205,487	270,564
15	44,717	45,331	52,016	30	235,107	228,912	304,385

TABLE XVI

percent (an actual average), so its compound rate of return to the investor is 11.4 percent.

The third fund is a no-load fund with a management expense ratio of 1.5 percent, so its compound rate of return is 12.5 per cent.

The table suggests that, all other things being equal, investors who expect to hold a fund for a long time and are choosing between a front-end load fund and a deferred declining-sales-charge fund with a higher management fee are better off paying the front-end load. Of course, if the fund company gives you a choice of front-end or rear-end load on the same fund, which is the trend, and you are a long-term investor you are better off with the declining-sales-charge option, unless you can negotiate a zero front-end commission.

If the choice is between a front-end load fund and a no-load fund, the decision depends on the difference in management fees. A no-load fund has the advantage for at least twenty-five years, even if its management expense ratio is one-quarter point higher.

Your best buy is a no-load fund with a low management fee, ignoring the value of service and advice you receive when buying a load fund. Very few funds meet this description.

Investors shouldn't shop on the basis of price alone. The decision to purchase a fund should be based on the securities in which the fund invests and the expertise of the manager. Arguments can be made for allowing costs to determine the choice of fund, but many people who haven't the time to continuously follow their investments are probably better off getting professional advice – and paying for it.

CHAPTER 11

How to Pick a Fund

INDIVIDUAL INVESTORS AND fund advisors spend hours agonizing over performance figures, attending information meetings and reading annual and quarterly reports and prospectuses searching for something that will help them pick one fund over another.

Unfortunately, there is no way you can know for certain that any one fund will outperform another. The best you can do is choose funds whose investment policies are compatible with your own and which have performed well over time, particularly in the same type of market conditions you currently face (or whose current managers have demonstrated acceptable performance under similar market conditions).

The first thing you have to do is determine what type of fund meets your objectives. If you want long-term capital growth tied to the Canadian economy, look at Canadian equity funds. If you want stable growth based on income within your RRSP, look at bond funds, mortgage funds or both.

Examine past performance

Most funds are sold on their past performance. But past performance is not a perfect indicator of future performance. It may be a fair indication of how a specific manager performed under certain market conditions but it is not a guarantee.

A performance figure is a fund's rate of return or average rate of return over a specific period of time. If you look at several ending dates you'll likely find different funds among the top performers. You should also realize that many funds have grown from a few million dollars to hundreds of millions, a growth that could impact on both the fund manager's investment strategy and performance. The management styles and stock market trading responsible for

LISTINGS FOR THE PERIOD ENDED JUNE 30, 1994

Canadian Equity Funds

RETURN	VOLATILITY	FUND NAME	RRSP / RRIF ELIGIBILITY	TOTAL ASSETS $M	NAVPS	DISTRIBUTIONS	FEES	MER	TOTAL RETURN			AVERAGE ANNUAL COMPOUND RETURN			
									1-MONTH	3-MONTH	6-MONTH	1-YEAR	3-YEAR	5-YEAR	10-YEAR
**	AV-	Admax Canadian Performance Fund	R	10.4	5.65		O	2.46*	-6.5	-7.7	-9.0	-2.5	6.1	NA	NA
***	AV-	All-Canadian CapitalFund	R	14.6	11.89		F	2.00*	-5.1	-4.6	0.4	7.8	9.8	7.0	8.0
***	AV-	All-Canadian Compound(C)	R	13.3	16.14		N	0.00*	-5.1	-4.6	0.4	8.1	9.7	7.0	8.0
NA	NA	All-Canadian ConsumerFund	R	1.2	3.49		F	1.97*	-6.2	-4.6	0.0	5.7	NA	NA	NA
****	AV+	Altafund Investment Corp.	R	136.5	17.39		N	2.28*	-3.7	2.4	4.6	2.3	23.1	NA	NA
****	AV	Altamira Capital Growth Fund	R	108.3	12.48	0.010	N	2.03*	-5.9	-4.4	-3.0	6.6	15.5	11.0	10.4
*****	AV+	Altamira Equity Fund	R	1616.1	27.82		N	2.37*	-4.8	-3.3	-1.1	0.4	29.8	24.0	NA
NA	NA	Altamira North American Recovery	R	109.3	11.08		N	2.37*	-6.3	-6.2	-3.3	NA	NA	NA	NA
****	AV+	Altamira Special Growth Fund	R	354.7	15.26		N	1.81*	-6.7	-10.6	-13.0	-9.8	23.2	17.4	NA
*	LOW	Associate Investors Ltd.	R	7.8	7.04	0.090	N	2.06	-4.8	-6.8	-7.2	0.2	5.6	3.3	8.6
*****	HIGH	ABC Fundamental Value Fund(R)	R	65.3	9.76		N	2.00	-4.7	-3.9	5.2	38.2	32.4	25.7	NA
**	AV-	AGF Canadian Equity Fund	R	466.5	10.47		O	2.38*	-7.0	-8.6	-9.4	1.2	6.7	1.8	7.9
****	AV+	AGF Growth Equity Fund Ltd.	R	384.7	18.68		O	2.38*	-7.2	-9.1	-8.1	3.0	23.2	12.9	12.0
****	AV+	AIC Advantage Fund	R	146.6	19.67		D	2.73*	-9.4	-13.9	-18.7	10.1	18.8	12.1	NA
**	AV-	AMI Private Capital Equity	R	2.4	12.15		N	1.75*	-5.5	-5.1	-4.7	4.3	6.5	2.4	NA
*	LOW	Batirente - Section Actions(R)	R	1.4	13.21		N	1.61	-5.5	-5.7	-7.7	-0.8	2.2	0.1	NA
*	AV	Beutel Goodman Canadian Equity Fund	R	14.6	11.36		N	2.50*	-5.6	-3.0	-2.3	8.3	4.7	NA	NA
***	LOW	Bissett Canadian Equity Fund(R)	R	7.2	19.72		N	1.41	-7.1	-7.3	-7.2	0.2	11.5	8.3	10.9
NA	NA	Bissett Small Cap Fund(R)	R	5.6	19.20		N	1.50	-7.5	-7.5	-6.5	6.7	NA	NA	NA
****	AV	Bullock Growth Fund	R	174.0	3.48		O	2.25	-6.5	-8.4	-5.9	2.4	15.1	8.1	8.2
NA	NA	BNP (Canada) Equity Fund	R	8.6	28.52	0.024	N	2.45	-6.1	-5.2	-6.3	-2.8	NA	NA	NA
**	AV+	BPI Canadian Equity Fund	R	9.5	12.10		O	2.81*	-5.7	-8.2	-5.1	-3.5	7.9	3.6	NA
***	LOW	BPI Canadian Equity Value Fund	R	214.8	6.51		O	2.45*	-5.5	-6.1	-6.3	-3.7	9.7	7.2	NA
****	AV	BPI Canadian Small Cap Fund	R	89.1	7.45		O	2.60*	-5.8	-3.6	-5.1	-1.6	17.1	10.0	NA
NA	NA	C.I. Canadian Growth Fund	R	334.5	6.12		O	2.45	-6.3	-5.3	-4.2	7.3	NA	NA	NA
***	AV+	C.I. Sector Canadian Fund	F	13.0	5.01		O	2.45	-6.2	-5.3	-4.2	6.4	9.2	2.4	NA
****	AV+	Cambridge Growth Fund (Sagit Mgnt)	R	83.4	8.76		O	2.66*	-6.8	-10.3	-14.5	-4.4	14.2	10.6	15.8
***	HIGH	Cambridge Special Equity (Sagit)	R	12.3	8.48		O	2.66*	-8.8	-12.1	-17.3	-14.8	8.5	0.2	NA
**	AV-	Canada Life Canadian Equity S-9	R	299.0	104.09		R	2.00	-4.2	-4.9	-5.9	0.9	7.8	3.6	10.0
****	AV+	Canada Trust Everest Special Equity	R	430.6	17.79		N	2.09	-7.3	-11.7	-15.0	-5.3	13.9	8.7	NA

SOURCE: FINANCIAL TIMES OF CANADA

TABLE XVII

superior performance when a fund was small may not work as well in a larger fund.

Performance information is widely available. The *Financial Times of Canada, The Globe and Mail Report on Business, The Financial Post, Les Affaires* and some of the major newspapers owned by Southam Corporation publish monthly performance tables. While the information varies among publications they all report performance figures covering short-term changes as well as one-year, three-year, five-year and ten-year annual compound rates of return which assume all income in reinvested. Average annual compound rates of return are a more accurate method of measuring performance than simply taking the average annual performance of the fund. Performance tables also include some sort of volatility measure or ranking. Some provide phone numbers of the fund management company or the name of the fund manager.

Both Southam and the Financial Times of Canada publish two products – computer software and detailed books sold in three-ring binders – widely used by mutual fund professionals and, to a lesser extent, by individual investors.

The Financial Times BellCharts mutual fund disk and the Southam Sourcedisk are software packages which can be used on an IBM or compatible computer. These disks contain mutual fund data that is updated monthly. They provide historical performance information in a format that allows investors to sort and to rank funds in hundreds of different ways. You can study all of the funds that are on the disks or you can narrow your study by tagging funds of particular interest or selecting funds by establishing criteria. You could, for example, rank Canadian equity funds with assets equal to or greater than $25 million and a five-year average annual compound performance of at least 10%. The Financial Times disk also allows you to compare funds on a scattergraph that charts both the volatility and returns of funds. Both disks also provide information on individual funds.

The Southam Sourcebook contains performance information as well as details covering such items as commission rates, trustee fees, the names of the fund managers and the addresses of the management companies. The Mutual Fund Book published by Financial Times BellCharts contains not only the historical performance, fees and administrative details of more than 800 funds, it also examines the market outlook, portfolio strategy and investment style of the fund managers.

A third mutual fund software package is from Portfolio Analytics Limited. Its Paltrak Pro computer disk database provides detailed information on about 900 funds.

Most people who work in the fund business emphasize the longer-term rates of return, arguing that most investors buy funds as long-term investments. They feel that many investors are misled by short-term performance. However, short-term performance is also important because it can act as an indicator of a change in a manager's investment strategy. For instance, if a top-performing fund started to lag behind its competition in a rising market, it might indicate that the manager is building cash in anticipation of a market correction. If your fund starts to fall behind other performers, you might want to investigate. It could mean a change in investment strategy or it could signal something more serious, such as a change in fund manager.

It makes sense to look at performance over various periods of time if you're holding for long-term growth. If a fund has good long- and short-term performance but poor medium-term performance, don't reject it outright. Try to determine why performance fluctuated. It's possible the manager called the market wrong for a relatively short period but then corrected the error. Even though the error in strategy was corrected, it will be reflected in the performance figures for several years.

When judging the performance of specialty funds, particularly volatile ones such as golds and Japanese funds, short-term performance figures are probably more important than long-term figures. You are more likely to buy specialty funds for a relatively short-term hold and your decision will probably be based on how the fund has done recently rather than over ten, five or even three years.

If you're considering a relatively new fund, you only have short-term performance to examine. Remember, there is little correlation between short-term and long-term performance. If you buy a fund for its short-term performance, don't be surprised if its long-term performance fails to meet your expectations. In fact, some investors buy funds that have good long-term performance but which have lagged the pack recently. Their view is that every dog has its day.

If you ask your broker, fund dealer or a fund company for information about how well a fund has performed relative to competing funds, you'll probably get a copy of a performance table from the *Financial Times* or similar table. However, some dealers prepare detailed studies of funds.

In addition to performance, you should also consider volatility, particularly when considering funds whose objectives are growth or a combination of growth and income. If you are trying to decide between two funds as long-term investments and they have similar performance histories, the fund with the lower volatility would be your choice.

On the other hand, if you're looking for a short-term trading position, you might want the fund that has shown the largest swings in performance as measured by the volatility rating. Funds which tended to have large swings in the past will likely be the funds that have large swings in the future. If you're nimble you can buy low and sell high.

Look at the fund's attributes

Another way to choose a fund is by examining the fund's attributes – specific characteristics such as its yield, cash component, size of companies in its portfolio – and choosing one whose attributes match your views on market. For example, if you believe interest rates will decline sharply you would look for a bond fund whose average maturity is ten years or greater rather than a fund which is primarily invested in treasury bills and bonds which mature within five years.

Investors who expect a period of economic expansion would choose funds which are growth oriented rather than invested in mature companies. Conversely, investors who expect a recession would invest in funds which have defensive characteristics, such as a high component of cash and high-yielding stocks.

Portfolio Analytics Limited of Toronto has looked at this issue closely, arriving at the conclusion that differences in fund performance result primarily from the allocation of assets and, within asset types, management style or strategy. It has also concluded that future performance will be affected more by a fund's current attributes than its past performance. By analysing the holdings within fund portfolios Portfolio Analytics determines the attributes of different funds, information which investors can then use in making their decisions.

Investors who want a diversified portfolio of funds would look at fund attributes so they can choose funds which complement, rather than duplicate, each other. For example, they might pick a fund invested in companies with small capitalization as a balance against a fund invested in mature, large-cap companies.

Who is the manager?

You and your fund advisor should also look at who is managing the fund and consider his or her experience. This information is available from most fund management companies. Indeed, many sales people place more emphasis on the manager than on the fund's performance record. After all, it doesn't make sense to buy a fund on the basis of its ten-year performance if the person who was responsible for that performance has left for another job. Similarly, it doesn't make sense to reject a fund with poor performance if a new manager with a superior track record has just been put in charge.

Besides looking at the manager, look at the management organization. Is there adequate back-up if the manager takes a vacation or quits? What type of analytical support is behind the manager? There is nothing wrong with investing in a fund whose manager has little back-up. Just be prepared to be nimble if the manager leaves.

When should I switch?

No manager is infallible. From time to time a manager may make a bad decision that has an impact on performance. A manager may build cash prematurely in a rising market and consequently underperform the competition. Or, he or she may not sell soon enough and tumble with the general market.

Don't make a decision to sell on the basis of short-term performance. You should, however, determine whether the manager has corrected any misjudgments and is back on track. It can be difficult to know whether the manager has, in fact, made an error. Some managers habitually "sell too soon," only to outperform their competition in the subsequent market downturn. Three to five years is probably the minimum period over which to judge a fund manager.

What you can expect

Pick up the financial pages of any newspaper and you'll likely see ads for mutual funds. Generally, the results they display are impressive. In 1989 when long-term rates were high, many showed ten-year average annual compound rates of return of 16 percent, 18 per cent, even 22 percent. Some ads for newer funds emphasize short-term performance that may be significantly higher. During the summer of 1992 few funds were advertising long-term rates because they were much lower.

There aren't any guarantees that future results will be similar to past performance. However, historically, people who have invested for long-term growth using equity funds have done better than people who invested in guaranteed investments. Moreover, people who have invested in equity funds have outpaced inflation.

Over the ten years ended June 30, 1987, the average annual compound rate of return for Canadian equity funds was 17.2 percent, while the average return for bond and mortgage funds was 11.1 per cent. In comparison, an investment in Government of Canada treasury bills would have given an average return of 11 per cent. Using the ten years to June 30, 1988, which includes the October 1987 crash, the average return for Canadian equity funds was 14.5 percent, still substantially above a T-bill return of 11.1 percent. For the ten years ended June 30, 1989, the average return for Canadian equity funds was 12.6 percent; for the ten years ended June 30, 1990, the return was only 9.5 percent. However, July 1980, was near a market cycle peak. The stock market declined 39.2 percent in the twelve months ended June 30, 1982. Even without a crystal ball it was predictable that the ten-year rate of 13.5 percent for the period ended June 30, 1992 would be higher than the June 1990 ten-year rate and the June 1991 ten-year rate of 8.5 percent.

No one can predict the rates of return that funds will achieve. But given the structure of the economy, it seems safe to say that people who buy equities for the long term will continue to do better than people who take less risk and buy fixed-income investments.

Legal registration of funds

Open-end funds are either mutual fund corporations, mutual fund trusts or insurance company variable life policies. Their common element is an underlying portfolio of securities or investments, which determines the share or unit value of the fund.

It doesn't really matter to most investors which of the three they own. But there are some subtle differences, particularly with insurance company variable life policies, that can have a bearing on making investment decisions.

For tax purposes, mutual fund trusts must "flow through" to investors all Canadian dividends, interest and capital gains. It would also flow foreign income through to investors but it would generally charge expenses against foreign income and interest income to reduce the potential tax liability of unitholders.

Mutual fund corporations also flow through Canadian dividends and capital gains. However, they are not allowed to flow through interest and foreign income. Rather, it is taxable in the fund's hands. But mutual fund corporations generally charge expenses against interest income and foreign income, thus cutting their tax liability.

There are some circumstances in which a mutual fund corporation's Canadian income can become taxable in the fund's hands rather than flow through to shareholders. If 25 percent or more of the shares of a mutual fund corporation are held by one shareholder, an unlikely event, its income would be taxable. Similarly, if 25 percent or more of its income is interest income, it would be taxable in the corporation's hands. This can happen if a fund manager, anticipating a declining stock market, holds a major portion of the portfolio in treasury bills and other short-term investments.

Having income taxed in the fund's hands is a disadvantage for RRSP holders, who would pay no tax if the income were flowed through. Even so, on a per-unit basis this is of little consequence, especially when weighed against the alternative of not preserving capital in a falling market.

Mutual fund corporations must hold annual meetings but trusts do not. This is not a significant difference since both mutual fund corporations and trusts must issue detailed annual and semi-annual financial statements to investors. Most of them issue quarterly reports as well. Trusts generally don't issue certificates, although many will on request. This is of little importance to most people. In fact, certificates can be a bother, particularly if you have distributions automatically reinvested to buy additional units in a fund. After a few years you could end up with a stack of certificates. Alternatively, you would be constantly having your certificates replaced to reflect your increased holdings.

In some circumstances having certificates can be helpful. If you borrow money from a bank using your fund holdings as security, the bank may want the certificate as security for the loan. However, the certificate isn't really necessary. You can assign the units as collateral so that the bank's name would appear on the fund's list of unitholders. Virtually all fund management companies have procedures covering this and can explain them to bank or trust company managers, if necessary.

All in all, it makes little difference whether you hold units in a mutual fund corporation or mutual fund trust.

In fact, in July 1994, after years of overtures to Ottawa by the funds industry, the Finance department announced a proposed change in the Income Tax Act which would allow fund companies to merge mutual fund corporations and trusts with similar objectives. In the past transfers from a corporation to a trust triggered capital gains. It is likely that over the next few years mutual fund corporations will be merged into mutual fund trusts so that all mutual funds will flow dividends, interest, and realized capital gains through to unitholders.

Creditor-proof funds

Insurance company segregated funds are effectively insurance policies on which the value varies with the underlying assets. On the death of the investor or at maturity, the holder of the policy or his or her estate receives either the market value of the policy or 75 percent of the value of contributions, whichever is greater. Moreover, as an insurance policy, the investment can be made creditor-proof under certain circumstances by designating a beneficiary within the immediate family. Also, these policies give holders the option of rolling the funds into an annuity at guaranteed rates, although these rates are generally quite low.

For tax purposes, dividends, interest and capital gains received by insurance company segregated funds are flowed to investors.

All funds have similar mechanisms to protect investors. The fund portfolio is the property of the investors, not the fund management company, and the securities are held by a custodian, generally a bank or trust company. The portfolio is not part of the assets of the fund management company and cannot be used by the manager to support its business. If the fund management company goes bankrupt, the investors in the funds are protected.

Avoiding commissions

Should you buy a no-load fund and avoid commissions? The answer depends on your own personal situation. In some cases the answer is "absolutely." In other cases it's a definite "no." In many cases it's a "maybe." It all depends on your objectives, how much work you do on your own and whether you need professional advice. Moreover, with the choice of funds available with deferred declining sales charges, redemption fees, or zero loads, the question is becoming academic in many cases, especially when management fees are comparable.

Some no-load fund groups have employees who can provide advice. But the majority of fund specialists sell load funds or funds with redemption fees and are paid commissions. If you decide to use a broker or fund specialist, make sure the person you pick has the expertise and can provide a level of service that justifies the commission you pay.

As far as performance is concerned, no-loads, as a group, are just as good as load funds. Both groups include funds that are excellent performers as well as funds that are poor performers. In fact, some investment managers manage both types of funds, but the funds are marketed through different distribution companies.

If you are a sophisticated, experienced investor who knows what you want, then by all means buy no-load funds and save yourself the commission (or negotiate the commission on a load fund down to a handling fee). Even if you aren't an investment wizard but have a good idea which funds suit your objectives – perhaps you want a bond fund for your RRSP or a mortgage fund for income – then check out the no-loads offered by the banks and trust companies with which you deal. Just make sure the portfolios are compatible with your view on the direction of interest rates.

The vast majority of no-loads are offered by banks and trust companies. However, a handful of investment counsellors such as Sceptre Investment Counsel Ltd. offer no-loads directly to the public. As well, several organizations such as the Canadian Medical Association and Ontario Teachers' Group offer families of funds to their members.

If you buy a fund from a bank or trust company the quality of advice you'll get, if any, depends on the expertise of the individual who comes to the counter. This can be a hit-or-miss situation, depending on the experience and education of the institution's employee. Recognizing the need for quality information, some banks and trust companies have made significant investments in training their employees.

Securities regulators have taken steps to improve the proficiency of bank and trust company funds salespeople. As well as the IFIC mutual fund course and the Canadian Securities Institute course, regulatory authorities accept for registration requirements courses offered by the Institute of Canadian Bankers and Trust Companies Institute.

The onus is on you to determine whether the person advising you has sufficient training and experience. It is generally a good idea to ask for the manager. And don't be too shy to ask what training he or she has. Just remember that if you use no-load funds you've assumed the responsibility of monitoring performance and making changes to your fund portfolio when necessary. You've also assumed the task of making sure the portfolio of funds you've chosen meets your needs and objectives.

CHAPTER 12

How to Pick an Advisor

THE MAJORITY OF FUND owners in Canada buy funds through an intermediary. It can be an investment dealer or stockbroker, a mutual fund specialist, a trust company employee, or an insurance agent selling insurance company segregated funds or mutual funds.

Some intermediaries will sell funds offered by several fund management companies; others will sell only a single group of funds. Firms that advertise themselves as independent dealers, such as Regal Capital Planners Ltd., offer funds from many of the major fund management companies. In contrast, sales representatives employed by Investors Group, or its subsidiary Investors Syndicate Ltd., will offer only the Investors funds, although this may be changing. Similarly, many insurance agents will sell only the specific family of funds that is affiliated with their insurance company. Stockbrokers will generally offer funds from the major fund management companies. In addition, some will offer funds affiliated with their firms. It's expected that brokerage houses owned by banks may soon be distributing bank-managed mutual funds along with other funds.

Should you use an advisor who offers a single family of funds or someone who offers many? All advisors will, or should, offer you the best they have. The question is whether a sales representative handling a single family of funds has the best. Similarly, many independents handle only a few fund groups which may or may not be the best for you. While many fund companies have top performers, none has a monopoly on top performance in all types of funds – RRSP equity, RRSP bond, foreign equity, specialty funds and so on. An independent salesperson who handles many funds has access to a wider range than a captive representative who has only a single family to offer. Further, many of the top-performing funds are available only through independent salespeople. But as the ranking table indicates, some of the funds sold only through captive sales forces have done quite well, as have some of the no-load funds.

Of course, there is nothing stopping you from dealing with more than one sales organization and indeed many people do have several dealers.

Much depends on the individual sales representative and whether he or she can tailor a fund portfolio to suit your needs. The key point is that if you are going to need advice and guidance, the salesperson you choose must be an expert. A mutual fund specialist, whether employed by an investment dealer, independent fund sales organization, insurance agency or part of a captive sales force should have a detailed understanding of how to use funds to meet clients' objectives. He or she should monitor fund performance closely and be in touch with fund management companies to be aware of any changes in strategy or investment personnel that may have an impact on client returns.

While there is a tendency among many fund salespeople not to second-guess portfolio managers, some salespeople demand detailed explanations of current investment policy. This helps them determine whether specific funds continue to meet the criteria on which they base their recommendations. Take the time to choose your fund advisor carefully and with thought. Making the wrong choice can be financially and emotionally expensive.

Licensing requirements

Sales of mutual funds are regulated by provincial securities commissions. Firms selling mutual funds must meet certain capital requirements and their officers and managers must demonstrate specific levels of expertise. Individuals selling mutual funds must also meet certain standards.

To receive registration to sell mutual funds, individuals must complete an investment course. Salespeople who are employed by investment dealers must have completed the Canadian Securities Course. This course covers the investment spectrum but includes a section on mutual funds. It also meets the requirement for licensing of people employed by mutual fund dealers. The Canadian Investment Funds Course is designed specifically for people seeking registration to sell mutual funds and as additional education for people who are registered to sell securities. The banking and trust companies associations have their own educational programs which meet licensing requirements for their employees.

The Canadian Investment Funds Course is sponsored by the education division of the Investment Funds Institute of Canada. IFIC is the umbrella organization of the fund industry and is recognized as such by provincial securities commissions. The educational standards of the industry are constantly being upgraded. However, the quality of people giving advice on mutual funds varies widely, just as in any other profession. It's up to you to determine whether a specific fund salesperson meets your needs.

If you do most of your own work and know specifically which funds you want, almost any dealer can handle your order at a discounted commission. If you only want your purchase order executed and nothing else, expect to pay between one-third and one-half of the maximum commission in the fund prospectus for the amount of money you're investing, although some firms will execute the order at zero commission plus a handling fee of $25. If you buy funds with a declining deferred redemption fee you will not get a break on the redemption fee whether you buy from a full service or discount broker.

If you want full service, including detailed advice and monitoring of your holdings, and you are buying funds sold only with an acquisition fee expect to pay higher commissions – up to, but not necessarily, the full rates. Full service should include an analysis of your investment objectives and needs along with recommendations on the funds that meet your requirements. Many sales representatives will confine their analysis to your investment needs; others will extend their analysis to every aspect of your finances including your life insurance needs, tax returns, pension plans and personal balance sheet.

You should determine in advance what type of ongoing service you can expect from a fund salesperson. Is his or her analysis of funds limited to reviewing rates of return? Or does the analysis include reviews of portfolio managers' investment strategies and comparisons with other funds? Many fund salespeople do this on their own, while others depend on specialists within their firms to do this work. It is essential that your advisor have access to this type of information on a continuous basis in order to advise you when conditions have changed. Your advisor should be able to give you detailed explanations behind all purchase recommendations, especially those that involve switching funds. He or she should also provide you with periodic statements of your holdings and their performance, generally monthly or quarterly, depending on how active you are in the market.

The use of personal computers has allowed many fund salespeople to develop their own report packages. These often include monthly statements showing how your funds have performed. Other reports include such items as projected returns using recent performance figures along with account histories and performance summaries of each fund held plus a detailed portfolio summary and performance comparison of clients' holdings.

Not every investor wants detailed reports. What it really comes down to is making sure that you are comfortable with the salesperson you choose. Do his or her recommendations fit your investment objectives? Do they take into consideration your other investment holdings? Have the risks been explained in detail? Will your situation be monitored constantly and, if so, how? Will you get service even if you don't make any subsequent purchases? Does your advisor have substantial investment or business experience? Unfortunately, many fund salespeople may not fully appreciate the risks involved in the strategies they recommend.

Financial planning

Many people selling funds call themselves financial planners. However, financial planning is unregulated except in Quebec. Anyone can call himself or herself a financial planner, whether or not they have any financial expertise. The fund industry is trying to set some standards. The Canadian Institute of Financial Planning, which is affiliated with IFIC, has developed a program of six correspondence courses. Successful completion of the course leads to the designation of chartered financial planner.

A voluntary association of financial planners, the Canadian Association of Financial Planners, has been formed as an industry group and has also set standards for membership. And provincial securities commissions have been considering registering financial planners as a separate category. Should the commissions proceed – and there is a wide range of opinion in the fund industry about whether they should – they will likely require that people who call themselves financial planners show their expertise either through completing specific courses or by demonstrating relevant experience.

CHAPTER 13

Inside the Prospectus

WHILE VIRTUALLY EVERY fund uses glossy sales material to promote itself, the offer to sell fund shares or units is made only through the fund's prospectus. This is a legal document that discloses all pertinent information about the fund.

When you first inquire about a fund you may be given the prospectus or, more likely, the condensed prospectus summary statement. No-load funds routinely send out prospectuses in response to requests for information. But many load funds do not because their salespeople prefer to stick with the more easily understood brochures.

When you actually get down to buying a fund, the seller is required by law to provide a prospectus, the latest annual financial statements and subsequent quarterly statements, if any. Generally, these will be mailed to you along with the slip confirming your purchase order.

Most people don't bother to read prospectuses and financial statements and, frankly, most people are not any worse off since they can get enough information from sales material or their salesperson. Nevertheless, you might take the time to at least skim through the prospectus.

Each fund actually files two prospectuses, the second being a shorter form or summary statement of the first. This summary prospectus includes the main points of the full prospectus in plain language. Real estate funds are the exception. They file only the full prospectus.

The shorter version was introduced in response to requests from the fund industry in the belief that a condensed version would not only save the funds money on postal and printing costs but would also more likely be read by investors.

If you request a prospectus or agree to invest in a fund, you'll almost certainly receive the shorter version. Even if you don't want to read it thoroughly, leaf through the first couple of pages of the section that summarizes the document.

There are a number of areas you can look at quickly. Make sure the fund's investment policies and objectives are compatible with yours. It's also important that you understand the sales charges, if any, and whether they are negotiable. You should also be aware of ongoing management fees. Every fund has management fees that, with the rare exception, are charged to the fund and not to individual investors. Management fees cover the cost of portfolio management and certain other expenses of running a fund. Since they can vary widely and have a significant impact on the rate of return you receive, you should look at the explanation of how these fees are calculated and paid.

Some funds absorb all expenses, such as legal and audit fees, as part of their management fees. Others charge certain expenses directly to the fund. If you want to compare directly expenses of different funds, check the management expense ratio. This takes into account all fees charged to the fund, excluding brokerage commissions, and allows for direct comparisons among funds in most cases. A few funds charge some ongoing sales fees directly to their clients.

The summary prospectus begins by telling you that it is only an outline of the information you should have before making a decision to buy and that additional information is available in the prospectus or annual information form, which you can get by writing to the issuer.

The summary prospectus also explains your statutory rights. Generally speaking, you can back out of an agreement to buy mutual fund shares or units within two days after receipt of the simplified prospectus or within forty-eight hours of receiving the confirmation of the purchase of such securities. Very few people use this right of rescission. But if you read the prospectus and you find that the fund's investment objectives aren't compatible with yours or that the fund is undesirable for any other reason, you have the right to withdraw from your agreement to purchase.

You have other rights, too. Some provinces provide for cancelling the purchase and allow for damages if the prospectus includes misrepresentations. There are time limits, however, on exercising these rights.

The next item in a prospectus is the name and address of the fund and information on its incorporation. This is followed by a brief summary of the fund's investment policies.

The summary statement may include a section outlining risks. This isn't included in all short-form prospectuses. Rather, it is required only if a fund is speculative or has significant risk factors. The value of all funds, except money market funds, will fluctuate with changes in the value of their underlying securities. This is disclosed in all summary prospectuses. However, not every fund calls this a risk factor.

Following the summary statement is a description of the shares or units, which provides information on dividend rights, voting rights and the like.

Other important items include how the manager calculates the price at which sales are offered and redeemed, how the shares will be distributed, as well as information on minimum purchases and sales charges, management fees, dividend records, the tax consequences of sales, rules governing dividends and redemptions. Every prospectus will provide the name and address of the auditor.

Since the rules on exactly where all this information must appear aren't rigid, some of this information may be found in the annual report, rather than the summary statement.

ii

CHAPTER 14

The Largest Funds

TO MAKE THE TASK OF choosing a fund easier, we have included a list of 200 of the largest funds offered in Canada within eight categories. This is not to say you should restrict your search to these 200 funds. But the list is representative of the almost 900 funds currently offered in Canada. Before you begin comparing funds, go through the following steps before deciding on a particular investment:

1. Get your financial house in order. Make sure your insurance needs are taken care of, your will is up to date, personal debts are paid off and your affairs are structured so you don't pay any more taxes than necessary. Eliminating your personal debts is the best high-return, no-risk investment you can make. Also, make sure you understand how different types of investment income are taxed so you can keep taxes to a minimum.

2. Next, list your specific investment objectives, such as saving for retirement, saving for your children's education or maximizing current income. With this in mind, choose the fund type or types that are most suitable for your goals. Remember, the shorter the time frame, the more conservative you should be. Conversely, if you can invest for the long term, it's to your advantage to take some risk.

3. Then, decide on the strategies that can help you meet your objectives. These might include opening an RRSP to save for retirement; beginning a dollar-averaging plan; opening a withdrawal plan; or even borrowing money to invest.

4. At this point, decide whether to make all your own investment decisions or to seek an advisor. If you decide to use an advisor, make sure he or she is an experienced specialist who stays on top of developments in the fund industry and understands your objectives.

5. Finally, understand all the costs associated with your investment and the criteria used to choose a specific fund. Costs

vary widely and can have a significant impact on rates of return. The time to investigate is before you buy a fund not after. Two other things: make sure that a fund's objective is compatible with your personal objectives and don't forget to compare a fund's performance with other funds that have similar objectives.

How the listings work

The funds are listed within six groups and ranked by assets which the funds managed on June 30, 1994. These lists give you much of the information you need to pick a suitable fund:

• Funds are ranked on their average monthly performance over the past thirty-six months. The top 10 percent in a category earn five stars. The bottom 10 percent earn one star.

• The variation in a fund's monthly rate of return, the standard deviation, is used to rank the volatility of funds in each category from HIGH to LOW.

• Whether the fund can be registered as an RRSP or as a RRIF.

• The assets under management expressed in millions of dollars. (We've also included the net asset value per share.)

• At what point the sales fee, if any, is applied and the commission options.

• The management expense ratio. This is the ratio of management and other administrative fees charged to the fund as a percentage of a fund's total assets.

• The total return, over the six months and one year periods to June 30, 1994, as a percentage change in the value of the investment with reinvestment of distributions.

• The compound returns represent the average annual returns with reinvestment of distributions over the three, five and ten year periods to June 30, 1994.

In chapter fifteen the funds are ranked by performance. In appendix two you'll find the total returns for 890 mutual funds in each twelve-month period ended June 30 going back to 1985. These periods include some of the strongest markets as well as some weak ones. This enables you to determine and compare how funds performed in both bull and bear markets. Finally, the fund management companies are listed in chapter sixteen so that you can call or write to the company for a prospectus and financial report.

Twenty-five Largest Canadian Equity Funds

Return	Vol.	Fund Name	RRSP Elig.	Assets $Mil.	NAVPS	Fees	MER	- Total Return % -		- Compound Return % -		
								6 mo.	1 yr.	3 yr.	5 yr.	10 yr.
★★★	LOW	Trimark RSP Equity Fund	R	1757.4	7.3	D	2.00*	-3.3	8.8	10.9	8.3	NA
★★★★★	AV+	Altamira Equity Fund	R	1616.1	27.8	N	2.37*	-1.1	0.4	29.8	24.0	NA
★★	LOW	Investors Retirement Mutual Fund	R	1572.5	11.7	B	2.1	-1.8	5.3	7.2	4.1	9.6
★★★	AV-	MD Equity Fund	R	1335.9	11.3	N	1.0	-1.4	11.0	12.2	7.2	12.5
★★★★	LOW	Investors Canadian Equity Fund	R	1318.9	8.9	B	2.1	-2.2	5.3	12.3	8.8	10.7
★★	AV+	Industrial Growth Fund	R	1244.0	15.7	O	2.48*	-4.1	4.2	8.0	3.9	10.0
★★	AV	Industrial Horizon Fund	R	1165.2	6.0	O	2.48*	-2.8	6.2	8.0	4.5	NA
★★★	AV-	Royfund Equity Ltd.	R	892.4	25.3	N	2.0	-3.4	5.0	9.7	4.4	9.8
★★★★	AV-	Trimark Canadian Fund	R	832.5	15.2	F	1.56*	-2.7	10.7	13.7	9.7	13.4
NA	NA	Trimark Select Canadian Growth Fund	R	692.5	6.6	O	2.60*	-1.7	9.2	NA	NA	NA
★★	AV	Fidelity Capital Builder Fund	R	648.3	16.6	O	2.21*	-6.8	-2.9	6.3	6.8	NA
★★★	AV-	Canada Trust Everest Stock Fund	R	618.8	14.0	N	1.9	-8.1	0.8	11.3	7.2	NA
★★★★	LOW	Royal Trust Canadian Stock Fund	R	589.5	13.3	N	1.93*	-3.7	2.5	7.1	3.8	7.9
★★★	AV-	Great-West Life Canadian Equity	R	527.4	150.5	N	2.6	-6.1	-3.0	11.3	7.8	NA
★★★	LOW	Investors Retirement Gth. Portfolio	R	490.8	6.5	B	0.2	-0.9	6.3	8.7	5.9	NA
★★★	AV	Manulife Vistafund 1 Equity Fund	R	474.5	12.9	F	1.63*	-1.4	-0.5	8.3	5.3	8.0
★★	AV	Manulife Vistafund 2 Equity Fund	R	474.5	12.4	R	2.38*	-1.8	-1.2	7.5	4.5	7.2
★★★	AV	London Life Canadian Equity	R	472.0	180.2	R	1.50*	-6.9	-1.5	9.8	4.2	10.1
★★★	AV-	AGF Canadian Equity Fund	R	466.5	10.5	O	2.38*	-9.4	1.2	6.7	1.8	7.9
★★★★	AV+	Canada Trust Everest Special Equity	R	430.6	17.8	N	2.1	-15.0	-5.3	13.9	8.7	NA
★	AV	Great-West Life Equity Index Invest	R	419.3	118.3	N	2.6	-7.0	1.6	5.9	2.7	7.5
NA	NA	Global Strategy Canada Growth Fund	R	419.2	17.3	O	2.9	-12.4	0.7	NA	NA	NA
★★★★	AV+	AGF Growth Equity Fund Ltd.	R	384.7	18.7	O	2.38*	-8.1	3.0	23.2	12.9	12.0
★	AV	CIBC Canadian Equity Fund	R	378.1	10.8	N	2.25*	-10.5	-4.7	1.9	2.0	NA
★★★	AV	Manulife Vistafund 1 Cap. Gains Gth	R	373.3	14.6	F	1.63*	-4.1	-2.7	12.6	7.9	10.7

RRSP eligibility: R = 100% eligible, F = eligible as foreign content, N = ineligible. Management expense ratio: An "m" indicates the ratio represents the management fee only. An "*" indicates additional fees might be charged directly to the investor. Fees: n = no sales fees. F = front-end load, D = deferred load, O = optional, B = Both, usually a front-end and back-end fee but can be a redemption fee and a deferred load.

Twenty-five Largest Special Equity Funds

Return	Vol.	Fund Name	RRSP Elig.	Assets $Mil.	NAVPS	Fees	MER	Total Return % 6 mo.	Total Return % 1 yr.	Compound Return % 3 yr.	Compound Return % 5 yr.	Compound Return % 10 yr.
*****	AV-	Altamira Resource Fund	R	506.3	15.2	N	2.36*	-0.5	-5.7	42.5	NA	NA
*	LOW	Investors Real Property Fund	R	392.1	4.5	B	2.1	1.2	-0.3	-0.1	2.4	6.2
****	AV+	Dynamic Precious Metals Fund	R	162.3	2.2	O	2.86*	7.7	23.1	28.3	16.0	NA
**	AV-	MD Realty Fund A Units	R	117.4	11.7	N	1.50m	0.5	-4.6	-12.4	-5.2	2.8
****	AV	Universal Canadian Resource Fund	R	99.3	11.1	O	2.77*	7.5	-0.1	35.8	15.7	9.7
***	AV	AGF Canadian Resources Fund	R	96.4	15.1	O	2.52*	-1.6	-9.2	24.2	14.4	8.0
***	AV	Royal Trust Energy Fund	R	82.9	13.5	N	2.17*	11.1	-7.7	27.3	15.9	9.6
*	AV-	MD Realty Fund B Units	F	66.4	11.3	N	1.50m	4.9	-1.1	-12.0	-5.0	2.5
NA	NA	Global Strategy Div. Gold Plus	R	53.8	7.5	O	2.6	1.3	NA	NA	NA	NA
**	LOW	Royal Trust Precious Metals Fund	R	44.8	13.0	N	2.70*	-5.5	1.0	12.7	5.1	NA
***	AV-	BPI Canadian Resource Fund Inc.	R	36.4	22.8	O	2.50*	-2.6	-9.4	26.3	16.8	10.2
NA	NA	Green Line Science & Tech. Fund	F	32.0	9.8	N	2.6	NA	NA	NA	NA	NA
NA	NA	Green Line Resource Fund	R	30.6	10.7	N	2.2	NA	NA	NA	NA	NA
****	AV	Prudential Natural Resource of Can.	R	29.6	8.6	F	1.77*	1.8	-7.8	33.4	20.5	NA
NA	NA	First Cdn. Resource Fund	R	28.9	9.5	N	2.26*	-11.6	NA	NA	NA	NA
*	LOW	Roycom-Summit TDF Fund	R	27.2	12.3	D	3.29*	5.1	3.9	5.1	6.4	7.8
**	AV	Goldtrust	R	23.4	9.1	F	2.5	5.9	22.0	24.2	13.8	NA
NA	NA	Scotia Precious Metals Fund	R	22.3	10.1	N	2.0	-7.1	NA	NA	NA	NA
*	LOW	Roycom-Summit Realty Fund	F	22.0	12.2	D	3.7	4.1	10.0	5.5	7.2	NA
****	AV+	Dominion Equity Resource Fund Inc.	R	20.9	11.5	R	1.8	4.6	-17.6	30.3	16.2	NA
*	LOW	Royal Lepage Commercial Real Estate	R	20.5	8.4	N	3.2	2.2	-0.4	-1.8	2.0	NA
***	HIGH	Cambridge Resource Fund	R	18.5	3.8	O	2.66*	4.7	-19.9	26.1	11.1	9.8
NA	NA	Scotia CanAm Growth Fund	R	12.1	9.7	N	1.25m	-3.9	NA	NA	NA	NA
***	AV+	Goldfund Ltd.	F	11.8	9.2	F	3.4	7.4	34.6	27.1	16.0	7.8
NA	NA	Universal World Precious Metals	F	11.0	5.0	O	2.00m*	NA	NA	NA	NA	NA

RRSP eligibility: R = 100% eligible. F = eligible as foreign content. N = ineligible. Management expense ratio: An "m" indicates the ratio represents the management fee only. An * indicates additional fees might be charged directly to the investor. Fees: n = no sales fees. F = front-end load, D = deferred load, O = optional, B = Both, usually a front-end and back-end fee but can be a redemption fee and a deferred load.

Twenty-five Largest U.S. Equity Funds

Return	Vol.	Fund Name	RRSP Elig.	Assets $Mil.	NAVPS	Fees	MER	– Total Return %– 6 mo.	1 yr.	– Compound Return % – 3 yr.	5 yr.	10 yr.
★★★★	AV	Fidelity Growth America Fund	F	541.1	18.1	O	2.18*	0.8	8.6	19.8	NA	NA
★★★★	LOW	Investors U.S. Growth Fund Ltd.	F	399.7	20.4	B	2.0	4.7	15.9	18.7	14.3	13.8
★★★	HIGH	Bullock American Fund	F	300.6	18.3	O	2.3	-15.0	-1.4	13.4	18.7	16.9
★★★	AV	Industrial American Fund	F	238.1	11.1	O	2.48*	0.5	11.0	13.5	9.3	11.9
★★★★★	AV+	Altamira Select American Fund	F	215.3	20.4	N	2.35*	-1.8	17.2	26.9	NA	NA
★★★	AV	Phillips, Hager & North U.S. Equity	F	211.2	41.5	N	1.1	-0.5	12.4	16.0	15.1	14.2
NA	NA	Royal Trust Zweig Strategic Growth	F	177.6	14.1	N	2.50*	2.7	13.1	NA	NA	NA
NA	NA	20/20 Aggressive Growth Fund	F	167.4	10.9	O	2.50*	-8.4	8.7	NA	NA	NA
★★★	AV+	AGF Special Fund Ltd.	F	156.3	9.2	O	2.32*	-3.3	7.8	13.3	10.5	12.1
★★★	AV-	London Life U.S. Equity	F	121.8	15.5	R	1.50*	-2.0	4.9	12.4	5.0	NA
★★★★	AV+	GBC North American Growth Fund Inc.	F	116.4	5.4	N	1.8	-9.2	4.6	21.3	10.6	12.2
★★★	AV	AGF American Growth Fund Ltd.	F	104.8	10.1	O	2.29*	-2.0	9.7	13.8	8.5	11.0
NA	NA	Universal U.S. Emerging Growth Fund	F	103.5	6.4	O	3.03*	-11.1	3.6	NA	NA	NA
★★★	AV	Royal Trust American Stock Fund	F	101.8	11.5	N	1.87*	0.1	8.7	13.7	12.1	12.5
★★	AV	Laurentian American Equity Fund Ltd	F	99.5	8.6	O	2.7	0.1	8.5	11.7	6.3	11.6
NA	NA	Canada Trust Everest AmeriGrowth	R	82.0	9.6	N	1.4	-4.1	0.4	NA	NA	NA
★★	AV	Elliott & Page American Growth Fund	F	71.3	12.5	O	1.73*	3.0	8.6	10.8	9.1	8.9
★★	LOW	BPI American Equity Value Fund	F	67.4	6.6	O	2.48*	-0.3	7.3	11.3	9.6	NA
NA	NA	NN Can-Am Fund	R	65.9	9.9	R	2.25*	-4.2	-0.5	NA	NA	NA
NA	NA	MD U.S. Equity Fund	F	61.9	13.1	N	1.0	-2.3	9.6	NA	NA	NA
★★★	LOW	20/20 U.S. Growth Fund	F	55.1	23.0	O	2.48*	-1.2	15.4	14.1	11.4	NA
NA	NA	C.I. American Fund	F	54.2	7.6	O	2.6	0.9	16.5	NA	NA	NA
★★★	LOW	Scotia American Equity Growth Fund	F	47.6	9.8	N	2.3	2.8	11.3	12.0	10.8	NA
NA	NA	Royfund U.S. Equity Fund	F	46.6	14.9	N	2.3	-0.2	11.1	NA	NA	NA
★	LOW	Green Line US Index Fund ($US)	N	42.9	8.1	N	0.6	-3.6	0.6	7.7	8.4	NA

RRSP eligibility: R = 100% eligible, F = eligible as foreign content, N = ineligible. Management expense ratio: An "m" indicates the ratio represents the management fee only. An * indicates additional fees might be charged directly to the investor. Fees: n = no sales fees. F = front-end load, D = deferred load, O = optional, B = Both, usually a front-end and back-end fee but can be a redemption fee and a deferred load.

Twenty-five Largest International Equity Funds

Return	Vol.	Fund Name	RRSP Elig.	Assets $Mil.	NAVPS	Fees	MER	– Total Return %–		– Compound Return % –		
								6 mo.	1 yr.	3 yr.	5 yr.	10 yr.
★★★	LOW	Templeton Growth Fund Ltd.	F	2428.6	7.7	O	1.89*	1.8	23.9	22.6	14.5	15.1
NA	NA	Fidelity Far East Fund	F	1641.0	21.4	O	2.54*	-16.4	24.7	NA	NA	NA
★★★★	AV	Trimark Select Growth Fund	F	1618.7	9.1	O	2.41*	3.2	19.2	21.7	15.0	NA
★★★★	AV	MD Growth Investments Ltd.	F	1509.3	7.3	N	1.0	-0.3	28.4	21.5	12.3	15.8
★★★★	AV	Trimark Fund	F	1149.8	17.8	F	1.54*	4.2	23.2	23.9	15.8	16.6
★★★★★	AV+	Investors Pacific International	F	930.2	11.5	B	2.2	-9.1	43.6	28.6	NA	NA
★★	LOW	Investors North American Growth	F	898.0	11.7	B	2.1	0.8	5.7	14.2	11.5	13.7
★★★★	AV+	C.I. Pacific Fund	F	777.5	17.2	O	2.6	-11.6	36.3	25.1	17.2	20.7
NA	NA	Templeton Emerging Markets Fund	F	717.5	8.2	O	3.1	-6.1	29.5	NA	NA	NA
★★★★	AV	C.I. Global Fund	F	674.7	9.4	O	2.6	-0.6	19.6	19.5	14.1	NA
NA	NA	Fidelity European Growth Fund	F	624.8	13.1	O	2.63*	2.5	22.7	NA	NA	NA
NA	NA	Altamira Asia Pacific Fund	F	589.2	16.4	N	2.38*	7.3	31.4	NA	NA	NA
NA	NA	AGF Asian Growth Fund Limited	F	550.0	13.5	O	2.65*	-11.0	38.7	NA	NA	NA
NA	NA	CIBC Far East Prosperity Fund	F	510.1	9.6	N	2.8	-20.5	NA	NA	NA	NA
★★	HIGH	Investors Japanese Growth Fund Ltd.	F	482.7	20.5	B	2.1	28.7	30.4	18.8	8.3	14.9
★★★	AV-	Investors Global Fund Ltd.	F	478.8	8.7	B	2.1	6.7	23.4	15.2	11.5	NA
★★★★	AV+	Templeton International Stock Fund	F	461.7	9.3	O	2.5	3.2	32.8	25.6	15.0	NA
NA	NA	C.I. Latin American Fund	F	444.3	10.8	O	2.9	-9.6	NA	NA	NA	NA
NA	NA	C.I. Emerging Markets Fund	F	443.6	8.6	O	2.9	-12.1	30.5	NA	NA	NA
★★★	AV-	Fidelity International Portfolio	F	426.1	17.2	O	2.57*	6.1	19.7	17.6	13.1	NA
★★	AV	Investors European Growth Fund	F	415.3	6.6	B	2.2	0.3	18.6	13.1	NA	NA
NA	NA	Investors World Growth Portfolio	F	400.6	6.8	B	0.4	3.9	18.5	NA	NA	NA
★★★	LOW	Cundill Value Fund Ltd.	F	324.7	16.8	F	2.0	7.2	23.4	19.2	10.2	12.4
★★	LOW	Laurentian Commonwealth Fund Ltd.	F	301.1	8.4	O	2.7	2.1	14.0	13.6	9.0	12.8
NA	NA	Trimark - The Americas Fund	F	289.9	5.6	O	2.85*	0.5	11.7	NA	NA	NA

RRSP eligibility: R = 100% eligible, F = eligible as foreign content, N = ineligible. Management expense ratio: An "m" indicates the ratio represents the management fee only. An * indicates additional fees might be charged directly to the investor. Fees: n = no sales fees. F = front-end load, D = deferred load, O = optional, B = Both, usually a front-end and back-end fee but can be a redemption fee and a deferred load.

Twenty-five Largest Balanced Funds

Return	Vol.	Fund Name	RRSP Elig.	Assets $Mil.	NAVPS	Fees	MER	Total Return % – 6 mo.	1 yr.	Compound Return % – 3 yr.	5 yr.	10 yr.
★★★	AV-	Royfund Balanced Fund	R	2071.3	6.8	N	2.3	-4.3	3.6	11.9	8.7	NA
★★★	AV	Industrial Income Fund	R	1833.9	8.1	O	2.01*	-10.1	-4.1	8.2	6.3	12.3
★	LOW	Investors Income Plus Portfolio	R	1304.9	5.2	B	0.2	-6.3	-0.8	6.5	6.9	NA
★★★	LOW	Investors Retirement Plus Portfolio	R	999.6	6.0	B	0.2	-3.0	3.8	8.2	6.9	NA
★★★★★	AV	Trimark Select Balanced Fund	R	998.8	6.5	O	2.39*	-4.7	5.3	11.7	NA	NA
★★★	AV	Dynamic Partners Fund	R	870.2	7.6	R	2.67*	-4.5	6.7	19.7	13.6	NA
★★★	AV-	London Life Diversified	R	758.1	101.7	R	1.50*	-6.7	-0.5	9.7	7.1	NA
★★★	AV	Canada Trust Everest Balanced Fund	R	752.6	13.3	N	2.1	-8.5	-0.5	8.9	7.4	NA
★	AV	20/20 Canadian Asset Allocation	R	738.2	4.3	O	2.42*	-7.1	4.6	8.2	7.3	NA
★★★	AV	CIBC Balanced Income and Growth	R	671.2	11.5	N	2.25*	-9.6	-2.8	5.5	5.6	NA
★★★	AV	Canada Life Managed Fund S-35	R	646.5	26.8	R	2.0	-6.5	1.3	9.0	6.4	10.5
★★★	AV	Manulife Vistafund 1 Diversified	R	617.3	13.5	F	1.63*	-6.2	-1.7	8.2	6.2	9.2
★★	AV	Manulife Vistafund 2 Diversified	R	617.3	13.0	R	2.38*	-6.5	-2.5	7.4	5.4	8.4
★★★	LOW	Royal Trust Advantage Balanced Fund	R	437.3	12.1	N	1.68*	-4.6	2.3	9.0	7.7	NA
NA	NA	Bullock Asset Strategy Fund	R	385.4	11.1	O	2.3	-6.7	1.6	NA	NA	NA
★★★	AV	Industrial Balanced Fund	R	375.5	5.6	O	2.55*	-7.7	-0.5	8.2	NA	NA
NA	NA	Investors Asset Allocation Fund	R	369.1	4.6	B	2.3	NA	NA	NA	NA	NA
★★★	LOW	Phillips, Hager & North Bal Pens Tr	R	343.2	11.6	N	N/A	-4.6	5.0	10.3	9.2	NA
★★	AV-	Fonds Desjardins Equilibre	R	318.4	11.4	N	2.0	-7.0	1.0	7.9	6.6	NA
★★★★	AV+	Altamira Growth & Income Fund	R	313.9	7.2	N	1.41*	-0.7	8.9	15.1	11.8	NA
NA	NA	Fidelity Asset Manager Fund	F	306.9	11.4	O	2.76*	-4.2	9.3	NA	NA	NA
NA	NA	MD Balanced Fund	R	303.1	11.5	N	1.0	-6.7	4.4	7.8	NA	NA
★★	AV-	Great-West Life Diversified RS Inv.	R	289.8	154.1	N	2.6	-6.2	-0.8	7.8	6.4	NA
★	AV+	First Cdn. Asset Allocation	R	277.2	10.4	N	1.86*	-11.0	-5.6	5.0	4.5	NA
★★	LOW	InvesNat Retirement Balanced Fund	R	276.9	5.4	N	2.97*	-6.8	-3.0	6.6	5.7	NA

RRSP eligibility: R = 100% eligible, E = eligible as foreign content, F = eligible, N = ineligible. Management expense ratio: An "m" indicates the ratio represents the management fee only. An * indicates additional fees might be charged directly to the investor. Fees: n = no sales fees. F = front-end load, D = deferred load, O = optional, B = Both, usually a front-end and back-end fee but can be a redemption fee and a deferred load.

Twenty-five Largest Bond and Mortgage Funds

Return	Vol.	Fund Name	RRSP Elig.	Assets $Mil.	NAVPS	Fees	MER	Total Return % – 6 mo.	1 yr.	Compound Return % – 3 yr.	5 yr.	10 yr.
★	AV-	Investors Mortgage Fund	R	3467.3	4.8	R	1.8	-5.6	-0.7	5.8	7.9	9.5
★★★	AV+	First Canadian Mortgage Fund	R	2407.7	11.4	N	1.02*	-5.0	0.9	7.6	9.9	10.6
★★	AV-	Investors Bond Fund	R	1639.7	4.3	R	1.8	-9.6	-2.6	8.0	8.1	10.9
★★★★	AV+	CIBC Mortgage Investment Fund	R	1590.8	11.3	N	1.50*	-4.3	1.2	8.1	9.7	10.0
NA	NA	Royfund Mortgage Fund	R	1538.8	10.6	N	1.7	-3.2	3.4	NA	NA	NA
★	LOW	Royal Trust Mortgage Fund	R	1230.5	10.3	N	1.94*	-4.9	-0.4	5.9	8.4	9.6
★★★	AV+	Global Strategy Diversified Bond	R	1225.4	10.7	O	2.1	-9.9	-3.3	9.9	NA	NA
★★	AV	Green Line Canadian Mortgage	R	1091.5	10.5	N	1.5	-4.8	1.0	7.4	9.5	10.0
★★★★	AV+	AGF Canadian Bond Fund	R	1010.4	4.7	O	1.37*	-13.0	-3.9	10.3	8.4	11.7
★★★★	AV+	Global Strategy World Bond Fund	F	988.1	10.0	O	2.1	-10.2	-4.3	11.1	8.2	NA
★★★★	HIGH	Industrial Mortgage Securities	R	973.9	1.3	O	1.98*	-7.9	-2.3	9.5	7.4	12.1
★★	AV+	Investors Income Portfolio Fund	R	888.6	5.0	R	0.2	-7.7	-1.8	6.7	7.7	NA
★★★	AV-	Canada Trust Everest Mortgage Fund	R	851.2	57.4	N	1.6	-2.4	3.4	7.7	9.3	10.1
NA	NA	Scotia Mortgage Fund	R	740.3	9.8	N	1.5	-5.1	1.4	NA	NA	NA
NA	AV	Royfund Bond Fund	R	716.6	5.1	N	1.5	-8.3	-1.1	9.3	8.8	10.7
★★★	AV+	Great-West Life Mortgage Investment	R	677.0	151.3	N	2.4	-6.2	-0.6	7.9	8.1	9.6
★★★	AV	Royal Trust Bond Fund	R	630.4	9.3	N	1.38*	-9.4	-1.5	9.3	8.6	11.2
★★★★	NA	Fidelity North American Income Fund	F	600.7	10.0	O	1.75*	-6.8	2.6	NA	NA	NA
NA	NA	InvesNat Mortgage Fund	R	596.4	10.0	N	1.33*	-2.6	3.3	NA	NA	NA
★★★	AV	Canada Trust Everest Bond Fund	R	568.0	10.4	N	1.3	-10.3	-2.8	9.1	8.6	NA
★★	AV	Great-West Life Canadian Bond Fund	R	566.5	147.2	N	2.4	-10.1	-3.6	8.0	7.4	10.0
★★★★★	AV	Phillips, Hager & North Bond Fund	R	473.3	8.2	N	0.6	-9.0	-0.5	10.4	9.9	13.2
★★	AV+	Altamira Income Fund	R	467.1	6.7	O	1.00*	-12.4	-3.1	11.2	10.8	11.9
★★	AV+	Spectrum Interest Fund	R	454.4	9.0	O	1.6	-12.2	-4.6	7.7	7.7	NA
★★	AV+	CIBC Canadian Bond Fund	R	426.9	9.9	N	1.50*	-14.0	-7.2	8.0	7.8	NA

RRSP eligibility: R = 100% eligible, F = eligible as foreign content, N = ineligible. Management expense ratio: An "m" indicates the ratio represents the management fee only. An * indicates additional fees might be charged directly to the investor. Fees: n = no sales fees. F = front-end load, D = deferred load, O = optional, B = Both, usually a front-end and back-end fee but can be a redemption fee and a deferred load.

Twenty-five Largest Money Market Funds

Return	Vol.	Fund Name	RRSP Elig.	Assets $Mil.	NAVPS	Fees	MER	— Total Return %—		— Compound Return % —		
								6 mo.	1 yr.	3 yr.	5 yr.	10 yr.
★★★★	AV	Green Line Canadian Money Mkt	R	1966.3	10.0	N	0.7	2.0	4.2	5.9	8.4	NA
★★★	AV	Royfund Canadian T-Bill Fund	R	1799.0	10.0	N	0.8	1.8	3.7	5.5	NA	NA
★★★	AV	First Canadian Money Market	R	1538.4	1.0	N	0.95*	1.7	3.6	5.4	7.7	NA
★★★	AV-	CIBC Premium T-Bill Fund	R	886.9	10.0	N	0.55*	1.9	3.8	5.4	NA	NA
★★	AV	Royal Trust Canadian Money Market	R	744.7	10.0	N	1.16*	1.7	3.4	5.2	7.6	NA
★	AV	CIBC Money Market Fund	R	694.9	10.0	N	1.20*	1.6	3.3	5.0	7.7	NA
★★	AV	Canada Trust Everest Money Market	R	596.5	10.0	N	0.8	1.8	3.6	5.2	8.0	NA
NA	NA	Scotia Premium T-Bill Fund	R	595.7	10.0	N	0.6	2.0	4.1	NA	NA	NA
★★★	AV	Royfund Money Market Fund	R	417.5	10.0	N	1.2	1.7	3.4	5.4	7.9	8.6
★★★	AV	AGF Money Market Account	R	408.2	10.0	O	0.83*	1.8	3.6	5.4	7.9	NA
★★	LOW	Investors Money Market Fund	R	369.9	1.0	R	1.08*	1.7	3.6	5.2	7.7	NA
★★★★	AV+	Elliott & Page Money Fund	R	344.7	10.0	F	0.56*	2.1	4.3	6.1	8.6	NA
★	AV-	CIBC Canadian T-Bill Fund	R	318.5	10.0	N	1.20*	1.6	3.1	4.8	NA	NA
NA	NA	Scotia Gov. of Can. Treasury Bill	R	294.8	10.0	N	0.8	1.9	3.8	NA	NA	NA
★★★	AV	MD Money Fund	R	277.8	58.1	N	0.5	1.9	4.0	5.6	7.9	8.3
★★★	AV	PH & N Canadian Money Market	R	267.0	10.0	N	0.5	2.0	4.1	5.9	8.4	NA
★★★	AV-	Natcan Treasury Bill Fund	R	255.8	10.0	N	0.87*	1.9	3.8	5.6	NA	NA
★	AV	Great-West Life Money Market Invest	R	251.7	145.4	N	1.7	1.5	3.1	4.9	7.4	8.1
★★	LOW	Spectrum Cash Reserve Fund	R	243.4	1.0	O	1.1	1.8	3.7	5.3	7.8	NA
★★★	LOW	Industrial Cash Management	R	242.5	10.0	F	0.50*	2.0	4.0	5.7	8.2	NA
★★★	AV-	InvesNat Money Market Fund	R	240.7	10.0	N	1.09*	1.8	3.7	5.5	NA	NA
★	LOW	Finsco T-Bill Fund	R	217.8	10.0	F	1.29*	1.7	3.4	5.0	7.5	NA
★★★★★	HIGH	Altamira Short Term Global Income	R	207.7	12.2	N	1.28*	8.0	11.6	12.2	NA	NA
★	AV	Fidelity Short Term Asset Fund	R	200.5	1.0	O	1.00*	1.7	3.3	5.2	NA	NA
★★★	AV-	Trimark Interest Fund	R	188.2	10.0	F	0.75*	1.9	3.8	5.5	8.1	NA

RRSP eligibility: R = 100% eligible. F = eligible as foreign content, N = ineligible. Management expense ratio: An "m" indicates the ratio represents the management fee only. An * indicates additional fees might be charged directly to the investor. Fees: n = no sales fees. F = front-end load, D = deferred load, O = optional, B = Both, usually a front-end and back-end fee but can be a redemption fee and a deferred load.

Twenty-five Largest Dividend Funds

Return	Vol.	Fund Name	RRSP Elig.	Assets $Mil.	NAVPS	Fees	MER	– Total Return %–		– Compound Return % –		
								6 mo.	1 yr.	3 yr.	5 yr.	10 yr.
★★	AV	Investors Dividend Fund	F	2482.0	10.3	B	2.0	-6.4	0.6	7.8	7.1	9.5
★★★★	AV	Investors Mutual of Canada Ltd.	F	442.9	9.8	B	2.0	-3.7	4.3	10.5	7.2	9.7
★★	AV-	Laurentian Dividend Fund Ltd.	R	303.0	7.8	O	2.70*	-6.9	1.0	6.6	5.5	9.4
NA	NA	Royfund Dividend Fund	R	293.3	11.1	N	1.8	-6.7	2.2	NA	NA	NA
★★★	LOW	AGF High Income Fund	R	290.5	9.4	O	1.42*	-4.3	3.6	8.3	7.9	8.3
NA	NA	CIBC Equity Income Fund	R	267.5	10.7	N	2.00*	-10.5	-1.4	NA	NA	NA
★★★★	HIGH	Industrial Dividend Fund Ltd.	R	197.9	9.6	O	2.52*	-2.8	7.1	11.2	3.4	9.8
★★★	AV	Green Line Dividend Fund	R	109.8	12.0	N	2.2	-5.6	1.4	8.8	7.9	NA
★★	LOW	Guardian Preferred Dividend Fund	R	96.6	8.4	O	1.24*	-5.0	1.0	7.8	6.1	NA
★★★	LOW	Dynamic Dividend Fund	R	81.4	5.3	O	1.80*	-4.8	3.0	9.0	7.2	NA
★★	AV	Spectrum Dividend Fund	R	56.0	10.9	O	1.6	-7.1	2.5	5.7	5.5	NA
NA	NA	MD Dividend Fund	R	48.4	10.0	N	1.0	-6.1	2.7	NA	NA	NA
★★★	AV+	20/20 Dividend Fund	R	46.3	11.4	O	2.08*	-6.8	3.6	8.4	6.9	NA
NA	NA	National Trust Dividend Fund	R	34.1	10.5	N	2.2	-6.7	4.1	NA	NA	NA
★★★	AV+	Phillips, Hager & North Div. Income	N	33.9	16.9	N	1.2	-6.5	5.4	8.5	6.9	9.9
★★★★★	AV+	Prudential Dividend Fund of Canada	R	29.4	5.5	F	1.53*	-2.5	9.2	16.0	7.8	NA
★★	AV-	Montreal Trust Excelsior Dividend	R	17.6	9.1	N	1.1	-5.2	2.6	7.2	6.4	NA
★	AV-	Royal Trust Growth and Income Fund	R	15.7	9.2	F	2.80*	-6.0	0.2	5.1	4.0	NA
★	AV-	BPI Income Fund	R	15.0	8.7	F	1.15*	-5.8	1.6	3.9	4.3	6.4
NA	NA	NatCan Dividend Fund	R	11.2	10.2	N	1.63*	-3.4	2.4	NA	NA	NA
NA	NA	Mawer Canadian Income Fund	F	10.5	9.6	N	1.1	-8.4	-1.0	NA	NA	NA
★★★★	AV	Corporate Investors Ltd.	R	8.3	13.2	F	1.35*	-6.8	6.8	10.6	6.0	8.8
NA	NA	Fonds Desjardins Dividendes	R	7.3	8.9	N	1.80m	NA	NA	NA	NA	NA
★★★★	AV-	Dynamic Dividend Growth Fund	R	7.2	4.4	O	1.80*	-5.8	5.2	9.5	5.2	NA
★	AV+	Trans-Canada Income Fund	R	5.4	5.0	O	2.66*	-5.1	6.5	1.3	1.4	9.5
NA	NA	Bissett Dividend Income Fund	F	3.1	10.9	N	1.5	-4.3	3.5	NA	NA	NA

RRSP eligibility: R = 100% eligible. F = eligible as foreign content, N = ineligible. Management expense ratio: An "m" indicates the ratio represents the management fee only. An "*" indicates additional fees might be charged directly to the investor. Fees: n = no sales fees. F = front-end load, D = deferred load, O = optional, B = Both, usually a front-end and back-end fee but can be a redemption fee and a deferred load.

CHAPTER 15

The Best Performers

	Top One-Year Performers	Category	Return
1	Sceptre Asian Growth Fund	International Equity	50.3
2	Multiple Opportunities Fund	Canadian Equity	47.0
3	Investors Pacific International	International Equity	43.6
4	BPI Global Small Companies	International Equity	43.1
5	Hyperion Asian Trust	International Equity	42.0
6	AGF Asian Growth Fund	International Equity	38.7
7	ABC Fundamental Value Fund	Canadian Equity	38.2
8	Regent Tiger Fund	International Equity	38.1
9	Beutel Goodman Intrn'l Equity	International Equity	37.5
10	C.I. Pacific Fund	International Equity	36.3
11	Regent International Fund	International Equity	36.1
12	C.I. Sector Pacific Fund	International Equity	35.7
13	Goldfund Ltd.	Special Equity	34.6
14	Templeton International Stock	International Equity	32.8
15	Regent Korea Fund	International Equity	32.7
16	Royal Trust Japanese Stock	International Equity	32.4
17	Altamira Asia Pacific Fund	International Equity	31.4
18	C.I. Emerging Markets Fund	International Equity	30.5
19	Investors Japanese Growth	International Equity	30.4
20	C.I. Sector Emerging Markets	International Equity	29.9
21	NAL-Investor Global Equity	International Equity	29.6
22	20/20 Asia Pacific Fund	International Equity	29.5
23	Sceptre International Fund	International Equity	29.5
24	Templeton Emerging Markets	International Equity	29.5
25	Universal World Equity Fund	International Equity	29.0
26	MD Growth Investments Ltd.	International Equity	28.4
27	Green Line Emerging Markets	International Equity	27.8

The one-year figures show the percentage rate of return, including dividends and capital gains distributions, for the twelve months ending June 30, 1994.

28	InvesNat Eur. Equity Fund	International Equity	27.6
29	Green Line International Equity	International Equity	27.5
30	General Trust of Canada Intl.	International Equity	27.4
31	Mackenzie Sentinel Global	International Equity	27.0
32	Mawer World Investment	International Equity	26.6
33	First Canadian Int'l Growth	International Equity	26.2
34	Guardian Global Equity (EAFE)	International Equity	26.2
35	Finsco Global Fund	International Equity	25.9
36	20/20 World Fund	Balanced	25.1
37	Canada Trust Everest International	International Equity	25.0
38	Fonds Desjardins International	International Equity	24.9
39	Guardian Pacific Rim Corp.	International Equity	24.8
40	Fidelity Far East Fund	International Equity	24.7
41	HRL Overseas Growth Fund	International Equity	24.7
42	Royfund International Equity	International Equity	24.6
43	Royal Trust European Growth	International Equity	24.5
44	Templeton Growth Fund Ltd.	International Equity	23.9
45	Mutual Premier International	International Equity	23.5
46	Cundill Value Fund Ltd.	International Equity	23.4
47	Investors Global Fund Ltd.	International Equity	23.4
48	Trimark Fund	International Equity	23.2
49	Dynamic Precious Metals Fund	Special Equity	23.1
50	BPI Global Equity Fund	International Equity	23.1
	Highest return for the period		50.3
	Lowest return among all funds for the period		-19.9
	Median return among all funds for the period		3.1
	Average return for all funds for the period		4.7
	Number of funds with one-year history		751

	Top Three-Year Funds	Category	Return
1	Marathon Equity Fund	Canadian Equity	42.7
2	Altamira Resource Fund	Special Equity	42.5
3	Universal Canadian Resource	Special Equity	35.8
4	Multiple Opportunities Fund	Canadian Equity	33.8
5	Prudential Natural Resource	Special Equity	33.4
6	ABC Fundamental Value Fund	Canadian Equity	32.4
7	Dynamic Cdn Growth Fund	Canadian Equity	30.8
8	Dominion Equity Resource	Special Equity	30.3
9	Altamira Equity Fund	Canadian Equity	29.8
10	Investors Pacific International	International Equity	28.6
11	Dynamic Precious Metals Fund	Special Equity	28.3
12	Royal Trust Energy Fund	Special Equity	27.3
13	Goldfund Ltd.	Special Equity	27.1
14	Hyperion Asian Trust	International Equity	27.0
15	Altamira Select American Fund	U.S. Equity	26.9
16	Sceptre International Fund	International Equity	26.8
17	BPI Canadian Resource Fund	Special Equity	26.3
18	Cambridge Resource Fund	Special Equity	26.1
19	Industrial Equity Fund Ltd.	Canadian Equity	25.7
20	Templeton International Stock	International Equity	25.6
21	C.I. Pacific Fund	International Equity	25.1
22	C.I. Sector Pacific Fund	International Equity	24.8
23	Prudential Precious Metals	Special Equity	24.5
24	Goldtrust	Special Equity	24.2
25	AGF Canadian Resources Fund	Special Equity	24.2
26	Trimark Fund	International Equity	23.9
27	University Avenue Cdn Fund	Canadian Equity	23.9
28	BPI American Equity Growth	U.S. Equity	23.4
29	AGF Growth Equity Fund Ltd.	Canadian Equity	23.2
30	Altamira Special Growth Fund	Canadian Equity	23.2
31	Altafund Investment Corp.	Canadian Equity	23.1
32	Templeton Growth Fund Ltd.	International Equity	22.6
33	Mawer New Canada Fund	Canadian Equity	22.5
34	Regent Tiger Fund	International Equity	22.1
35	Regent International Fund	International Equity	21.9
36	Trimark Select Growth Fund	International Equity	21.7
37	MD Growth Investments Ltd.	International Equity	21.5

The three-year, five-year and ten-year rates are the average annual compound rates of return, including dividends and capital gains, for periods ending June 30, 1994.

38	GBC North American Growth	U.S. Equity	21.3
39	Fidelity Growth America Fund	U.S. Equity	19.8
40	Dynamic Partners Fund	Balanced	19.7
41	20/20 World Fund	Balanced	19.5
42	C.I. Global Fund	International Equity	19.5
43	Cundill Value Fund Ltd.	International Equity	19.2
44	C.I. Sector Global Fund	International Equity	19.2
45	Canada Life U.S.&Int. Eqty S-34	International Equity	19.1
46	Finsco Global Fund	International Equity	18.9
47	Investors Japanese Growth	International Equity	18.8
48	Fonds Desjardins International	International Equity	18.8
49	Saxon World Growth	International Equity	18.8
50	AIC Advantage Fund	Canadian Equity	18.8
	Highest return for the period		42.7
	Lowest return among all funds for the period		-12.4
	Median return among all funds for the period		8.2
	Average return of all funds for the period		10.0
	Number of funds with three-year history		594

	Top Five-Year Performers	Category	Return
1	ABC Fundamental Value Fund	Canadian Equity	25.7
2	Multiple Opportunities Fund	Canadian Equity	24.0
3	Altamira Equity Fund	Canadian Equity	24.0
4	Prudential Natural Resource	Special Equity	20.5
5	Marathon Equity Fund	Canadian Equity	20.4
6	Dynamic Cdn Growth Fund	Canadian Equity	19.9
7	Bullock American Fund	U.S. Equity	18.7
8	Sceptre International Fund	International Equity	18.3
9	BPI American Equity Growth	U.S. Equity	17.8
10	Altamira Special Growth Fund	Canadian Equity	17.4
11	C.I. Pacific Fund	International Equity	17.2
12	Mawer New Canada Fund	Canadian Equity	17.1
13	C.I. Sector Pacific Fund	International Equity	16.9
14	BPI Canadian Resource Fund	Special Equity	16.8
15	GBC Canadian Growth Fund	Canadian Equity	16.3
16	Dominion Equity Resource	Special Equity	16.2
17	Dynamic Precious Metals Fund	Special Equity	16.0
18	Goldfund Ltd.	Special Equity	16.0
19	Royal Trust Energy Fund	Special Equity	15.9
20	Trimark Fund	International Equity	15.8
21	Universal Canadian Resource	Special Equity	15.7
22	ABC Fully-Managed Fund	Balanced	15.3
23	PH&N U.S. Equity	U.S. Equity	15.1
24	Templeton International Stock	International Equity	15.0
25	Trimark Select Growth Fund	International Equity	15.0
26	Canada Life U.S.&Int. Eqty S-34	International Equity	14.6
27	Templeton Growth Fund Ltd.	International Equity	14.5
28	AGF Canadian Resources Fund	Special Equity	14.4
29	Investors U.S. Growth Fund	U.S. Equity	14.3
30	C.I. Global Fund	International Equity	14.1
31	Goldtrust	Special Equity	13.8
32	C.I. Sector Global Fund	International Equity	13.8
33	Fonds Desjardins International	International Equity	13.7
34	Dynamic Partners Fund	Balanced	13.6
35	Investors Special Fund Ltd.	International Equity	13.2
36	Fidelity International Portfolio	International Equity	13.1
37	Guardian American Equity	U.S. Equity	13.1

The three-year, five-year and ten-year rates are the average annual compound rates of return, including dividends and capital gains, for periods ending June 30, 1994.

38	Empire International Fund	International Equity	13.1
39	Regent International Fund	International Equity	13.0
40	General Trust of Canada U.S. Equity	U.S. Equity	13.0
41	Mawer World Investment	International Equity	13.0
42	Talvest U.S. Growth Fund Ltd.	U.S. Equity	13.0
43	AGF Growth Equity Fund Ltd.	Canadian Equity	12.9
44	Prudential Precious Metals	Special Equity	12.8
45	Capstone Int. Investment Trust	International Equity	12.7
46	McLean Budden Am. Growth	U.S. Equity	12.4
47	MD Growth Investments Ltd.	International Equity	12.3
48	Guardian Vantage U.S. Equity	U.S. Equity	12.3
49	BPI International Equity Fund	International Equity	12.2
50	Cornerstone Global Fund	International Equity	12.2
	Highest return for the period		25.7
	Lowest return among all funds for the period		-5.2
	Median return among all funds for the period		7.7
	Average return of all funds for the period		7.8
	Number of funds with five-year history		524

	Top Ten-Year Performers	Category	Return
1	C.I. Pacific Fund	International Equity	20.7
2	Bullock American Fund	U.S. Equity	16.9
3	Trimark Fund	International Equity	16.6
4	MD Growth Investments Ltd.	International Equity	15.8
5	Cambridge Growth Fund	Canadian Equity	15.8
6	Canada Life U.S.&Int. Eqty S-34	International Equity	15.1
7	Templeton Growth Fund Ltd.	International Equity	15.1
8	Investors Japanese Growth	International Equity	14.9
9	AGF Japan Fund Ltd.	International Equity	14.7
10	Imperial Growth Cdn Equity	Canadian Equity	14.4
11	PH&N U.S. Equity	U.S. Equity	14.2
12	General Trust of Canada U.S. Equity	U.S. Equity	14.0
13	Investors U.S. Growth Fund	U.S. Equity	13.8
14	Investors North Am. Growth	International Equity	13.7
15	Cambridge Balanced Fund	Balanced	13.7
16	Montreal Trust Excelsior Intl	International Equity	13.4
17	Trimark Canadian Fund	Canadian Equity	13.4
18	Cassels Blaikie American Fund	U.S. Equity	13.3
19	PH&N Bond Fund	Canadian Bond	13.2
20	National Life Fixed Income	Canadian Bond	12.9
21	Universal Americas Fund	International Equity	12.8
22	Laurentian Commonwealth	International Equity	12.8
23	Confed Life C	Canadian Bond	12.8
24	Investors Special Fund Ltd.	International Equity	12.7
25	Trans-Canada Equity Fund	Canadian Equity	12.6
26	Royal Trust American Stock	U.S. Equity	12.5
27	Dynamic Income Fund	Canadian Bond	12.5
28	United Canadian Equity Fund	Canadian Equity	12.5
29	MD Equity Fund	Canadian Equity	12.5
30	Cundill Value Fund Ltd.	International Equity	12.4
31	Confed Fixed Income	Canadian Bond	12.3
32	Industrial Income Fund	Balanced	12.3
33	GBC North American Growth	U.S. Equity	12.2
34	Empire Equity Growth Fund 3	Canadian Equity	12.2
35	AGF Special Fund Ltd.	U.S. Equity	12.1
36	Industrial Mortgage Securities	Canadian Mortgage	12.1

The three-year, five-year and ten-year rates are the average annual compound rates of return, including dividends and capital gains, for the periods ending June 30, 1994.

37	AGF Growth Equity Fund Ltd.	Canadian Equity	12.0
38	United American Growth	U.S. Equity	12.0
39	National Life Equities Fund	Canadian Equity	12.0
40	Altamira Income Fund	Canadian Bond	11.9
41	Industrial American Fund	U.S. Equity	11.9
42	Universal Canadian Bond Fund	Canadian Bond	11.9
43	Talvest U.S. Growth Fund Ltd.	U.S. Equity	11.8
44	Equitable Life Seg. Accum Inc	Canadian Bond	11.8
45	Dynamic Fund of Canada	Canadian Equity	11.8
46	CDA Common Stock Fund	Canadian Equity	11.8
47	AGF Canadian Bond Fund	Canadian Bond	11.7
48	United Canadian Growth Fund	Canadian Equity	11.6
49	Laurentian American Equity	U.S. Equity	11.6
50	United American Equity Fund	International Equity	11.5
51	Cambridge Global Fund	International Equity	11.5
	Highest return for the period		20.7
	Lowest return among all funds for the period		2.5
	Median return among all funds for the period		10.0
	Average return of all funds for the period		10.2
	Number of funds with ten-year history		197

CHAPTER 16

Directory of Fund Management Companies

20/20 Group Financial Inc.
2010 Winston Park Drive
Oakville, Ontario L6H 5R7
(905) 829-2020 (800) 268-8690
Fax: (905) 829-3863
20/20 Aggressive Growth
20/20 American Tactical Asset
  Allocation
20/20 Asia Pacific
20/20 Canadian Asset Allocation
20/20 Canadian Growth
20/20 Dividend
20/20 European Asset Allocation
20/20 Foreign RSP Bond
20/20 High Yield
20/20 Income
20/20 Latin America
20/20 Money Market
20/20 Multimanager Emerging
  Markets
20/20 RSP Aggressive Equity
20/20 RSP Int'l Equity Allocation
20/20 U.S. Growth
20/20 World Bond
20/20 World

**Admax Regent International
  Management Ltd.**
200 King Street West 8th Floor
Toronto, Ontario M5H 3Z8
(416) 971-8416 (800) 667-2369
Fax: (416) 594-8863
Admax American Performance
Admax Asset Allocation
Admax Canadian Income
Admax Canadian Performance
Admax Cash Performance
Admax Global Health Sciences
Polymetric Performance
Regent Dragon 888
Regent Europa Performance
Regent International
Regent Korea
Regent Nippon
Regent Tiger
Regent World Income
U.S. Polymetric Performance

AGF Management Limited
Toronto-Dominion Bank Tower
31st Floor, P.O. Box 50
Toronto-Dominion Centre
Toronto, Ontario M5K 1E9
(416) 367-1900 (800) 268-8583
Fax: (416) 865-4155
AGF American Growth Fund Ltd.
AGF Asian Growth Fund Ltd.
AGF Canadian Bond
AGF Canadian Equity
AGF Canadian Resources
AGF China Focus Fund Ltd. A
AGF China Focus Fund Ltd. B
AGF China Focus Fund Ltd. C
AGF European Growth Fund Ltd. A
AGF European Growth Fund Ltd. B
AGF European Growth Fund Ltd. C
AGF Global Government Bond
AGF Growth Equity Fund Ltd.
AGF High Income
AGF Japan Fund Ltd.
AGF Money Market Account
AGF Special Fund Ltd.
AGF Strategic Income
AGF U.S. Dollar Money Market
AGF U.S. Income
Corporate Investors Ltd.
Corporate Investors Stock Fund Ltd.

AIC Limited
1 Markland Street
Hamilton, Ontario L8P 2J5
(905) 529-5500 (800) 263-2144
Fax: (905) 529-0966
AIC Advantage
AIC Value
AIC World

All-Canadian Management Inc.
P.O. Box 7320
Ancaster, Ontario L9G 3N6
(905) 648-2025
Fax: (905) 648-5422
All-Canadian Capitalfund
All-Canadian Compound
All-Canadian Consumer
All-Canadian Resources Corporation

Altamira Investment Services Inc.
250 Bloor Street East Suite 200
Toronto, Ontario M4W 1E6
(416) 925-1623 (800) 263-2824
Fax: (416 925-8415
Altafund Investment Corp.
Altamira Asia Pacific
Altamira Balanced
Altamira Bond
Altamira Capital Growth
Altamira Diversified
Altamira Equity
Altamira European Equity
Altamira Global Bond
Altamira Growth & Income
Altamira Income
Altamira North American Recovery
Altamira Resource
Altamira Select American
Altamira Short-Term Global Income
Altamira Special Growth
Altamira U.S. Larger Company

AMI Partners Inc.
26 Wellington Street East
Suite 900
Toronto, Ontario M5E 1S2
(416) 865-1985
Fax: (416) 865-9241
AMI Private Capital Equity
AMI Private Capital Income
AMI Private Capital Money Market
AMI Private Capital Optimix

Bank of Montreal Investment Management Limited
100 King Street West P.O. Box 1
Toronto, Ontario M5X 1A1
(416) 927-6000
Fax: (416)867-7305
First Canadian Asset Allocation
First Canadian Bond
First Canadian Equity Index
First Canadian Growth
First Canadian International Bond
First Canadian International Growth
First Canadian Money Market
First Canadian Mortgage
First Canadian Resource
First Canadian Special Growth
First Canadian U.S. Growth

Beutel Goodman Managed Funds Inc.
20 Eglinton Avenue West
Suite 1109
Toronto, Ontario M4R 1K8
(416) 932-6400
Fax: (416) 485-8194
Beutel Goodman American Equity
Beutel Goodman Balanced
Beutel Goodman Canadian Equity

(Beutel Goodman continued)
Beutel Goodman Income
Beutel Goodman International Equity
Beutel Goodman Money Market

Bissett & Associates Investment Management Ltd.
500 4th Avenue S.W. Suite 1120
Calgary, Alberta T2P 2V6
(403) 266-4664
Fax: (403) 237-2334
Bissett American Equity
Bissett Bond
Bissett Canadian Equity
Bissett Dividend Income
Bissett Money Market
Bissett Retirement
Bissett Small Cap

BNP (Canada) Valeurs Mobiliers Inc.
1981 McGill College Avenue
5th Floor
Montreal, Quebec H3A 2W8
(514) 285-2920
Fax: (514) 285-7598
BNP (Canada) Bond
BNP (Canada) Canadian
  Money Market
BNP (Canada) Equity
BNP (Canada) US $ Money Market

BPI Capital Management Corporation

10 Bay Street Suite 1001
Toronto, Ontario M5J 2R8
(416) 861-9811 (800) 263-2427
Fax: (416) 861-9415
BPI American Equity Growth
BPI American Equity Value
BPI Balanced
BPI Bond
BPI Canadian Bond
BPI Canadian Equity
BPI Canadian Equity Value
BPI Canadian Resource Inc
BPI Canadian Small Cap
BPI Global Balanced
BPI Global Equity
BPI Global Real Estate Securities
BPI Global Small Companies
BPI Income
BPI International Equity
BPI Money Market
BPI North American Tactical Asset
   Allocation RSP
BPI One Decision Balanced
BPI Short Term Interest
BPI T-Bill
BPI World Tactical Asset
   Allocation RSP
BPI RSP Bond

Caldwell Securities Ltd.

55 University Avenue Suite 340
Toronto, Ontario M5J 2H7
(416) 862-7755
Fax: (416) 862-2498
Caldwell Securities Associate
Caldwell Securities International

Canada Life Investment Management Ltd.

330 University Ave
Toronto, Ontario M5G 1R8
(416) 597-1456 (800) 387-4447
Fax: (416) 597-9674
Canada Life Canadian Equity S-9
Canada Life Fixed Income S-19
Canada Life International Bond S-36
Canada Life Managed S-35
Canada Life Money Market S-29
Canada Life U.S. & International
   Equity S-34

Canadian Airline Pilots Association

250 Bloor Street East Suite 200
Toronto, Ontario M4W 1E6
(416) 925-1623 (800) 263-2824
Gyro Bond
Gyro Equity

Canadian Anaesthetists Mutual Accumulating Fund Ltd.

94 Cumberland Street Suite 503
Toronto, Ontario M5R 1A3
(416) 925-7331 (800) 267-4713
Canadian Anaesthetists Mutual
   Accumulating

Canadian Dental Association

100 Consilium Place Suite 710
Toronto, Ontario M1H 3G8
(416) 296-9401 (800) 591-9401
CDA Balanced
CDA Bond and Mortgage
CDA Common Stock
CDA Money Market
CDA RSP Aggressive Equity

Canadian International Fund Management Inc.

151 Yonge Street Eighth Floor
Toronto, Ontario M5C 2Y1
(416) 364-1145 (800) 563-5181
C.I. American
C.I. Canadian Balanced
C.I. Canadian Bond
C.I. Canadian Growth
C.I. Emerging Asian
C.I. Emerging Markets
C.I. European
C.I. Global Bond RSP
C.I. Global Equity RSP
C.I. Global
C.I. Latin American
C.I. Money Market
C.I. New World Income
C.I. Pacific
C.I. Sector Canadian
C.I. Sector Emerging Markets
C.I. Sector European
C.I. Sector Global
C.I. Sector North American
C.I. Sector Pacific
C.I. Sector Short-Term
C.I. World Bond

Capstone Consultants Limited

One University Ave Suite 401
Toronto, Ontario M5J 2P1
(416) 863-0687/863-0005
Fax: (416) 863-0841
Capstone Cash Management
Capstone International Investment
  Trust
Capstone Investment Trust

Cassels Blaikie & Co. Limited

33 Yonge Street Suite 200
Toronto, Ontario M5E 1S8
(416) 941-7500
Fax: (416) 867-9821
Cassels Blaikie American
Cassels Blaikie Canadian
Cassels Blaikie International

Chou Associates Management

70 Dragoon Crescent
Scarborough, Ontario M1V 1N4
(416) 299-6749
Fax: (416) 299-6749
Chou Associates
Chou RRSP

CIBC Securities Inc.

Commerce Court Postal Station
P.O. Box 51
Toronto, Ontario M5L 1A2
(416) 980-3863 (800) 268-5666
Fax: (416) 351-4440
CIBC Balanced Income and Growth
CIBC Canadian Bond
CIBC Canadian Equity
CIBC Canadian Income
CIBC Canadian T-Bill
CIBC Capital Appreciation
CIBC Equity Income
CIBC Far East Prosperity
CIBC Global Equity
CIBC Money Market
CIBC Mortgage Investment
CIBC Premium T-Bill
CIBC U.S. Dollar Money Market
CIBC U.S. Equity
Hyperion Asian Trust
Hyperion Aurora Trust

(CIBC continued)
Hyperion European Trust
Hyperion Fixed Income Trust
Hyperion Managed Trust
Hyperion Value Line Equity Trust

Clean Environment Mutual Funds Inc.
70 University Avenue Suite 650
Toronto, Ontario M5J 2M4
(416) 599-9567 (800) 461-4570
Fax: (416) 599-6493
Clean Environment Balanced
Clean Environment Equity
Clean Environment Income
Clean Environment International Equity

Colonia Life Insurance Company
2 Street Clair Avenue East
Toronto, Ontario M4T 2V6
(416) 960-3601
Fax: (416) 323-0934
Colonia Bond
Colonia Equity
Colonia Money Market
Colonia Mortgage
Colonia Special Growth

Confederation Funds Management Inc.
1 Mount Pleasant Rd 9th Floor
Toronto, Ontario M4Y 2Y5
(416) 323-8999 (800) 263-2820
Fax: (416) 323-2254
Confed Growth
Confed Mortgage

Confederation Life Insurance Company
1 Mount Pleasant Rd 10th Floor
Toronto, Ontario M4Y 2Y5
(416) 323-8111
Fax: (416) 323-4191
Confed Equity
Confed Fixed Income
Confed Life B
Confed Life C

CSA Management Enterprises Ltd.
145 King Street West Suite 2700
Toronto, Ontario M5H 1J8
(416) 865-0326 (800) 363-3463
Fax: (416) 865-9636
Goldfund Ltd.
Goldtrust

Canada Trust Fund Services Inc.
161 Bay Street 3rd Floor
Toronto, Ontario M5J 2T2
(800) 668-8888
Canada Trust Everest Amerigrowth
Canada Trust Everest Asiagrowth
Canada Trust Everest Balanced
Canada Trust Everest Bond
Canada Trust Everest Eurogrowth
Canada Trust Everest International
Canada Trust Everest Money Market
Canada Trust Everest Mortgage
Canada Trust Everest North American
Canada Trust Everest Special Equity
Canada Trust Everest Stock
Canada Trust Everest U.S. Equity
Canada Trust Income Investments
Canada Trust Investment-Equity
Canada Trust Investment-Income

Desjardins Trust Inc.
1 Complexe Desjardins C.P. 34
Montreal, Quebec H5B 1E4
(514) 286-5883
Fonds Desjardins Actions
Fonds Desjardins Croissance
Fonds Desjardins Dividendes
Fonds Desjardins Environnement
Fonds Desjardins Equilibre
Fonds Desjardins Hypotheques
Fonds Desjardins International
Fonds Desjardins Monetaire
Fonds Desjardins Obligations

Dominion Equity Resource Fund Inc.
Suite 1710, 205 - 5th Ave S.W.
Calgary, Alberta T2P 2V7
(403) 531-2657
Dominion Equity Resource Fund

Elliott & Page Limited
120 Adelaide Street West
Suite 1120
Toronto, Ontario M5H 1V1
(416) 365-8300 (800) 363-6647
Fax: (416) 365-0520
Elliott & Page American Growth
   Fund Ltd.
Elliott & Page Balanced
Elliott & Page Bond
Elliott & Page Equity
Elliott & Page Money
Elliott & Page T-Bill

Empire Life Insurance Company
259 King Street East
Kingston, Ontario K7L 3A8
(613) 548-1881
Fax: (613) 548-4104
Empire Balanced
Empire Bond
Empire Elite Equity 5
Empire Equity Growth 3
Empire International
Empire Money Market
Empire Premier Equity 1

Equitable Life Insurance Company
1 Westmount Road North
Waterloo, Ontario N2J 4C7
(519) 886-5110 (800) 387-0588
Fax: (519) 886-5314
Equitable Life Canadian Bond
Equitable Life Canadian Stock
Equitable Life Seg. Common Stock
Equitable Life Seg. Accum Inc.

Ethical Funds Inc.
300 The East Mall
Toronto, Ontario M9B 6B7
(416) 232-1262 (800) 267-5019
Fax: (416) 237-9681
Ethical Balanced
Ethical Growth
Ethical Income
Ethical Money Market
Ethical North American Equity

Fidelity Investments Canada Limited
Ernst & Young Tower
222 Bay Street Suite 900
Toronto, Ontario M5K 1P1
(416) 307-5200 (800) 263-4077
Fax: (416) 307-5290
Fidelity Asset Manager
Fidelity Capital Builder
Fidelity Emerging Markets Bond
Fidelity European Growth
Fidelity Far East
Fidelity Global Bond
Fidelity Government Bond
Fidelity Growth & Income
Fidelity Growth America
Fidelity International Portfolio
Fidelity Japanese Growth
Fidelity Latin American Growth
Fidelity North American Income
Fidelity Short Term Asset
Fidelity Small Cap

Finsco Services Limited
110 Yonge Street Suite 500
Toronto, Ontario M5C 1T4
(416) 368-6161 (800) 268-8697
Fax: (416) 368-8300
Finsco Global
Finsco Money Market
Finsco T-Bill
Finsco U.S. Money Market (US $)
Jarislowsky Finsco American Equity
Jarislowsky Finsco Balanced
Jarislowsky Finsco Bond
Jarislowsky Finsco Canadian Equity

First Marathon Securities Ltd.
P.O. Box 21 The Exchange Tower
2 First Canadian Place Suite 3100
Toronto, Ontario M5X 1J9
(416) 869-3707
Fax: (416) 869-3319
Marathon Equity

Fonds des Professionnels du Quebec Inc.
2 Complexe Desjardins #3020
Montreal, Quebec H5B 1G8
(514) 350-5055 (800) 363-6713
Fax: (514) 350-5051
Fonds des Professionnels Balanced
Fonds des Professionnels Bond
Fonds des Professionnels Canadian Equity
Fonds des Professionnels International Equity
Fonds des Professionnels Short Term

GBC Asset Management Inc.
55 University Avenue Suite 616
Toronto, Ontario M5J 2H7
(800) 668-7383
Fax: (416) 366-6833
GBC Canadian Bond
GBC Canadian Growth
GBC International Growth
GBC Money Market
GBC North American Growth

Global Strategy Financial Inc.

33 Bloor Street East Suite 1600
Toronto, Ontario M4W 3T8
(416) 966-3676 (800) 387-1229
Fax: (416) 927-9168
Global Strategy Asia
Global Strategy Bond
Global Strategy Canada Growth
Global Strategy Diversified Americas
Global Strategy Diversified Asia
Global Strategy Diversified Bond
Global Strategy Diversified Europe
Global Strategy Diversified Gold Plus
Global Strategy Diversified Growth
Global Strategy Diversified Japan Plus
Global Strategy Diversified Latin
Global Strategy Diversified Savings
Global Strategy Europe
Global Strategy
Global Strategy Income Plus
Global Strategy Japan Plus
Global Strategy Latin
Global Strategy Real Estate Securities
Global Strategy T-Bill Savings
Global Strategy U.S. Growth
Global Strategy U.S. Savings (US $)
Global Strategy World Bond

Goodman & Company Ltd.

55th Floor Scotia Plaza
40 King Street West
Toronto, Ontario M5H 4A9
(416) 363-5621 (800) 268-8186
Fax: (416)363-1417
Dynamic American
Dynamic Canadian Growth
Dynamic Dividend
Dynamic Dividend Growth
Dynamic Europe

(Goodman continued)

Dynamic Far East
Dynamic of Canada
Dynamic Global Bond
Dynamic Global Green
Dynamic Global Partners
Dynamic Government Income
Dynamic Income
Dynamic International
Dynamic Managed Portfolio Inc.
Dynamic Money Market
Dynamic Partners
Dynamic Precious Metals

Gordon Daly Grenadier Securities

224 Richmond Street West
Toronto, Ontario M5V 1V6
(416) 593-0144 (800) 268-9165
Fax: (416) 593-4922
First Heritage

Great-West Life Assurance Company

60 Osborne Street North
Winnipeg, Manitoba R3C 3A5
(204) 946-1190 (800) 665-0049
Fax: (204) 946-8622
Great-West Life Canadian Bond
Great-West Life Canadian Equity
Great-West Life Diversified RS Invest.
Great-West Life Equity Index Invest.
Great-West Life Equity/Bond Invest.
Great-West Life Money Market Invest.
Great-West Life Mortgage Invest.

Groupe Financier Concorde
850 Place d'Youville
Quebec, Quebec G1R 3P6
(418) 694-0000
Fax: (418) 694-2075
Concorde Croissance
Concorde Hypotheques
Concorde Monetaire
Concorde Revenu

**Guardian Group of Funds
Limited**
Commerce Court West
Suite 3100 P.O. Box 201
Toronto, Ontario M5L 1E8
(416) 364-8341 (800) 668-7327
Fax: (416) 947-0601
Guardian American Equity Fund Ltd.
Guardian Balanced
Guardian Canada Bond
Guardian Canadian Equity
Guardian Canadian Money Market
Guardian Enterprise
Guardian Global Equity
Guardian Growth Equity
Guardian International Balanced
Guardian International Income
Guardian North American
Guardian Pacific Rim Corporation
Guardian Preferred Dividend Fund Ltd.
Guardian U.S. Money Market (US $)
Guardian Vantage U.S. Equity

Guardian Timing Services Inc.
130 Adelaide Street West
Suite 3303
Toronto, Ontario M5H 3P5
(416) 960-4890
Fax: (416) 364-3752
Canadian Protected
First American
Protected American

**Hercules International
Management LLC**
BCE Place 181 Bay Street
Suite 400
Toronto, Ontario M5J 2V8
(800) 567-4525
Fax: (416) 369-7756
Hercules European Value
Hercules Latin American Value
Hercules North American Growth and
Income
Hercules Pacific Basin Value
Hercules World Bond

Hodgson Roberton Laing Limited
One Queen Street East
Suite 1920
Toronto, Ontario M5C 2Y5
(416) 368-1428 (800) 268-9622
Fax: (416) 869-1653
HRL Balanced
HRL Bond
HRL Canadian
HRL Instant $$
HRL Overseas Growth

Hongkong Bank Securities Inc.
885 West Georgia Street
Suite 400
Vancouver, B.C. V6C 3E9
(604) 641-2950 (800) 565-3883
Fax: (604) 641-1925
Hongkong Bank Asian Growth
Hongkong Bank Balanced
Hongkong Bank Equity
Hongkong Bank Money Market
Hongkong Bank Mortgage

**I.A. Michael Investment
Counsel Ltd.**
8 King Street East Suite 500
Toronto, Ontario M5C 1B5
(416) 365-9696 Fax: (416)
365-9705
ABC Fully-Managed
ABC Fundamental Value

**Imperial Life Assurance
Company of Canada**
95 Street Clair Avenue West
Toronto, Ontario M4V 1N7
(416) 324-1617
Fax: (416) 324-1670
Imperial Growth Canadian Equity
Imperial Growth Diversified
Imperial Growth Money Market
Imperial Growth North American Equity

**Industrial Alliance Life
Insurance Company**
1081 Chemin St- Louis C.P. 1907
Quebec, Quebec G1K 7M3
(418) 684-5000 (800) 268-8882
Fax: (418) 688-0705
Industrial Alliance Ecoflex A
Industrial Alliance Ecoflex B
Industrial Alliance Ecoflex D
Industrial Alliance Ecoflex H
Industrial Alliance Ecoflex M

**Integra Capital Management
Corporation**
55 University Avenue
Suite 1100 P.O. Box 42
Toronto, Ontario M5J 2H7
(416) 367-0404
Fax: (416) 367-0351
Integra Balanced
Integra Short-Term Investment

InvesNat Mutual Funds
600 de la Gauchetiere ouest
6th Floor
Montreal, Quebec H3B 4L2
(514) 394-8671 (800) 363-3511
Fax: (514) 394-6610
InvesNat American Equity
InvesNat Canadian Equity
InvesNat European Equity
InvesNat Money Market
InvesNat Mortgage
InvesNat Retirement Balanced
InvesNat Short Term Government Bond
InvesNat U.S. Money Market (US $)

Investors Group Financial Services Inc.

One Canada Centre
447 Portage Avenue
Winnipeg, Manitoba R3C 3B6
(204) 943-0361
Fax: (204) 943-0021
Investors Asset Allocation
Investors Bond
Investors Canadian Equity
Investors Corporate Bond
Investors Dividend
Investors European Growth
Investors Global Bond
Investors Global Fund Ltd.
Investors Growth Plus Portfolio
Investors Growth Portfolio
Investors Income Plus Portfolio
Investors Income Portfolio
Investors Japanese Growth Fund Ltd.
Investors Money Market
Investors Mortgage
Investors Mutual of Canada Ltd.
Investors North American Growth
   Fund Ltd.
Investors Pacific International
Investors Real Property
Investors Retirement Growth Portfolio
Investors Retirement Mutual
Investors Retirement Plus Portfolio
Investors Special Fund Ltd.
Investors Summa Fund Ltd.
Investors U.S. Growth Fund Ltd.
Investors World Growth Portfolio

John D. Hillery Investment Counsel Inc.

2842 Bloor St West Suite 203
Etobicoke, Ontario M8X 1B1
(416) 234-0846
Fax: (416) 234-0846
Margin of Safety

Jones Heward Investment Management Inc.

Aetna Canada Centre
145 King Street West Suite 1920
Toronto, Ontario M5H 3Z9
(416) 359-5000 (800) 361-1392
Fax: (416) 359-5040
Jones Heward American
Jones Heward Bond
Jones Heward Canadian Balanced
Jones Heward Fund Ltd.

Laurentian Funds Management Inc.

95 Street Clair Avenue West
Toronto, Ontario M4V 1N7
(416) 324-1617
Fax: (416) 324-1670
Laurentian American Equity Fund Ltd.
Laurentian Canadian Balanced
Laurentian Canadian Equity Fund Ltd.
Laurentian Commonwealth Fund Ltd.
Laurentian Dividend Fund Ltd.
Laurentian Global Balanced
Laurentian Government Bond
Laurentian Income
Laurentian International Fund Ltd.
Laurentian Money Market
Laurentian Special Equity

Leith Wheeler Investment Counsel Ltd.

400 Burrard Street, Suite 1500
Vancouver, British Columbia
V6C 3A6
(604) 683-3391
Fax: (604) 683-0323
Leith Wheeler Balanced
Leith Wheeler Canadian Equity
Leith Wheeler Fixed Income
Leith Wheeler Money Market
Leith Wheeler U.S. Equity

Leon Frazer & Associates Limited

8 King Street East Suite 2001
Toronto, Ontario M5C 1B6
(416) 864-1120
Fax: (416) 864-1494
Associate Investors Ltd.

London Life Insurance Company

255 Dufferin Avenue
London, Ontario N6A 4K1
(519) 432-5281
Fax: (519) 432-9035
London Life Bond
London Life Canadian Equity
London Life Diversified
London Life Money Market
London Life Mortgage
London Life U.S. Equity

Loring Ward Investment Counsel Ltd.

360 Main Street Suite 1501
Winnipeg, Manitoba R3C 3Z3
(204) 957-1730 (800) 267-1730
Fax: (204) 947-2103
Optima Strategy Equity Section
Optima Strategy Global Fixed Income
Optima Strategy Income Section
Optima Strategy International Equity
Optima Strategy Short Term Invest
Optima Strategy U.S. Equity

M. K. Wong Management Ltd.

26 Wellington Street East
Suite 640
Toronto, Ontario M5E 1S2
(604) 669-4555 (416) 361-3370
Fax: (604) 669-2756
Lotus Bond
Lotus Canadian Equity
Lotus
Lotus Income
Lotus International Bond

Mackenzie Financial Corporation

150 Bloor Street West
Suite M111
Toronto, Ontario M5S 3B5
(416) 922-5322 (800) 387-0615
Fax: (416) 922-0399
Industrial American
Industrial Balanced
Industrial Bond
Industrial Cash Management
Industrial Dividend Fund Ltd.
Industrial Equity Fund Ltd.
Industrial Future
Industrial Growth

(Mackenzie continued)
Industrial Horizon
Industrial Income
Industrial Mortgage Securities
Industrial Pension
Industrial Short-Term
Industrial Strategic Capital Protection
Ivy Canadian
Ivy Capital Protection
Ivy Capital Protection 1994
Ivy Foreign Equity
Ivy Growth and Income
Ivy Mortgage
Ivy Short-Term
Mackenzie Equity
Mackenzie Sentinal Global
Mackenzie Sentinel American Equity
Mackenzie Sentinel Canada Bond
Mackenzie Sentinel Canada Equity
Mackenzie Sentinel Canada Money
   Market
Universal Americas
Universal Canadian Bond
Universal Canadian Equity Fund Ltd.
Universal Canadian Resource
Universal Far East
Universal Japan
Universal U.S. Emerging Growth
Universal World Asset Allocation
Universal World Balanced RRSP
Universal World Emerging Growth
Universal World Equity
Universal World Precious Metals

MagnaTrends Asset
  Management Inc.
4 King Street West Suite 301
Toronto, Ontario M5X 1J7
(416) 865-1090
Fax: (416) 363-1954
Century DJ

Majendie Securities Ltd.
200 Burrard Street Suite 320
Vancouver, B.C. V6C 3L6
(604) 682-6446
Fax: (604) 662-8594
Top Fifty Equity
Top Fifty T-Bill/Bond
Top Fifty U.S. Equity

Manulife Financial
500 King Street North
Waterloo, Ontario N2J 4C6
(519) 747-7000
Fax: (519) 747-6895
Manulife Vistafund Bond 1
Manulife Vistafund Bond 2
Manulife Vistafund Capital Gains
   Growth 1
Manulife Vistafund Capital Gains
   Growth 2
Manulife Vistafund Diversified 1
Manulife Vistafund Diversified 2
Manulife Vistafund Equity 1
Manulife Vistafund Equity 2
Manulife Vistafund 1 Short Term Sec
Manulife Vistafund 2 Short Term Sec

Maritime Life Assurance Company

2701 Dutch Village Road
P.O. Box 1030
Halifax, Nova Scotia B3J 2X5
(902) 453-4300
Fax: (902) 453-7041
Maritime Life Balanced
Maritime Life Bond
Maritime Life Growth
Maritime Life Money Market

Mawer Investment Management

603 7th Avenue South West
Suite 600 Manulife House
Calgary, Alberta T2P 2T5
(403) 262-4673
Fax: (403) 262-4099
Mawer Canadian Balanced
    Retirement Savings
Mawer Canadian Bond
Mawer Canadian Diversified
    Investment
Mawer Canadian Equity
Mawer Canadian Income
Mawer Canadian Money Market
Mawer New Canada
Mawer U.S. Equity
Mawer World Investment

McLean Budden Ltd.

390 Bay Street Suite 1000
Toronto, Ontario M5H 2Y2
(416) 862-9800
McLean Budden American Growth
McLean Budden Balanced
McLean Budden Equity Growth
McLean Budden Fixed Income
McLean Budden Money Market

MD Management Limited

1867 Alta Vista Drive
Ottawa, Ontario K1G 3Y6
(613) 731-4552 (800) 267-4022
Fax: (613) 526-1352
MD Balanced
MD Bond
MD Dividend
MD Equity
MD Growth Investments Ltd.
MD Money
MD Realty A Units
MD Realty B Units
MD Select
MD U.S. Equity

Metropolitan Life Insurance Company of Canada

99 Bank Street
Ottawa, Ontario K1P 5A3
(613) 560-7700 (800) 267-0407
Fax: (613) 560-6926
Metlife MVP Balanced
Metlife MVP Bond
Metlife MVP Equity
Metlife MVP Growth
Metlife MVP Money Market
Metlife MVP U.S. Equity

Middlefield Group

One First Canadian Place
58th Floor P.O. Box 192
Toronto, Ontario M5X 1A6
(416) 362-0714
Fax: (416) 362-7925
Middlefield Growth

MOF Management Ltd.
609 Granville Street 20th Floor
P.O. Box 10379
Vancouver, B.C. V7Y 1G8
(604) 643-7416 (800) 663-6370
Fax: (604) 687-6532
Multiple Opportunities
Special Opportunities Fund Ltd.

Montreal Trust Services Inc.
1800 McGill College Avenue
12th Floor
Montreal, Quebec H3A 3K9
(514) 982-7000 (800) 463-7777
Fax: (514) 982-7069
Montreal Trust Excelsior Balanced
Montreal Trust Excelsior Dividend
Montreal Trust Excelsior Equity
Montreal Trust Excelsior Income
Montreal Trust Excelsior International
Montreal Trust Excelsior Money Market
Montreal Trust Excelsior Mortgage
Montreal Trust Excelsior Total Return

Mutual Investco Inc.
227 King Street South
Waterloo, Ontario N2J 4C5
(519) 888-2290
Fax: (519) 888-3646
Mutual Amerifund
Mutual Bond
Mutual Canadian Indexfund
Mutual Diversifund 25
Mutual Diversifund 40
Mutual Diversifund 55
Mutual Equifund
Mutual Money Market
Mutual Premier American
Mutual Premier Blue Chip

(Mutual Investco continued)
Mutual Premier Bond
Mutual Premier Growth
Mutual Premier International
Mutual Premier Mortgage

National Bank Securities Inc.
600 de la Gauchetiere Ouest,
6th Floor
Montreal, Quebec H3B 4L2
(514) 394-8671 (800) 363-3511
Fax: (514) 394-6610
Natcan American Equity
Natcan Canadian Bond
Natcan Canadian Equity
Natcan Dividend
Natcan Treasury Bill

National Life of Canada
522 University Avenue
Toronto, Ontario M5G 1Y7
(416) 585-2122 (800) 265-6919
Fax: (416) 598-0728
National Life Balanced
National Life Equities
National Life Fixed Income
National Life Global Equities
National Life Money Market

Natrusco Investment Funds Limited
1 Financial Place
1 Adelaide Street East 9th Floor
Toronto, Ontario M5C 2W8
(416) 361-3863
Fax: (416) 361-5563
National Trust American Equity
National Trust Balanced
National Trust Dividend

(Natrusco Investment continued)
National Trust Equity
National Trust Income
National Trust Money Market
National Trust Mortgage
National Trust Special Equity

Nigel Stephens Counsel Inc.
1200 Sheppard Avenue East
Suite 402
North York, Ontario M2K 2S5
(416) 502-9300
Fax: (416) 502-9394
Pursuit American
Pursuit Canadian Equity
Pursuit Income
Pursuit Money Market

NN Life Insurance Company of Canada
One Concorde Gate
Don Mills, Ontario M3C 3N6
(416) 391-2200
Fax: (416) 391-8415
NN Balanced
NN Bond
NN Can-am
NN Can-asian
NN Canadian 35 Index
NN Canadian Growth
NN Money Market
NN T-Bill

North American Life Assurance Company
5650 Yonge Street North
North York, Ontario M2M 4G4
(416) 229-4515 (800) 668-1503
Fax: (416) 229-6594
CCPE Diversified Growth
CCPE Fixed Income
CCPE Growth R
NAL-Investor Bond
NAL-Investor Diversified
NAL-Investor Equity
NAL-Investor Global Equity
NAL-Investor Money Market
NAL-Investor U.S. Equity

North American Trust Company
151 Yonge Street 3rd Floor
Toronto, Ontario M5C 2W7
(416) 947-5179
Fax: (416) 367-8483
Cornerstone Balanced
Cornerstone Bond
Cornerstone Canadian Growth
Cornerstone Global
Cornerstone Government Money
Cornerstone U.S. Fund Ltd

OHA Investment Management Ltd.
150 Ferrand Drive
Don Mills, Ontario M3C 1H6
(416) 429-2661 (800) 268-9597
Fax: (416) 429-5945
OHA Balanced
OHA Bond
OHA Canadian Equity
OHA Foreign Equity
OHA Short Term

Ontario Teachers Group
57 Mobile Drive
Toronto, Ontario M4A 1H5
(416) 752-9410 (800) 263-9541
Fax: (416) 752-6649
Ontario Teachers Group Balanced
Ontario Teachers Group Diversified
Ontario Teachers Group Fixed Value
Ontario Teachers Group Global
Ontario Teachers Group Growth
Ontario Teachers Group Mortgage Inc

Orbit Mutual
Fund Management Ltd.
4141 Sherbrooke St W. Suite 303
Montreal, Quebec H32 1B8
(514) 932-3000
Fax: (514) 989-2132
Orbit World

Peter Cundill & Associates Ltd.
1100 Melville Street
1200 Sun Life Plaza
Vancouver, BC V6E 4A6
(604) 685-4231 (800) 663-0156
Fax: (604) 689-9532
Cundill Security
Cundill Value Fund Ltd.

Phillips, Hager & North Ltd.
1055 West Hastings Street
Suite 1700
Vancouver, BC V6E 2H3
(604) 691-6781 (800) 661-6141
Fax: (604) 685-5712
Phillips, Hager & North Bond
Phillips, Hager & North Balanced
Phillips, Hager & North Canadian
  Equity

(PH&N continued)
Phillips, Hager & North Canadian
  Money Market
Phillips, Hager & North Dividend
  Income
Phillips, Hager & North North
  American Equity
Phillips, Hager & North RSP/RIF Equity
Phillips, Hager & North Short Term
  Bond and Mortgage
Phillips, Hager & North U.S. Equity
Phillips, Hager & North $U. S. Money
  Market
Phillips, Hager & North Vintage

Placements Optimum du
St-Laurent Inc.
425 boul Maisonneuve ouest
Suite 1620
Montreal, Quebec H3A 3G5
(514) 288-1620 (800) 363-7675
Fax: (514) 288-4280
Optimum Fonds d'Actions
Optimum Fonds d'Obligations
Optimum Fonds Equilibre
Optimum Fonds d'Epargne

Primerica Financial Services
350 Burnhamthorpe Road
Suite 300
Mississauga, Ontario L5B 3J1
(905) 848-7731
Fax: (905) 270-7096
Common Sense Asset Builder 1

Prosperity Capital Corporation

20 Toronto Street Suite 400
Toronto, Ontario M5C 2B8
(416) 867-3863
Fax: (416) 360-5615
Prosperity American Performance

Prudential Fund Management Canada Ltd.

200 Consilium Place 6th Floor
Scarborough, Ontario M1H 3E6
(416) 296-3287
Fax: (416) 296-3186
Prudential Diversified Investment
Prudential Dividend
Prudential Growth Fund Canada Ltd.
Prudential Income
Prudential Money Market
Prudential Natural Resource
Prudential Precious Metals

Royal Bank of Canada

4th Floor 200 Bay Street
Royal Bank Plaza North Tower
Toronto, Ontario M5J 2J2
(416) 974-6640
Fax: (416) 974-4076
Royfund Balanced
Royfund Bond
Royfund Canadian T-Bill
Royfund Dividend
Royfund Equity Ltd.
Royfund Growth
Royfund International Equity
Royfund International Income
Royfund Money Market
Royfund Mortgage
Royfund U.S. Equity
Royfund U.S. Money Market (US$)

Royal Life Insurance Company of Canada

277 Lakeshore Road East
Oakville, Ontario L6J 1H9
(905) 842-6200 (800) 263-1747
Fax: (905) 842-6294
Royal Life Balanced
Royal Life Equity
Royal Life Income
Royal Life Money Market

Royal Trust Investment Services Inc.

Royal Trust Tower
77 King Street West 5th Floor
Toronto, Ontario M5W 1P9
(416) 981-7001 (800) 463-3863
Fax: (416) 981-7120
Royal Lepage Commercial Real Estate
Royal Trust Advantage Balanced
Royal Trust Advantage Growth
Royal Trust Advantage Income
Royal Trust American Stock
Royal Trust Asian Growth
Royal Trust Bond
Royal Trust Canadian Money Market
Royal Trust Canadian Special Growth
Royal Trust Canadian Stock
Royal Trust Canadian T-Bill
  Money Market
Royal Trust Energy
Royal Trust European Growth
Royal Trust Growth and Income
Royal Trust International Bond
Royal Trust Japanese Stock
Royal Trust Mortgage
Royal Trust Precious Metals
Royal Trust U.S. Money Market (US$)
Royal Trust Zweig Strategic Growth

Roycom Advisors Inc.
120 Adelaide Street West
Suite 2012
Toronto, Ontario M5H 1T1
(416) 363-3730 (800) 565-1979
Fax: (416) 363-4972
Roycom-Summit Realty
Roycom-Summit TDF

Sagit Investment Management Ltd.
789 West Pender St Suite 900
Vancouver, BC V6C 1H2
(604) 685-3193 (800) 663-1003
Fax: (604) 681-7536
Cambridge American Growth
Cambridge Americas
Cambridge Balanced
Cambridge Global
Cambridge Growth
Cambridge Pacific
Cambridge Resource
Cambridge Special Equity
Trans-Canada Bond
Trans-Canada Equity
Trans-Canada Income
Trans-Canada Money Market
Trans-Canada Pension

Saxon Funds
20 Queen St West Suite 1904
P.O. Box 95
Toronto, Ontario M5H 3R3
(416) 979-1818
Fax: (416) 979-7424
Saxon Balanced
Saxon Small Cap
Saxon Stock
Saxon World Growth

Sceptre Investment Counsel Limited
26 Wellington St East Suite 1200
Toronto, Ontario M5E 1W4
(416) 360-4826
Fax: (416) 367-8716
Sceptre Asian Growth
Sceptre Balanced
Sceptre Bond
Sceptre Equity
Sceptre International
Sceptre Money Market

Scotia Securities Inc.
One Richmond St West 7th Floor
Toronto, Ontario M5H 3W4
(416) 866-4574 (800) 268-9269
Fax: (416) 866-2018
Scotia American Equity Growth
Scotia Canadian Equity Growth
Scotia Canam Growth
Scotia Canam Income
Scotia Defensive Income
Scotia Global Growth
Scotia Govt of Canada Treasury Bill
Scotia Income
Scotia Money Market
Scotia Mortgage
Scotia Precious Metals
Scotia Premium T-Bill
Scotia Stock & Bond

Sogefonds MFQ Inc.
625 St. Amable
Quebec, Quebec G1R 2G5
(418) 644-4225 (800) 463-5549
Fonds Ficadre Actions
Fonds Ficadre Equilibree
Fonds Ficadre Money Market
Fonds Ficadre Obligations

Spectrum Bullock Financial Services
15th Floor 55 University Avenue
Toronto, Ontario M5J 2H7
(416) 360-2200 (800) 263-1851
Bullock American
Bullock Asian Dynasty A
Bullock Asian Dynasty B
Bullock Asian Dynasty C
Bullock Asset Strategy
Bullock Emerging Markets A
Bullock Emerging Markets B
Bullock Emerging Markets C
Bullock Global Bond A
Bullock Global Bond B
Bullock Global Bond C
Bullock Growth
Bullock Optimax USA A
Bullock Optimax USA B
Bullock Optimax USA C
Canadian Investment Fund Ltd.
Spectrum Canadian Equity
Spectrum Cash Reserve
Spectrum Diversified
Spectrum Dividend
Spectrum Government Bond
Spectrum Interest
Spectrum International Bond
Spectrum International Equity
Spectrum Savings

St. Laurent Financial Corp.
425 de Maisonneuve boul ouest
Suite 1740
Montreal, Quebec H3A 3G5
(514) 288-7545
Fax: (514) 288-4200
Batirente - Section Actions
Batirente - Section Diversifiee
Batirente - Section Marche Monetaire
Batirente - Section Obligations

Standard Life Assurance Company
1245 Sherbrooke Street West
Montreal, Quebec H3G 1G3
(514) 499-6829 (800) 665-6237
Fax: (514) 499-4466
Standard Life Balanced Mutual
Standard Life Bond Mutual
Standard Life Equity Mutual
Standard Life Money Market
Standard Life Ideal Investment - Balanced
Standard Life Ideal Investment - Bond
Standard Life Ideal Investment - Equity
Standard Life Ideal Investment -
    Money Market

Stanley Investment Management Ltd.
304 Bay Street Suite 810
P.O. Box 10
Toronto, Ontario M5H 4A5
(416) 350-3232
Fax: (416) 350-3239
Resolute Growth

Strata Mutual Funds Ltd.

101 Frederick Street
P.O. Box 9032
Kitchener, Ontario N2G 4R8
(519) 888-6700 (800) 265-2273
Fax: (519) 888-2071
Strata Canadian
Strata Government Bond
Strata Growth
Strata Income
Strata Money Market
Strata Tactical
Stratafund 40
Stratafund 60

Talvest Fund Management Inc.

One Queen Street East
Suite 2000
Toronto, Ontario M5C 2W5
(800) 268-8258
Fax: (416) 364-4472
Talvest Bond
Talvest Diversified
Talvest Foreign Pay Canadian Bond
Talvest Global Diversified
Talvest Global Growth
Talvest Growth Fund Inc.
Talvest Income
Talvest Money
Talvest New Economy
Talvest U.S. Diversified
Talvest U.S. Growth

Toronto-Dominion Securities Inc.

Toronto-Dominion Centre
P.O. Box 100
Toronto-Dominion Bank Tower
20th Floor
Toronto, Ontario M5K 1G8
(416) 982-6160 (800) 268-8166
Fax: (416) 982-6625
Green Line Asian Growth
Green Line Balanced Growth
Green Line Balanced Income
Green Line Blue Chip Equity
Green Line Canadian Bond
Green Line Canadian Equity
Green Line Canadian Government Bond
Green Line Canadian Index
Green Line Canadian Money Market
Green Line Canadian Mortgage
Green Line Canadian T-Bill
Green Line Dividend
Green Line Emerging Markets
Green Line Global Government Bond
Green Line Global RSP Bond
Green Line Global Select
Green Line International Equity
Green Line Mortgage-Backed
Green Line North American Growth
Green Line Resource
Green Line Science & Technology
Green Line Short Term Income
Green Line U.S. Index
Green Line U.S. Money Market (US$)
Green Line Value

Templeton Management Ltd.
4 King Street West
P.O. Box 4070 Station A
Toronto, Ontario M5W 1M3
(416) 364-4672 (800) 387-0830
Fax: (416) 364-4708
Templeton Balanced
Templeton Emerging Markets
Templeton Global Income
Templeton Global Smaller Companies
Templeton Growth Fund Ltd.
Templeton Heritage Bond
Templeton Heritage Retirement
Templeton International Stock
Templeton Treasury Bill

Total Return Management Inc.
500 Rene Levesque Boulevard
Suite 1000
Montreal, Quebec H2Z 1W7
(514) 954-0066
Fax: (514) 875-4230
CIS Commax Hedge
CIS Global Telecommunications
Total Return Fund Inc.

Tradex Management Inc.
124 O'Connor Street Suite 504
Ottawa, Ontario K1P 5M9
(613) 233-3394 (800) 567-3863
Fax: (613) 233-8191
Tradex Bond
Tradex Equity Fund Limited

**Trimark Investment
  Management Inc.**
One First Canadian Place
Suite 5600 P.O. Box 487
Toronto, Ontario M5X 1E5
(416) 362-7181 (800) 387-9841
Fax: (416) 368-6331
Trimark - The Americas
Trimark Canadian
Trimark Fund
Trimark Government Income
Trimark Income Growth
Trimark Interest
Trimark RSP Equity
Trimark Select Balanced
Trimark Select Canadian Growth
Trimark Select Growth

Trust General du Canada
1100 University Street
Montreal, Quebec H3B 2G7
(514) 871-7530 (800) 463-6643
Fax: (514) 871-8525
General Trust of Canada Balanced
General Trust of Canada Bond
General Trust of Canada Canadian
  Equity
General Trust of Canada Growth
General Trust of Canada International
General Trust of Canada Money
  Market
General Trust of Canada Mortgage
General Trust of Canada U.S. Equity
Vision Europe

Trust Pret et Revenu du Canada
850 Place d'Youville
Quebec, Quebec G1R 3P6
(418) 694-0000
Fax: (418) 694-2075
Trust Pret & Revenu American
Trust Pret & Revenu Bond
Trust Pret & Revenu Canadian
Trust Pret & Revenu H
Trust Pret & Revenu Money Market
Trust Pret & Revenu Retirement

**United Financial
  Management Ltd.**
200 King Street West Suite 1202
Toronto, Ontario M5H 3W8
(416) 598-7777 (800) 263-1867
Fax: (416) 598-7821
United American Equity
United American Growth Fund Ltd.
United Canadian Bond
United Canadian Equity
United Canadian Growth
United Canadian Interest
United Canadian Mortgage
United Canadian Portfolio of Funds
United Global Equity
United Global Growth
United Global Portfolio of Funds
United Global Telecommunications
United U.S. Dollar Money Market

**University Avenue
  Management Ltd.**
110 Yonge Street Suite 1701
Toronto, Ontario M5C 1T4
(416) 366-7319
Fax: (416) 366-2700
University Avenue Bond
University Avenue Canadian
University Avenue Growth

Working Opportunity Fund
Suite 2901 1055 W. Georgia St.
P.O. Box 11170 Royal Centre
Vancouver, BC V6E 3R5
(604) 688-9631
Fax: (604) 669-7605
Working Opportunity

**Working Ventures Investment
  Services Inc.**
65 Street Clair Avenue East
9th Floor
Toronto, Ontario M4T 2Y3
(416) 922-5479 (800) 268-8244
Fax: (416) 929-4390
Working Ventures Canadian Fund Inc.

The Growth of an Investment

This table shows:

1. How an investment of $100 a month (ignoring acquisition fees) would have grown if invested in a typical Canadian equity fund during the ten years ended June 30, 1994 and,

2. A withdrawal plan in which $100,000 (ignoring any acquisition or redemption fees) was invested at June 30, 1984 and $1,000 a month was withdrawn for the subsequent ten years.

Month	Return	Cumulative Contribution	Value of Plan	Cumulative Withdrawal	Value of Plan
1984-07	-4.8%	$100	$95	$1,000	$94,344
84-08	9.0%	$200	$213	$2,000	$102,009
84-09	1.3%	$300	$317	$3,000	$102,493
84-10	-2.0%	$400	$408	$4,000	$99,569
84-11	0.3%	$500	$510	$5,000	$98,995
84-12	2.3%	$600	$623	$6,000	$100,397
1985-01	7.9%	$700	$781	$7,000	$107,517
85-02	-0.7%	$800	$874	$8,000	$105,908
85-03	-0.7%	$900	$967	$9,000	$104,304
85-04	2.5%	$1,000	$1,094	$10,000	$106,082
85-05	6.1%	$1,100	$1,266	$11,000	$111,693
85-06	0.7%	$1,200	$1,376	$12,000	$111,675
85-07	0.9%	$1,300	$1,490	$13,000	$111,900
85-08	1.5%	$1,400	$1,614	$14,000	$112,735
85-09	-4.7%	$1,500	$1,633	$15,000	$106,565
85-10	1.9%	$1,600	$1,767	$16,000	$107,801
85-11	6.9%	$1,700	$1,995	$17,000	$114,396
85-12	3.4%	$1,800	$2,167	$18,000	$117,457
1986-01	0.6%	$1,900	$2,280	$19,000	$117,302
86-02	-0.7%	$2,000	$2,363	$20,000	$115,634
86-03	6.1%	$2,100	$2,614	$21,000	$121,889
86-04	-0.6%	$2,200	$2,697	$22,000	$120,324
86-05	0.8%	$2,300	$2,821	$23,000	$120,490
86-06	-1.3%	$2,400	$2,881	$24,000	$118,033

Month	Return	Cumulative Contribution	Value of Plan	Cumulative Withdrawal	Value of Plan
86-07	-3.2%	$2,500	$2,886	$25,000	$113,439
86-08	4.5%	$2,600	$3,122	$26,000	$117,762
86-09	-0.2%	$2,700	$3,215	$27,000	$116,664
86-10	1.1%	$2,800	$3,350	$28,000	$117,057
86-11	1.5%	$2,900	$3,501	$29,000	$117,965
86-12	-1.2%	$3,000	$3,559	$30,000	$115,749
1987-01	7.0%	$3,100	$3,915	$31,000	$123,027
87-02	3.4%	$3,200	$4,151	$32,000	$126,369
87-03	6.8%	$3,300	$4,540	$33,000	$134,108
87-04	0.6%	$3,400	$4,668	$34,000	$134,099
87-05	1.0%	$3,500	$4,814	$35,000	$134,540
87-06	2.0%	$3,600	$5,013	$36,000	$136,421
87-07	4.9%	$3,700	$5,366	$37,000	$142,332
87-08	-0.3%	$3,800	$5,452	$38,000	$141,141
87-09	-2.1%	$3,900	$5,437	$39,000	$137,375
87-10	-15.4%	$4,000	$4,686	$40,000	$115,427
87-11	-0.4%	$4,100	$4,767	$41,000	$114,156
87-12	3.7%	$4,200	$5,049	$42,000	$117,589
1988-01	-1.3%	$4,300	$5,080	$43,000	$115,183
88-02	3.4%	$4,400	$5,356	$44,000	$118,254
88-03	3.6%	$4,500	$5,653	$45,000	$121,685
88-04	1.0%	$4,600	$5,812	$46,000	$122,103
88-05	-1.6%	$4,700	$5,819	$47,000	$119,358
88-06	4.1%	$4,800	$6,164	$48,000	$123,462
88-07	-1.1%	$4,900	$6,197	$49,000	$121,308
88-08	-1.7%	$5,000	$6,190	$50,000	$118,414
88-09	0.3%	$5,100	$6,310	$51,000	$117,953
88-10	3.1%	$5,200	$6,606	$52,000	$120,722
88-11	-3.1%	$5,300	$6,497	$53,000	$116,127
88-12	2.4%	$5,400	$6,757	$54,000	$118,118
1989-01	5.7%	$5,500	$7,250	$55,000	$124,045
89-02	-0.5%	$5,600	$7,311	$56,000	$122,558
89-03	-0.2%	$5,700	$7,400	$57,000	$121,540
89-04	1.7%	$5,800	$7,630	$58,000	$122,823
89-05	3.1%	$5,900	$7,966	$59,000	$125,736
89-06	2.5%	$6,000	$8,264	$60,000	$127,989
89-07	5.1%	$6,100	$8,795	$61,000	$133,740
89-08	0.9%	$6,200	$8,978	$62,000	$134,162
89-09	-0.9%	$6,300	$9,000	$63,000	$132,171
89-10	-0.4%	$6,400	$9,063	$64,000	$130,806
89-11	1.6%	$6,500	$9,311	$65,000	$132,084
89-12	0.5%	$6,600	$9,459	$66,000	$131,924

Month	Return	Cumulative Contribution	Value of Plan	Cumulative Withdrawal	Value of Plan
1990-01	-5.7%	$6,700	$9,011	$67,000	$123,534
90-02	1.0%	$6,800	$9,203	$68,000	$123,937
90-03	0.4%	$6,900	$9,336	$69,000	$123,542
90-04	-7.3%	$7,000	$8,744	$70,000	$113,648
90-05	7.4%	$7,100	$9,496	$71,000	$121,204
90-06	-0.6%	$7,200	$9,542	$72,000	$119,684
90-07	0.5%	$7,300	$9,690	$73,000	$119,448
90-08	-4.5%	$7,400	$9,353	$74,000	$113,277
90-09	-4.0%	$7,500	$9,074	$75,000	$107,903
90-10	-2.2%	$7,600	$8,975	$76,000	$104,733
90-11	2.5%	$7,700	$9,305	$77,000	$106,549
90-12	1.8%	$7,800	$9,578	$78,000	$107,679
1991-01	0.8%	$7,900	$9,753	$79,000	$107,683
91-02	4.9%	$8,000	$10,333	$80,000	$112,089
91-03	2.1%	$8,100	$10,648	$81,000	$113,567
91-04	-0.6%	$8,200	$10,686	$82,000	$112,078
91-05	2.7%	$8,300	$11,075	$83,000	$114,254
91-06	-1.3%	$8,400	$11,033	$84,000	$111,967
91-07	2.4%	$8,500	$11,396	$85,000	$113,779
91-08	-0.6%	$8,600	$11,432	$86,000	$112,309
91-09	-1.5%	$8,700	$11,361	$87,000	$109,817
91-10	3.5%	$8,800	$11,862	$88,000	$112,824
91-11	-1.7%	$8,900	$11,756	$89,000	$110,046
91-12	2.7%	$9,000	$12,177	$90,000	$112,193
1992-01	4.6%	$9,100	$12,845	$91,000	$116,546
92-02	2.1%	$9,200	$13,212	$92,000	$118,116
92-03	-4.1%	$9,300	$12,764	$93,000	$112,425
92-04	-3.0%	$9,400	$12,477	$94,000	$108,208
92-05	2.0%	$9,500	$12,831	$95,000	$109,557
92-06	-0.2%	$9,600	$12,901	$96,000	$108,474
92-07	1.4%	$9,700	$13,189	$97,000	$109,211
92-08	-0.5%	$9,800	$13,220	$98,000	$107,804
92-09	0.3%	$9,900	$13,360	$99,000	$107,296
92-10	-0.3%	$10,000	$13,419	$100,000	$106,139
92-11	0.1%	$10,100	$13,529	$101,000	$105,386
92-12	4.7%	$10,200	$14,273	$102,000	$109,532
1993-01	3.9%	$10,300	$14,934	$103,000	$112,967
93-02	4.5%	$10,400	$15,714	$104,000	$117,251
93-03	14.3%	$10,500	$18,074	$105,000	$133,167
93-04	1.2%	$10,600	$18,389	$106,000	$133,912
93-05	5.4%	$10,700	$19,485	$107,000	$140,292
93-06	8.5%	$10,800	$21,250	$108,000	$151,383

Month	Return	Cumulative Contribution	Value of Plan	Cumulative Withdrawal	Value of Plan
93-07	-5.6%	$10,900	$20,147	$109,000	$142,023
93-08	7.4%	$11,000	$21,741	$110,000	$151,670
93-09	-5.0%	$11,100	$20,749	$111,000	$143,249
93-10	4.7%	$11,200	$21,837	$112,000	$149,206
93-11	-0.3%	$11,300	$21,876	$113,000	$147,961
93-12	6.6%	$11,400	$23,436	$114,000	$156,953
1994-01	2.0%	$11,500	$24,007	$115,000	$159,261
94-02	-4.5%	$11,600	$23,020	$116,000	$151,250
94-03	-2.6%	$11,700	$22,517	$117,000	$146,469
94-04	-2.3%	$11,800	$22,101	$118,000	$142,296
94-05	-0.2%	$11,900	$22,162	$119,000	$141,213
94-06	-6.3%	$12,000	$20,870	$120,000	$131,549

Survey of Annual Fund Performance

(for periods ending June 30)

Fund	1994	1993	1992	1991	1990	1989	1988	1987	1986	1985
Canadian Equity Funds										
Admax Cdn Performance Fund	-2.5	17.5	4.3	-1.4	.....	.....	.....	.....	.....	.....
All-Canadian CapitalFund	7.8	22.2	0.4	3.3	2.8	7.0	-9.3	15.3	16.7	17.6
All-Canadian Compound	8.1	21.6	0.4	3.3	2.7	7.1	-9.3	15.3	16.8	17.6
All-Canadian ConsumerFund	5.7	.....	6.5	9.6	9.1	9.0	6.7	9.0	6.1	20.0
Altafund Investment Corp.	2.3	57.5	15.9	.....	.....	.....	.....	.....	.....	.....
Altamira Capital Growth Fund	6.6	20.8	19.7	3.0	6.2	12.0	-14.5	19.6	10.0	26.2
Altamira Equity Fund	0.4	52.9	42.4	13.7	17.9	32.7	.....	.....	.....	.....
Altamira North American Recovery	.....	.....	.....	.....	.....	.....	.....	.....	.....	.....
Altamira Special Growth Fund	-9.8	54.2	34.4	14.3	4.6	8.0	-14.8	12.5	.....	.....
Associate Investors Ltd.	0.2	12.8	4.1	4.7	-4.6	14.6	-1.3	14.9	12.4	33.1
ABC Fundamental Value Fund	38.2	66.5	1.0	27.1	6.2	.....	.....	.....	.....	.....
AGF Canadian Equity Fund	1.2	19.5	0.4	-1.2	-9.1	9.2	-7.0	12.0	27.2	35.5
AGF Growth Equity Fund Ltd.	3.0	59.1	14.1	2.4	-4.1	4.4	-17.0	20.3	33.2	21.5
AIC Advantage Fund	10.1	30.3	17.0	14.5	-8.0	11.8	-9.2	16.6	.....	.....
AMI Private Capital Equity	4.3	17.0	-1.0	-3.4	-3.3	15.2	.....	.....	.....	.....
Batirente - Section Actions	-0.8	10.3	-2.5	-1.4	-4.4	13.4	.....	.....	.....	.....
Beutel Goodman Cdn Equity Fund	8.3	9.6	-3.3	.....	.....	.....	.....	.....	.....	.....
Bissett Canadian Equity Fund	0.2	32.5	4.4	5.3	1.9	12.2	-6.5	12.9	25.8	26.9
Bissett Small Cap Fund	6.7	101.7	.....	.....	.....	.....	.....	.....	.....	.....
Bullock Growth Fund	2.4	42.3	4.8	5.6	-8.3	7.1	-5.6	4.5	34.0	5.6
BNP (Canada) Equity Fund	-2.8	19.5	.....	.....	.....	.....	.....	.....	.....	.....
BPI Canadian Equity Fund	-3.5	35.9	-4.1	-4.5	-0.6	4.5	-15.0	6.4	.....	.....
BPI Canadian Equity Value Fund	-3.7	30.6	4.9	7.5	-0.1	.....	.....	.....	.....	.....
BPI Canadian Small Cap Fund	-1.6	52.1	7.4	10.8	-9.8	3.4	.....	.....	.....	.....
C.I. Canadian Growth Fund	7.3	.....	.....	.....	.....	.....	.....	.....	.....	.....
C.I. Sector Canadian Fund	6.4	31.7	-7.1	-6.5	-7.3	7.3	.....	.....	.....	.....
Cambridge Growth Fund	-4.4	42.8	9.2	6.3	4.4	12.4	-0.4	26.8	40.7	31.6
Cambridge Special Equity	-14.8	81.3	-17.4	-19.3	-1.7	17.7	-7.1	.....	.....	.....
Canada Life Canadian Equity S-9	0.9	18.5	4.7	0.7	-5.2	16.9	1.3	14.0	23.0	31.0
Canada Trust Everest Special Eqty	-5.3	45.5	7.2	5.6	-3.0	14.7	-19.0	.....	.....	.....
Canada Trust Everest Stock Fund	0.8	30.1	5.2	2.8	-0.3	.....	.....	.....	.....	.....
Canada Trust Investment-Eqty	-0.1	29.2	-1.2	2.5	-0.5	12.6	-9.3	.....	.....	.....
Canadian Investment Fund	-0.1	10.2	-2.6	-1.5	0.4	15.4	-7.7	11.1	15.2	27.4
Canadian Protected Fund	-5.1	30.7	3.8	7.0	6.4	5.8	8.8	6.4	21.7	.....
Chou RRSP Fund	3.1	9.0	5.4	-0.6	-5.5	15.3	7.1	.....	.....	.....
Clean Environment Equity Fund	5.0	31.2	.....	.....	.....	.....	.....	.....	.....	.....
Colonia Equity Fund	-3.3	14.4	.....	.....	.....	.....	.....	.....	.....	.....
Colonia Special Growth Fund	.....	.....	.....	.....	.....	.....	.....	.....	.....	.....
Concorde Croissance	1.5	14.2	.....	.....	.....	.....	.....	.....	.....	.....

NOTE: An interruption in the historical flow of data indicates that the fund's objectives changed during that twelve month period. If current information is not provided the fund company did not submit the net asset value per share for the fund for June 30, 1994.

Fund	1994	1993	1992	1991	1990	1989	1988	1987	1986	1985
Confed Equity Fund	3.3	12.5	7.8	-1.1	-6.8	15.8	-1.6	16.4	15.7	31.4
Confed Growth Fund	4.8	13.2	6.8	-0.4	-7.0	14.6	-3.4	16.3	24.9	34.0
Confed Life B	4.0	13.6	9.2	0.3	-5.9	17.0	-0.5	17.6	16.9	32.8
Cornerstone Cdn Growth	-3.9	18.6	12.9	3.3	-8.5	13.0	-9.8	.....	.....	.....
Corporate Investors Stock Fund	-1.5	43.6	8.5	5.1	-8.0	-9.8	-31.4	13.9	43.0	26.4
Cundill Security Fund	17.9	25.2	-16.2	-1.8	-4.5	9.7	2.1	22.6	10.3	24.2
CAMAF(Cdn-Anaest)	-1.8	16.3	-3.2	1.7	0.6	11.9	-3.5	20.4	22.0	27.2
CCPE Growth Fund R	4.8	10.5	-1.8	3.5	-2.6	18.9	-4.1	18.1	.....	.....
CDA Aggressive Equity Fund	.....	.....	.....	.....	.....	.....	.....	.....	.....	.....
CDA Common Stock Fund	3.2	23.0	3.8	5.1	-2.2	16.8	-4.8	22.4	25.7	31.4
CIBC Canadian Equity Fund	-4.7	18.5	-6.2	1.4	2.8	.....	.....	.....	.....	.....
CIBC Capital Appreciation Fund	-6.2	44.2	.....	.....	.....	.....	.....	.....	.....	.....
Dynamic Canadian Growth Fund	1.7	106.8	6.4	16.3	-4.6	4.1	-28.6	23.9	.....	.....
Dynamic Fund of Canada	-6.9	51.9	5.9	2.3	1.2	12.5	-1.9	25.3	15.2	23.0
Elliott & Page Equity Fund	-2.0	28.0	13.1	8.6	-6.4	20.7	.....	.....	.....	.....
Empire Elite Equity Fund 5	-1.7	22.0	9.4	1.2	-2.0	10.3	-13.7	17.0	24.2	43.9
Empire Equity Growth Fund 3	3.5	26.8	1.3	6.1	-4.1	18.2	0.9	7.2	44.2	27.3
Empire Premier Equity Fund 1	1.6	21.7	4.4	3.0	-1.8	14.6	3.5	16.9	23.5	31.9
Equitable Life Canadian Stock	4.0	.....	.....	.....	.....	.....	.....	.....	.....	.....
Equitable Life Seg. Common Stock	6.9	14.5	1.8	1.5	-5.6	10.9	-10.1	21.8	21.4	27.0
Ethical Growth Fund	-1.7	19.2	-0.8	7.3	4.0	16.0	10.9	9.5	.....	.....
Fidelity Capital Builder Fund	-2.9	26.5	-2.1	13.9	1.3	14.3	.....	.....	.....	.....
First Canadian Equity Index	2.4	17.2	0.5	-0.5	-3.7	11.0	.....	.....	.....	.....
First Cdn. Growth Fund	.....	.....	.....	.....	.....	.....	.....	.....	.....	.....
First Cdn. Special Growth Fund	.....	.....	.....	.....	.....	.....	.....	.....	.....	.....
Fonds de Prof. Cdn. Equity	-1.7	14.3	-0.3	4.7	-4.0	14.7	.....	.....	.....	.....
Fonds Desjardins Actions	-3.1	20.3	-0.8	3.2	-4.7	15.2	-11.0	.....	.....	.....
Fonds Desjardins Croissance	.....	.....	.....	.....	.....	.....	.....	.....	.....	.....
Fonds Desjardins Environnement	0.2	10.6	1.9	.....	.....	.....	.....	.....	.....	.....
Fonds Ficadre Actions	3.0	12.3	2.3	-2.7	-15.0	2.7	-25.6	.....	.....	.....
General Trust of Canada Cdn Eqty	-1.1	12.8	-2.3	2.3	-5.8	10.9	-8.2	14.8	19.7	26.1
General Trust of Canada Growth	-2.6	45.6	15.9	2.7	-10.5	25.2	.....	.....	.....	.....
Global Strategy Canada Growth	0.7	18.2	.....	.....	.....	.....	.....	.....	.....	.....
Great-West Life Canadian Equity	-3.0	33.0	6.8	3.7	1.8	9.9	-12.5	.....	.....	.....
Great-West Life Eqty Index Invest	1.6	17.9	-0.8	0.0	-3.9	11.2	-6.8	22.5	14.0	24.1
Green Line Blue Chip Equity Fund	0.1	10.9	4.2	1.8	-1.0	15.2	.....	.....	.....	.....
Green Line Canadian Equity Fund	1.7	26.3	-1.7	1.4	-5.6	19.0	.....	.....	.....	.....
Green Line Canadian Index Fund	2.7	19.1	-0.1	0.4	-3.5	11.5	-6.2	23.4	.....	.....
Green Line Value Fund	.....	.....	.....	.....	.....	.....	.....	.....	.....	.....
Guardian Canadian Equity Fund	-2.4	22.4	-2.6	-2.4	-4.2	7.1	-7.6	14.4	34.8	23.8
Guardian Enterprise Fund	-0.2	26.5	-1.8	1.5	5.7	2.5	-1.9	5.0	29.0	24.8
Guardian Growth Equity Fund	1.2	41.4	7.2	4.2	6.5	.....	.....	.....	.....	.....
Gyro Equity Fund	-2.0	34.2	-1.3	-3.4	-0.7	9.0	-1.0	28.4	.....	.....
GBC Canadian Growth Fund	-4.1	49.0	16.9	15.2	10.4	.....	.....	.....	.....	.....
Hongkong Bank Equity Fund	4.7	43.8	-1.3	2.7	-2.1	.....	.....	.....	.....	.....
Hyperion Aurora Trust	.....	.....	.....	.....	.....	.....	.....	.....	.....	.....
HRL Canadian Fund	1.6	15.7	-4.8	5.4	0.1	12.8	-2.6	.....	.....	.....
Imperial Growth Canadian Equity	1.5	19.3	5.4	3.1	-5.9	27.4	17.3	31.3	23.1	28.9
Industrial Alliance Ecoflex Fund A	6.1	.....	.....	.....	.....	.....	.....	.....	.....	.....
Industrial Equity Fund Ltd.	3.6	91.9	-0.2	-12.6	-13.0	-2.9	-0.5	31.4	18.1	16.8
Industrial Future Fund	5.3	37.5	-5.3	-0.9	-2.6	11.0	.....	.....	.....	.....
Industrial Growth Fund	4.2	32.5	-8.8	-1.5	-2.5	8.4	4.5	27.7	16.4	27.1
Industrial Horizon Fund	6.2	21.5	-2.3	0.4	-1.7	10.1	15.2	.....	.....	.....
Industrial Pension Fund	11.4	26.1	-7.2	-9.8	-7.9	3.5	4.3	23.4	20.8	30.6
Industrial Strategic Cap Protection	3.5	18.9	.....	.....	.....	.....	.....	.....	.....	.....
Investors Canadian Equity Fund	5.3	28.6	4.7	6.6	1.0	8.5	-5.7	10.1	27.8	25.4
Investors Retirement Gth. Portfolio	6.3	17.9	2.4	2.7	1.0	.....	.....	.....	.....	.....
Investors Retirement Mutual Fund	5.3	18.1	-0.8	1.9	-2.7	12.7	4.6	20.4	13.6	26.7
Investors Summa Fund Ltd.	3.2	14.3	5.7	1.8	-3.2	12.5	-3.1	.....	.....	.....
InvesNat Equity Fund	-2.1	20.5	4.9	3.4	1.4	.....	.....	.....	.....	.....
Ivy Canadian Fund	3.8	.....	.....	.....	.....	.....	.....	.....	.....	.....

Fund	1994	1993	1992	1991	1990	1989	1988	1987	1986	1985
Ivy Capital Protection Fund	-0.7	.....	.....	.....	.....	.....	.....	.....	.....	.....
Ivy Capital Protection Fund 1994	.....	.....	.....	.....	.....	.....	.....	.....	.....	.....
Jarislowsky Finsco Canadian Equity	1.9	6.9	-1.5	3.6	-0.8	13.5	-9.2	13.3	.....	.....
Jones Heward Fund Ltd.	-5.1	41.8	8.8	4.5	-9.7	10.7	-3.8	11.8	29.4	31.6
Laurentian Canadian Equity Fund	-0.5	16.8	1.3	1.6	-11.1	16.9	-2.6	11.1	20.6	25.9
Laurentian Special Equity Fund	11.7	24.6	1.8	3.4	.....	.....	.....	.....	.....	.....
Leith Wheeler Canadian Equity	.....	.....	.....	.....	.....	.....	.....	.....	.....	.....
London Life Canadian Equity	-1.5	27.2	5.7	1.1	-8.2	15.0	-0.3	21.0	19.0	28.7
Lotus (MKW) Canadian Equity	.....	.....	.....	.....	.....	.....	.....	.....	.....	.....
Mackenzie Equity Fund	9.9	24.7	-7.5	-8.6	-7.1	6.5	4.8	20.8	23.1	29.6
Mackenzie Sentinel Canada Equity	13.3	46.0	-7.6	-6.2	-4.4	6.1	-15.6	42.1	.....	.....
Manulife Vistafund 1 Cap. Gains Gth	-2.7	35.3	8.3	2.3	0.3	11.8	-8.0	24.3	14.4	28.6
Manulife Vistafund 1 Equity Fund	-0.5	21.5	5.1	3.7	-1.9	10.5	-6.1	20.3	9.8	22.5
Manulife Vistafund 2 Cap. Gains Gth	-3.4	34.2	7.5	1.5	-0.4	11.0	-8.7	23.4	13.6	27.7
Manulife Vistafund 2 Equity Fund	-1.2	20.6	4.3	2.9	-2.7	9.7	-6.8	19.4	9.0	21.6
Marathon Equity Fund	11.3	105.7	26.9	-7.3	-5.9	35.6	-33.0	3.7	.....	.....
Maritime Life Growth Fund	-2.6	25.0	0.1	-1.0	-4.0	13.5	-11.1	15.2	24.7	34.8
Mawer Canadian Equity Fund	-2.7	21.5	.....	.....	.....	.....	.....	.....	.....	.....
Mawer New Canada Fund	16.2	49.1	6.1	7.8	11.3	9.4	.....	.....	.....	.....
McLean Budden Equity Growth	1.0	19.6	6.0	1.3	-3.6	.....	.....	.....	.....	.....
Metlife MVP Equity Fund	1.1	13.4	-3.3	-1.4	-0.5	12.9	-11.8	.....	.....	.....
Metlife MVP Growth Fund	10.6	.....	.....	.....	.....	.....	.....	.....	.....	.....
Middlefield Growth Fund	-10.2	57.2	4.9	.....	.....	.....	.....	.....	.....	.....
Montreal Trust Excelsior Equity	5.9	17.7	-0.2	5.8	-2.0	10.1	-4.0	22.1	14.5	22.3
Multiple Opportunities Fund	47.0	66.5	-2.1	-3.9	27.3	-35.9	-27.2	93.5	.....	.....
Mutual Canadian Indexfund	3.5	9.2	-0.9	1.0	-0.4	10.4	.....	.....	.....	.....
Mutual Equifund	0.8	15.3	-2.0	-1.9	-8.2	20.4	-6.2	8.2	26.7	.....
Mutual Premier Blue Chip Fund	1.0	.....	.....	.....	.....	.....	.....	.....	.....	.....
Mutual Premier Growth Fund	2.6	.....	.....	.....	.....	.....	.....	.....	.....	.....
MD Equity Fund	11.0	29.3	-1.8	0.9	-0.4	11.1	6.1	20.5	20.5	33.9
MD Select Fund	.....	.....	.....	.....	.....	.....	.....	.....	.....	.....
National Life Equities Fund	6.0	23.8	3.1	8.7	-2.6	12.5	-1.3	23.7	17.5	34.3
National Trust Canadian Equity	-4.3	18.5	5.1	6.7	0.8	10.8	-9.7	14.6	24.9	31.0
National Trust Special Equity Fund	-0.9	.....	.....	.....	.....	.....	.....	.....	.....	.....
NatCan Canadian Equity Fund	-1.9	.....	.....	.....	.....	.....	.....	.....	.....	.....
NAL-Investor Equity Fund	-4.5	20.2	-0.7	4.1	-0.8	12.0	-7.6	.....	.....	.....
NN Canadian Growth	0.5	16.8	0.0	4.7	-6.5	9.9	-16.6	20.3	14.6	34.2
NN Canadian 35 Index	3.2	8.4	-1.0	1.2	-1.3	.....	.....	.....	.....	.....
Ontario Teachers Group Div.	1.4	17.3	-3.1	-0.8	-0.8	16.9	-4.7	17.3	21.3	34.8
Ontario Teachers Group Growth	1.7	17.6	-4.2	-0.6	0.9	16.9	-4.6	17.6	24.9	38.4
Optima Strategy Canadian Equity	7.6	7.0	3.6	1.4	-2.9	15.5	-9.4	11.9	19.8	31.0
Optimum Fonds d'Actions	.....	.....	.....	.....	.....	.....	.....	.....	.....	.....
OHA Canadian Equity Fund	-15.1	.....	.....	.....	.....	.....	.....	.....	.....	.....
PH&N RSP/RIF Equity	6.4	16.5	0.6	1.1	5.2	17.9	-6.3	16.5	29.0	29.3
PH&N Cdn. Equity	5.7	16.1	-1.2	1.3	4.1	18.2	-2.9	16.1	29.7	28.1
PH&N Vintage	4.9	23.0	8.2	10.5	13.3	17.2	-10.2	25.2	.....	.....
Polymetric Performance Fund	-1.1	9.4	-2.7	.....	.....	.....	.....	.....	.....	.....
Prudential Growth Fund Canada	-7.9	50.5	8.7	-0.9	-4.0	10.8	-14.6	28.0	23.7	27.8
Pursuit Canadian Equity Fund	-3.1	31.1	5.8	10.3	-8.9	0.6	.....	.....	.....	.....
Resolute Growth Fund	.....	.....	.....	.....	.....	.....	.....	.....	.....	.....
Royal Life Equity Fund	5.0	12.8	4.0	11.6	.....	.....	.....	.....	.....	.....
Royal Trust Cdn Special Growth	0.9	.....	.....	.....	.....	.....	.....	.....	.....	.....
Royal Trust Canadian Stock Fund	2.5	16.2	3.2	2.6	-4.3	15.1	-5.7	17.6	11.2	24.6
Royfund Equity Ltd.	5.0	27.5	-1.4	-6.3	0.1	10.2	-8.4	11.8	34.9	35.0
Royfund Growth Fund	0.7	.....	.....	.....	.....	.....	.....	.....	.....	.....
Saxon Small Cap	6.8	38.4	6.0	-1.9	-13.4	9.1	-9.1	11.9	.....	.....
Saxon Stock Fund	-2.0	51.9	0.1	1.6	-5.4	2.0	-12.9	5.5	.....	.....
Sceptre Equity Fund	22.7	15.0	-2.2	3.2	0.1	13.4	4.8	.....	.....	.....
Scotia Canadian Equity Growth	-3.0	16.7	7.9	7.6	-2.4	9.9	-10.9	.....	.....	.....
Spectrum Canadian Equity Fund	3.9	14.5	-1.4	2.6	-4.3	10.1	-3.3	.....	.....	.....
Standard Life Equity Mutual Fund	4.5	.....	.....	.....	.....	.....	.....	.....	.....	.....

Fund	1994	1993	1992	1991	1990	1989	1988	1987	1986	1985
Standard Life Ideal Equity Fund	4.0	14.3	4.2	5.0	0.9	7.7	-8.9	.....	.....	.....
Strata Canadian Fund	.....	.....	.....	.....	.....	.....	.....	.....	.....	.....
Strata Growth Fund	0.7	15.8	6.8	2.8	-5.1	.....	.....	.....	.....	.....
Talvest Growth Fund Inc.	1.3	10.6	2.4	10.6	-1.3	8.8	-0.6	25.7	15.4	27.5
Talvest New Economy	.....	.....	.....	.....	.....	.....	.....	.....	.....	.....
Templeton Heritage Retirement	10.4	10.9	-0.6	-3.4	-1.0	.....	.....	.....	.....	.....
Top Fifty Equity Fund	-2.4	8.3	3.0	2.2	-5.3	.....	.....	.....	.....	.....
Tradex Equity Fund Ltd.	5.8	20.6	-3.3	0.6	1.0	12.1	-3.2	20.4	20.7	26.1
Trans-Canada Equity Fund	-0.4	35.2	-11.8	1.4	-1.0	11.0	-0.9	26.5	47.0	34.3
Trans-Canada Pension Fund	2.6	36.2	-9.5	6.4	1.4	10.2	-6.0	15.4	23.2	25.6
Trimark Canadian Fund	10.7	22.8	8.0	5.1	3.1	16.9	1.6	19.6	18.1	31.5
Trimark RSP Equity Fund	8.8	17.5	6.6	8.0	1.4	.....	.....	.....	.....	.....
Trimark Select Canadian Growth	9.2	.....	.....	.....	.....	.....	.....	.....	.....	.....
Trust Pret & Revenu Canadian	-0.8	21.5	8.9	3.1	-3.2	12.5	-14.8	17.8	11.1	12.2
United Canadian Equity Fund	5.5	29.2	8.5	9.6	-4.2	16.1	-2.2	4.8	22.4	43.1
United Canadian Growth Fund	4.6	43.9	10.7	3.3	-11.8	13.1	-9.7	13.8	28.9	31.9
Universal Canadian Equity Fund	10.5	34.9	-7.2	-6.5	-7.0	7.6	11.0	17.2	24.3	31.1
University Avenue Canadian Fund	-4.1	56.4	26.8	14.6	.....	.....	.....	.....	.....	.....
Working Opportunity Fund	1.6	0.8	.....	.....	.....	.....	.....	.....	.....	.....
Working Ventures Canadian Fund	1.2	2.9	5.0	8.5	.....	.....	.....	.....	.....	.....
20/20 Canadian Growth Fund	7.9	9.7	2.9	7.7	1.9	.....	.....	.....	.....	.....
20/20 RSP Aggressive Equity	.....	.....	.....	.....	.....	.....	.....	.....	.....	.....
HIGHEST IN GROUP	47.0	106.8	42.4	27.1	27.3	35.6	17.3	93.5	47.0	43.9
AVERAGE IN GROUP	2.4	27.7	3.1	2.8	-1.9	11.6	-5.9	18.4	22.0	28.1
LOWEST IN GROUP	-15.1	0.8	-17.4	-19.3	-15.0	-35.9	-33.0	3.7	6.1	5.6

Special Equity Funds

Fund	1994	1993	1992	1991	1990	1989	1988	1987	1986	1985
All-Canadian Resources Corp.	11.3	54.9	-7.4	-8.9	-15.4	-2.7	-12.4	50.3	-8.1	0.1
Altamira Resource Fund	-5.7	108.8	47.0	8.7	.....	.....	.....	.....	.....	.....
AGF Canadian Resources Fund	-9.2	117.2	-2.8	-11.8	15.8	-6.1	-15.5	69.4	-15.4	-3.5
BPI Canadian Resource Fund Inc.	-9.4	102.3	9.8	7.4	0.5	2.7	-14.0	25.0	5.9	4.1
BPI Global Real Estate Securities	.....	.....	.....	.....	.....	.....	.....	.....	.....	.....
Cambridge Resource Fund	-19.9	202.4	-17.3	-8.4	-7.8	-2.2	-7.7	27.7	17.9	10.6
CIS Global Telecommunications	.....	.....	.....	.....	.....	.....	.....	.....	.....	.....
Dominion Equity Resource Fund	-17.6	163.0	2.1	-7.3	3.1	-37.9	-30.7	39.0	.....	.....
Dynamic Precious Metals Fund	23.1	75.0	-1.9	-3.6	3.1	-12.7	-7.2	73.2	.....	.....
First Cdn. Resource Fund	.....	.....	.....	.....	.....	.....	.....	.....	.....	.....
First Heritage Fund	-3.8	57.6	-3.8	-11.2	-5.1	4.0	-14.4	.....	.....	.....
Global Strategy Div. Gold Plus	.....	.....	.....	.....	.....	.....	.....	.....	.....	.....
Goldfund Ltd.	34.6	65.5	-7.8	-1.1	3.4	-20.4	-20.0	63.8	7.8	-10.6
Goldtrust	22.0	67.2	-6.1	-3.2	3.1	-18.2	-21.0	56.8	17.4	-7.1
Green Line Resource Fund	.....	.....	.....	.....	.....	.....	.....	.....	.....	.....
Green Line Science & Tech. Fund	.....	.....	.....	.....	.....	.....	.....	.....	.....	.....
Investors Real Property Fund	-0.3	-2.1	2.1	5.3	7.3	11.6	9.2	10.2	10.0	9.9
MD Realty Fund A Units	-4.6	-25.9	-5.1	-0.1	14.4	14.8	7.7	19.9	5.4	10.1
MD Realty Fund B Units	-1.1	-27.3	-5.4	-0.7	14.4	14.8	7.5	19.1	4.1	8.7
Prudential Nat'l Resource of Can.	-7.8	125.6	14.1	-6.4	14.4	18.7	.....	.....	.....	.....
Prudential Precious Metals of Can.	15.4	62.5	3.0	-15.7	12.2	2.1	.....	.....	.....	.....
Royal Lepage Comm. Real Estate	-0.4	-2.9	-2.1	8.6	7.6	.....	.....	.....	.....	.....
Royal Trust Energy Fund	-7.7	115.6	3.6	-7.4	9.4	5.2	-11.4	66.6	-23.3	0.1
Royal Trust Precious Metals Fund	1.0	40.9	0.6	-3.1	-7.6	.....	.....	.....	.....	.....
Roycom-Summit Realty Fund	10.0	0.6	6.3	7.5	12.1	10.7	11.9	.....	.....	.....
Roycom-Summit TDF Fund	3.9	4.7	6.7	7.0	9.9	12.5	14.5	.....	.....	.....
Scotia CanAm Growth Fund	.....	.....	.....	.....	.....	.....	.....	.....	.....	.....
Scotia Precious Metals Fund	.....	.....	.....	.....	.....	.....	.....	.....	.....	.....
Universal Canadian Resource Fund	-0.1	177.2	-9.5	-14.0	-3.6	-8.8	-4.0	53.9	-13.2	4.2
Universal World Precious Metals	.....	.....	.....	.....	.....	.....	.....	.....	.....	.....
HIGHEST IN GROUP	34.6	202.4	47.0	8.7	15.8	18.7	14.5	73.2	17.9	10.6
AVERAGE IN GROUP	1.6	70.6	1.2	-2.8	4.6	-0.7	-6.7	44.2	0.8	2.4
LOWEST IN GROUP	-19.9	-27.3	-17.3	-15.7	-15.4	-37.9	-30.7	10.2	-23.3	-10.6

Fund	1994	1993	1992	1991	1990	1989	1988	1987	1986	1985
U.S. Equity Funds										
Admax American Performance	2.0	6.1	7.5	-2.5	.....	.....	.....	.....	.....	.....
Altamira Select American Fund	17.2	40.7	24.1	.....	.....	.....	.....	.....	.....	.....
Altamira U.S. Larger Company	.....	.....	.....	.....	.....	.....	.....	.....	.....	.....
AGF American Growth Fund Ltd.	9.7	22.1	9.9	-2.6	5.0	21.2	-15.0	8.4	27.0	33.3
AGF Special Fund Ltd.	7.8	20.8	11.8	4.7	8.2	15.3	-8.2	10.5	31.2	23.4
AIC Value Fund	9.1	27.2	16.6	3.7	.....	.....	.....	.....	.....	.....
Beutel Goodman American Equity	11.3	30.1	7.9	.....	.....	.....	.....	.....	.....	.....
Bissett American Equity Fund	7.6	13.2	12.6	6.8	4.0	8.1	-11.5	13.2	13.9	.....
Bullock American Fund	-1.4	19.8	23.5	22.4	32.1	15.8	-20.7	21.2	56.0	16.8
Bullock Optimax U.S.A. Fund 'A'	.....	.....	.....	.....	.....	.....	.....	.....	.....	.....
Bullock Optimax U.S.A. Fund 'B'	.....	.....	.....	.....	.....	.....	.....	.....	.....	.....
Bullock Optimax U.S.A. Fund 'C'	.....	.....	.....	.....	.....	.....	.....	.....	.....	.....
BPI American Equity Growth Fund	17.2	53.2	4.6	7.0	12.7	-17.9	-18.0	.....	.....	.....
BPI American Equity Value Fund	7.3	17.1	9.8	7.4	7.0	.....	.....	.....	.....	.....
C.I. American Fund	16.5	.....	.....	.....	.....	.....	.....	.....	.....	.....
C.I. Sector North American	16.0	.....	.....	.....	.....	.....	.....	.....	.....	.....
Cambridge American Growth	1.4	4.8	.....	.....	.....	.....	.....	.....	.....	.....
Canada Trust Everest AmeriGrowth	0.4	.....	.....	.....	.....	.....	.....	.....	.....	.....
Canada Trust Everest U.S. Equity	0.6	19.4	6.8	.....	.....	.....	.....	.....	.....	.....
Cassels Blaikie Am. Fund ($US)	-5.9	8.5	5.6	2.5	28.0	24.9	-14.8	11.9	51.2	36.4
Century DJ Fund	2.8	9.5	4.6	3.3	17.7	5.2	-25.1	14.3	.....	.....
Chou Associates Fund	4.8	24.2	16.9	5.1	-4.1	18.6	-5.2	.....	.....	.....
Cornerstone U.S. Fund	7.8	13.7	10.9	0.5	15.1	11.4	-27.7	6.1	27.6	14.9
CIBC U.S. Equity Fund	3.6	16.9	16.6	.....	.....	.....	.....	.....	.....	.....
Dynamic American Fund	4.3	15.7	11.8	-4.0	7.5	16.4	-8.1	22.7	22.3	31.1
Elliott & Page American Growth	8.6	15.7	8.3	-0.9	14.7	8.9	-21.6	17.8	35.1	11.9
Ethical North American Equity	3.6	14.1	6.4	3.2	-3.6	9.3	-10.7	12.9	24.3	28.2
Fidelity Growth America Fund	8.6	28.4	23.2	.....	.....	.....	.....	.....	.....	.....
Fidelity Small Cap America Fund	.....	.....	.....	.....	.....	.....	.....	.....	.....	.....
First American	-7.4	32.9	.....	.....	.....	.....	.....	.....	.....	.....
First Cdn. U.S. Growth Fund	.....	.....	.....	.....	.....	.....	.....	.....	.....	.....
General Trust of Canada U.S. Eqty	2.8	35.2	20.0	-0.3	10.5	19.2	-20.9	18.3	39.9	29.6
Global Strategy Div. Americas	3.0	12.6	3.4	1.0	6.9	10.0	-18.1	.....	.....	.....
Global Strategy U.S. Growth	-3.2	.....	.....	.....	.....	.....	.....	.....	.....	.....
Green Line US Index Fund ($US)	0.6	11.2	11.7	5.5	13.7	18.2	-8.6	.....	.....	.....
Guardian American Equity Fund	11.8	22.7	16.1	4.2	11.3	12.3	-13.1	12.5	22.3	10.5
Guardian North American Fund	11.9	23.1	16.2	0.3	5.7	14.5	-24.0	3.1	25.2	13.3
Guardian Vantage U.S. Equity	9.4	18.9	14.9	6.7	12.1	.....	.....	.....	.....	.....
GBC North AmFund Inc.	4.6	36.3	25.0	-5.5	-1.8	16.1	-7.2	11.2	29.0	23.7
Hyperion Value Line Equity Trust	-3.3	35.7	16.9	.....	.....	.....	.....	.....	.....	.....
Imperial Growth North Am. Eqt.	11.8	21.1	8.2	-12.1	-5.7	12.1	-6.8	24.2	24.3	28.0
Industrial American Fund	11.0	19.4	10.5	-1.1	7.7	8.3	-6.3	18.4	26.3	29.9
Investors U.S. Growth Fund Ltd.	15.9	18.6	21.7	8.1	7.7	15.8	-14.4	18.5	25.3	27.2
InvesNat Am.Equity Fund (US$)	-4.3	.....	.....	.....	.....	.....	.....	.....	.....	.....
Jarislowsky Finsco American Equity	1.9	10.9	12.2	6.0	9.1	5.6	-14.8	11.9	.....	.....
Jones Heward American Fund	2.6	26.2	9.4	3.6	5.2	20.9	-17.5	14.6	39.0	20.2
Laurentian American Equity Fund	8.5	18.2	8.6	-4.3	1.6	15.6	-8.5	15.2	42.2	27.7
Leith Wheeler U.S. Equity Fund	.....	.....	.....	.....	.....	.....	.....	.....	.....	.....
London Life U.S. Equity	4.9	18.4	14.3	-2.9	-7.5	18.6	.....	.....	.....	.....
Mackenzie Sentinel Am. Equity	9.1	17.8	9.7	-3.8	10.2	19.7	.....	.....	.....	.....
Margin of Safety Fund	7.6	14.1	3.9	16.3	5.2	.....	.....	.....	.....	.....
Mawer U.S. Equity Fund	4.7	.....	.....	.....	.....	.....	.....	.....	.....	.....
McLean Budden Am. Growth Fund	6.2	8.4	15.3	15.1	17.6	.....	.....	.....	.....	.....
Metlife MVP U.S. Equity Fund	7.2	.....	.....	.....	.....	.....	.....	.....	.....	.....
Mutual Amerifund	9.2	17.1	6.4	-2.6	3.4	10.4	-3.6	9.6	.....	.....
Mutual Premier American Fund	9.0	.....	.....	.....	.....	.....	.....	.....	.....	.....
MD U.S. Equity Fund	9.6	.....	.....	.....	.....	.....	.....	.....	.....	.....
National Trust American Equity	4.9	.....	.....	.....	.....	.....	.....	.....	.....	.....
NatCan American Equity ($US)	0.3	.....	.....	.....	.....	.....	.....	.....	.....	.....

Fund	1994	1993	1992	1991	1990	1989	1988	1987	1986	1985
NAL-Investor U.S. Equity Fund	.....	.....	.....	.....	.....	.....	.....	.....	.....	.....
NN Can-Am Fund	-0.5	.....	.....	.....	.....	.....	.....	.....	.....	.....
Optima Strategy U.S. Equity	.....	.....	.....	.....	.....	.....	.....	.....	.....	.....
PH&N U.S. Equity	12.4	23.2	12.8	9.7	17.6	13.1	-10.6	8.1	28.8	32.4
Prosperity American Performance	.....	.....	.....	.....	.....	.....	.....	.....	.....	.....
Pursuit American Fund ($US)	-7.3	-5.8	13.3	24.6	15.1	9.0	.....	.....	.....	.....
Royal Trust American Stock Fund	8.7	19.6	12.9	1.8	18.2	16.1	-15.6	16.8	31.8	21.9
Royal Trust Zweig Strat. Growth	13.1	27.3	.....	.....	.....	.....	.....	.....	.....	.....
Royfund U.S. Equity Fund	11.1	29.3	.....	.....	.....	.....	.....	.....	.....	.....
Scotia American Equity Growth	11.3	16.7	8.3	6.8	11.5	-5.9	-22.9	.....	.....	.....
Talvest U.S. Growth Fund Ltd.	4.8	15.0	16.7	8.7	20.4	14.4	-15.0	6.6	25.8	26.6
Top Fifty U.S. Equity Fund	-3.1	27.0	.....	.....	.....	.....	.....	.....	.....	.....
Trust Pret & Revenu American	4.6	7.6	20.4	3.1	13.6	11.2	-22.3	15.0	35.4	24.2
U.S. Polymetric Performance	3.1	8.8	.....	.....	.....	.....	.....	.....	.....	.....
United American Growth Fund	7.3	22.7	13.1	12.6	2.3	19.8	-17.1	6.4	32.2	29.2
Universal U.S. Emerging Growth	3.6	44.1	.....	.....	.....	.....	.....	.....	.....	.....
University Avenue Growth Fund	-0.5	-6.3	-6.1	2.0	0.6	18.1	-19.7	32.8	.....	.....
20/20 Aggressive Growth Fund	8.7	.....	.....	.....	.....	.....	.....	.....	.....	.....
20/20 U.S. Growth Fund	15.4	21.9	5.5	5.1	10.0	.....	.....	.....	.....	.....
HIGHEST IN GROUP	17.2	53.2	25.0	24.6	32.1	24.9	0.0	32.8	56.0	36.4
AVERAGE IN GROUP	5.9	19.8	12.1	3.9	9.2	12.9	-14.8	14.2	31.1	24.6
LOWEST IN GROUP	-7.4	-6.3	-6.1	-12.1	-7.5	-17.9	-27.7	3.1	13.9	10.5

International Equity Funds

Fund	1994	1993	1992	1991	1990	1989	1988	1987	1986	1985
Admax Global Health Sciences	16.2	.....	.....	.....	.....	.....	.....	.....	.....	.....
Altamira Asia Pacific Fund	31.4	.....	.....	.....	.....	.....	.....	.....	.....	.....
Altamira Diversified Fund	17.9	7.3	12.2	-10.2	-9.3	5.7	-22.4	2.7	42.3	.....
Altamira European Equity Fund	.....	.....	.....	.....	.....	.....	.....	.....	.....	.....
AGF Asian Growth Fund Limited	38.7	21.3	.....	.....	.....	.....	.....	.....	.....	.....
AGF China Focus Fund 'A'	.....	.....	.....	.....	.....	.....	.....	.....	.....	.....
AGF China Focus Fund 'B & C'	.....	.....	.....	.....	.....	.....	.....	.....	.....	.....
AGF European Growth Ltd 'B & C'	.....	.....	.....	.....	.....	.....	.....	.....	.....	.....
AGF European Growth 'A'	.....	.....	.....	.....	.....	.....	.....	.....	.....	.....
AGF Japan Fund Ltd.	21.8	32.9	-13.0	-16.3	16.1	-6.8	4.6	31.8	92.9	15.9
AIC World Fund	.....	.....	.....	.....	.....	.....	.....	.....	.....	.....
Beutel Goodman Int'l Equity	37.5	.....	.....	.....	.....	.....	.....	.....	.....	.....
Bullock Asian Dynasty 'A'	.....	.....	.....	.....	.....	.....	.....	.....	.....	.....
Bullock Asian Dynasty 'B'	.....	.....	.....	.....	.....	.....	.....	.....	.....	.....
Bullock Asian Dynasty 'C'	.....	.....	.....	.....	.....	.....	.....	.....	.....	.....
Bullock Emerging Markets 'A'	.....	.....	.....	.....	.....	.....	.....	.....	.....	.....
Bullock Emerging Markets 'B'	.....	.....	.....	.....	.....	.....	.....	.....	.....	.....
Bullock Emerging Markets 'C'	.....	.....	.....	.....	.....	.....	.....	.....	.....	.....
BPI Global Equity Fund	23.1	5.3	18.4	-2.5	17.8	11.3	-17.8	14.7	.....	.....
BPI Global Small Companies Fund	43.1	.....	.....	.....	.....	.....	.....	.....	.....	.....
BPI International Equity Fund	19.6	12.6	13.3	-0.4	17.3	.....	.....	.....	.....	.....
C.I. Emerging Asian Fund	.....	.....	.....	.....	.....	.....	.....	.....	.....	.....
C.I. Emerging Markets Fund	30.5	13.4	.....	.....	.....	.....	.....	.....	.....	.....
C.I. European Fund	13.7	-4.6	.....	.....	.....	.....	.....	.....	.....	.....
C.I. Global Equity RSP Fund	.....	.....	.....	.....	.....	.....	.....	.....	.....	.....
C.I. Global Fund	19.6	17.3	21.7	2.2	10.8	3.0	-11.4	19.0	.....	.....
C.I. Latin American Fund	.....	.....	.....	.....	.....	.....	.....	.....	.....	.....
C.I. Pacific Fund	36.3	24.6	15.4	-7.0	21.4	2.0	-8.0	34.8	110.1	11.9
C.I. Sector Emerging Markets	29.9	.....	.....	.....	.....	.....	.....	.....	.....	.....
C.I. Sector European Fund	13.3	.....	.....	.....	.....	.....	.....	.....	.....	.....
C.I. Sector Global Fund	19.5	17.3	20.7	2.3	10.4	2.1	.....	.....	.....	.....
C.I. Sector Pacific Fund	35.7	24.2	15.3	-7.0	20.6	1.9	.....	.....	.....	.....
Caldwell Securities International	19.9	1.1	.....	.....	.....	.....	.....	.....	.....	.....
Cambridge Americas Fund	-1.6	21.3	12.6	-0.2	10.0	2.9	-14.7	.....	.....	.....
Cambridge Global Fund	8.5	18.9	8.7	-6.9	-2.7	6.5	9.0	20.0	30.8	28.1
Cambridge Pacific Fund	14.3	19.5	-0.4	1.4	18.4	.....	.....	.....	.....	.....

Fund	1994	1993	1992	1991	1990	1989	1988	1987	1986	1985
Canada Life U.S. & Int. Eqty S-34	18.9	18.7	19.7	3.0	13.3	17.5	-7.7	13.3	31.7	27.8
Canada Trust Everest AsiaGrowth	.....	.....	.....	.....	.....	.....	.....	.....	.....	.....
Canada Trust Everest EuroGrowth	.....	.....	.....	.....	.....	.....	.....	.....	.....	.....
Canada Trust Everest International	25.0	11.6	3.1	-5.2	26.0	30.0	.....	.....	.....	.....
Canada Trust Everest North Am.	-1.0	29.8	5.0	2.9	-2.0	11.9	-9.3	10.8	26.8	25.2
Capstone Int. Investment Trust	13.0	19.1	12.9	4.5	14.5	10.4	-6.2	.....	.....	.....
Cassels Blaikie International Fund	18.2	5.3	5.2	-19.5	16.9	-2.5	-24.5	15.6	.....	.....
Clean Environment Int'l Equity	.....	.....	.....	.....	.....	.....	.....	.....	.....	.....
Cornerstone Global Fund	20.5	13.7	10.5	1.3	16.0	7.9	-20.6	.....	.....	.....
Cundill Value Fund Ltd.	23.4	25.1	9.7	-5.7	1.6	10.4	10.3	16.6	22.6	13.6
CIBC Far East Prosperity Fund	.....	.....	.....	.....	.....	.....	.....	.....	.....	.....
CIBC Global Equity Fund	14.7	9.4	23.4	-10.7	13.4	5.8	.....	.....	.....	.....
Dynamic Europe 1992 Fund	21.2	-1.3	8.1	-17.4	.....	.....	.....	.....	.....	.....
Dynamic Far East Fund	.....	.....	.....	.....	.....	.....	.....	.....	.....	.....
Dynamic Global Green Fund	-8.3	25.1	-0.4	-11.4	16.4	3.7	-13.9	.....	.....	.....
Dynamic Global Partners Fund	.....	.....	.....	.....	.....	.....	.....	.....	.....	.....
Dynamic International Fund	8.5	28.2	9.5	10.9	-9.6	-2.6	-27.7	47.0	.....	.....
Empire International Fund	15.7	16.7	17.3	3.2	13.2	.....	.....	.....	.....	.....
Fidelity European Growth Fund	22.7	6.6	.....	.....	.....	.....	.....	.....	.....	.....
Fidelity Far East Fund	24.7	29.1	.....	.....	.....	.....	.....	.....	.....	.....
Fidelity International Portfolio	19.7	23.2	10.3	-7.4	22.8	11.6	.....	.....	.....	.....
Fidelity Japanese Growth Fund	.....	.....	.....	.....	.....	.....	.....	.....	.....	.....
Fidelity Latin American Growth	.....	.....	.....	.....	.....	.....	.....	.....	.....	.....
Finsco Global Fund	25.9	15.2	15.8	-7.3	.....	.....	.....	.....	.....	.....
First Canadian Int'l Growth	26.2	.....	.....	.....	.....	.....	.....	.....	.....	.....
Fonds de Professionnels Intl Equity	.....	.....	.....	.....	.....	.....	.....	.....	.....	.....
Fonds Desjardins International	24.9	16.3	15.3	-2.1	15.8	17.1	-16.9	.....	.....	.....
General Trust of Canada Intl.	27.4	12.0	13.0	-10.2	21.5	5.3	.....	.....	.....	.....
Global Strategy Asia Fund	.....	.....	.....	.....	.....	.....	.....	.....	.....	.....
Global Strategy Div. Japan Plus	.....	.....	.....	.....	.....	.....	.....	.....	.....	.....
Global Strategy Diversified Asia	.....	.....	.....	.....	.....	.....	.....	.....	.....	.....
Global Strategy Diversified Europe	6.0	.....	.....	.....	.....	.....	.....	.....	.....	.....
Global Strategy Diversified Latin	.....	.....	.....	.....	.....	.....	.....	.....	.....	.....
Global Strategy Europe	4.5	7.8	11.0	-13.1	14.4	11.6	-25.8	.....	.....	.....
Global Strategy Fund	6.7	16.0	3.3	-7.3	12.1	11.3	-17.3	24.7	.....	.....
Global Strategy Japan Plus Fund	20.1	13.6	1.4	-10.0	19.7	12.1	-8.9	.....	.....	.....
Global Strategy Latin Fund	.....	.....	.....	.....	.....	.....	.....	.....	.....	.....
Global Strategy Real Estate Sec.	1.4	12.5	-8.1	-14.3	.....	.....	.....	.....	.....	.....
Green Line Asian Growth Fund	.....	.....	.....	.....	.....	.....	.....	.....	.....	.....
Green Line Emerging Markets	27.8	.....	.....	.....	.....	.....	.....	.....	.....	.....
Green Line Global Select Fund	.....	.....	.....	.....	.....	.....	.....	.....	.....	.....
Green Line International Equity	27.5	.....	.....	.....	.....	.....	.....	.....	.....	.....
Green Line North Amer. Growth	.....	.....	.....	.....	.....	.....	.....	.....	.....	.....
Guardian Global Equity (EAFE)	26.2	6.4	0.7	-12.1	10.0	8.8	-13.9	12.7	52.7	20.6
Guardian Pacific Rim Corporation	24.8	28.6	-2.8	-6.2	2.0	-2.1	.....	.....	.....	.....
GBC International Growth Fund	13.6	11.8	2.0	-12.5	.....	.....	.....	.....	.....	.....
Hercules European Value Fund	.....	.....	.....	.....	.....	.....	.....	.....	.....	.....
Hercules Latin American Value	.....	.....	.....	.....	.....	.....	.....	.....	.....	.....
Hercules N. Am. Growth and Inc.	.....	.....	.....	.....	.....	.....	.....	.....	.....	.....
Hercules Pacific Basin Value Fund	.....	.....	.....	.....	.....	.....	.....	.....	.....	.....
Hongkong Bank Asian Growth	.....	.....	.....	.....	.....	.....	.....	.....	.....	.....
Hyperion Asian Trust	42.0	16.7	23.6	-11.6	.....	.....	.....	.....	.....	.....
Hyperion European Trust	17.5	0.5	29.4	.....	.....	.....	.....	.....	.....	.....
HRL Overseas Growth Fund	24.7	.....	.....	.....	.....	.....	.....	.....	.....	.....
Investors European Growth Fund	18.6	-2.0	24.5	.....	.....	.....	.....	.....	.....	.....
Investors Global Fund Ltd.	23.4	8.4	14.3	-6.4	20.5	3.0	-14.9	.....	.....	.....
Investors Growth Portfolio Fund	17.7	22.8	8.5	-1.1	7.1	.....	.....	.....	.....	.....
Investors Japanese Growth Fund	30.4	37.7	-6.7	-9.4	-1.7	-2.6	4.5	31.8	87.9	7.2
Investors North American Growth	5.7	23.7	13.9	7.1	7.9	21.8	-9.8	18.8	25.5	28.5
Investors Pacific International	43.6	17.0	26.4	.....	.....	.....	.....	.....	.....	.....
Investors Special Fund Ltd.	-0.6	36.4	11.8	9.5	12.0	18.3	-10.0	16.6	21.3	17.7

Fund	1994	1993	1992	1991	1990	1989	1988	1987	1986	1985
Investors World Growth Portfolio	18.5	.....	.....	.....	.....	.....	.....	.....	.....	.....
InvesNat European Equity Fund	27.6	.....	.....	.....	.....	.....	.....	.....	.....	.....
Ivy Foreign Equity Fund	10.2	.....	.....	.....	.....	.....	.....	.....	.....	.....
Laurentian Commonwealth Fund	14.0	15.8	11.2	-1.7	6.6	14.4	-3.7	21.4	30.4	24.2
Laurentian Global Balanced Fund	8.8	15.6	7.2	-2.6	.....	.....	.....	.....	.....	.....
Laurentian International Fund Ltd	18.0	17.7	8.2	-4.8	9.4	9.9	-5.2	10.4	32.3	21.1
Mackenzie Sentinel Global Fund	27.0	17.2	1.3	-15.3	10.0	4.7	-21.3	.....	.....	.....
Mawer World Investment Fund	26.6	5.1	25.0	0.7	10.1	.....	.....	.....	.....	.....
Montreal Trust Excelsior Intl	19.5	19.6	10.1	-1.3	12.6	7.3	-15.7	18.7	37.7	36.0
Mutual Premier International Fund	23.5	.....	.....	.....	.....	.....	.....	.....	.....	.....
MD Growth Investments Ltd.	28.4	14.9	21.3	-9.6	10.1	8.7	-5.2	25.3	37.5	36.8
National Life Global Equities Fund	.....	.....	.....	.....	.....	.....	.....	.....	.....	.....
NAL-Investor Global Equity Fund	29.6	20.7	.....	.....	.....	.....	.....	.....	.....	.....
NN Can-Asian Fund	.....	.....	.....	.....	.....	.....	.....	.....	.....	.....
Ontario Teachers Group Global	7.6	17.1	6.3	.....	.....	.....	.....	.....	.....	.....
Orbit World Fund	18.6	14.2	6.3	1.9	9.2	.....	.....	.....	.....	.....
OHA Foreign Equity Fund	20.9	.....	.....	.....	.....	.....	.....	.....	.....	.....
PH&N North American Equity	7.3	.....	.....	.....	.....	.....	.....	.....	.....	.....
Regent Europa Performance Fund	3.0	.....	.....	.....	.....	.....	.....	.....	.....	.....
Regent International Fund	36.1	20.3	10.5	-13.2	17.4	-1.6	.....	.....	.....	.....
Regent Korea Fund	32.7	8.7	.....	.....	.....	.....	.....	.....	.....	.....
Regent Nippon Fund	11.2	.....	.....	.....	.....	.....	.....	.....	.....	.....
Regent Tiger Fund	38.1	16.4	13.3	-8.9	.....	.....	.....	.....	.....	.....
Royal Trust Asian Growth Fund	.....	.....	.....	.....	.....	.....	.....	.....	.....	.....
Royal Trust European Growth	24.5	5.7	18.9	-11.8	0.3	3.4	.....	.....	.....	.....
Royal Trust Japanese Stock Fund	32.4	32.8	-16.9	-8.5	-4.7	-6.9	-4.7	42.4	87.7	.....
Royfund International Equity Fund	24.6	.....	.....	.....	.....	.....	.....	.....	.....	.....
Saxon World Growth	16.0	32.6	9.1	-5.3	-5.1	29.1	-10.8	31.6	.....	.....
Sceptre Asian Growth Fund	50.3	.....	.....	.....	.....	.....	.....	.....	.....	.....
Sceptre International Fund	29.5	27.0	23.9	-4.7	19.1	19.5	-4.4	.....	.....	.....
Scotia Global Growth Fund	.....	.....	.....	.....	.....	.....	.....	.....	.....	.....
Special Opportunities Fund	6.7	26.1	-11.4	5.8	.....	.....	.....	.....	.....	.....
Spectrum International Equity	17.2	9.1	19.7	-5.1	11.2	6.9	-17.7	.....	.....	.....
Talvest Global Diversified Fund	19.7	11.2	17.6	-8.0	14.9	6.1	.....	.....	.....	.....
Talvest Global Growth Fund Inc.	19.1	.....	.....	.....	.....	.....	.....	.....	.....	.....
Templeton Emerging Markets	29.5	19.6	.....	.....	.....	.....	.....	.....	.....	.....
Templeton Global Smaller Companies	18.1	23.9	10.1	-0.9	8.1	.....	.....	.....	.....	.....
Templeton Growth Fund Ltd.	23.9	16.3	28.0	-4.0	11.0	15.4	-10.4	19.3	31.8	28.2
Templeton International Stock	32.8	24.1	20.1	-5.7	7.9	.....	.....	.....	.....	.....
Total Return Fund Inc.	1.5	21.3	13.4	0.7	-1.2	.....	.....	.....	.....	.....
Trimark - The Americas Fund	11.7	.....	.....	.....	.....	.....	.....	.....	.....	.....
Trimark Fund	23.2	28.6	20.0	0.7	8.6	14.9	-0.5	17.5	31.2	26.5
Trimark Select Growth Fund	19.2	25.9	20.3	0.0	11.4	.....	.....	.....	.....	.....
United American Equity Fund	2.0	7.0	13.8	8.4	3.6	25.7	-14.9	11.7	34.2	32.9
United Global Equity Fund	12.5	13.5	13.4	.....	.....	.....	.....	.....	.....	.....
United Global Growth Fund	21.0	20.4	14.5	-2.5	-14.5	11.4	-18.9	4.3	27.4	30.3
United Global Telecommunications	.....	.....	.....	.....	.....	.....	.....	.....	.....	.....
Universal Americas Fund	12.1	22.0	13.6	0.0	9.4	8.8	-5.8	18.9	26.6	27.3
Universal Far East Fund	.....	.....	.....	.....	.....	.....	.....	.....	.....	.....
Universal Japan Fund	.....	.....	.....	.....	.....	.....	.....	.....	.....	.....
Universal World Asset Allocation	.....	.....	.....	.....	.....	.....	.....	.....	.....	.....
Universal World Emerging Growth	.....	.....	.....	.....	.....	.....	.....	.....	.....	.....
Universal World Equity Fund	29.0	18.5	1.9	-14.1	8.6	2.8	-1.4	32.1	.....	.....
Vision Europe Fund	16.4	-2.2	.....	.....	.....	.....	.....	.....	.....	.....
20/20 Asia Pacific Fund	29.5	.....	.....	.....	.....	.....	.....	.....	.....	.....
20/20 Latin America	.....	.....	.....	.....	.....	.....	.....	.....	.....	.....
20/20 Multimanager Emerging Mkts	.....	.....	.....	.....	.....	.....	.....	.....	.....	.....
20/20 RSP Int'l Equity Allocation										
HIGHEST IN GROUP	50.3	37.7	29.4	10.9	26.0	30.0	10.3	47.0	110.1	36.8
AVERAGE IN GROUP	20.4	16.8	11.2	-4.7	10.0	8.5	-10.6	20.9	43.9	24.2
LOWEST IN GROUP	-8.3	-4.6	-16.9	-19.5	-14.5	-6.9	-27.7	2.7	21.3	7.2

Fund	1994	1993	1992	1991	1990	1989	1988	1987	1986	1985
Balanced Funds										
Admax Asset Allocation Fund	5.6	.....	.....	.....	.....	.....	.....	.....	.....	.....
Altamira Balanced Fund	-4.4	33.4	9.0	-0.9	-5.0	8.6	-13.6	11.6	21.1	.....
Altamira Growth & Income Fund	8.9	18.5	18.3	10.8	3.5	12.3	12.6	12.3	.....	.....
ABC Fully-Managed Fund	20.2	38.2	-1.1	17.7	5.3	22.5			.....	.....
AMI Private Capital Optimix	2.0	13.8	8.3	5.3	1.3	11.3	.....	.....	.....	.....
Batirente - Section Diversifiee	-1.1	13.5	12.9	8.7	0.2	13.5	.....	.....	.....	.....
Beutel Goodman Balanced Fund	5.2	11.2	8.4	.....	.....	.....	.....	.....	.....	.....
Bissett Retirement Fund	1.9	20.4	.....	.....	.....	.....	.....	.....	.....	.....
Bullock Asset Strategy Fund	1.6	.....	7.7	5.6	0.7	9.3	.....	.....	.....	.....
BPI Balanced Fund	-2.4	21.0	11.6	6.2	-0.2	10.6	.....	.....	.....	.....
BPI Global Balanced Fund	10.2	30.1	10.3	1.0	-0.2	0.7	.....	.....	.....	.....
BPI North American TAA RSP Fund	-2.8	.....	.....	.....	.....	.....	.....	.....	.....	.....
BPI One Decision Balanced Fund	-2.1	20.2	7.1	4.1	1.2	.....	.....	.....	.....	.....
BPI World TAA RSP Fund	5.3	.....	.....	.....	.....	.....	.....	.....	.....	.....
C.I. Canadian Balanced	8.4	.....	.....	.....	.....	.....	.....	.....	.....	.....
Caldwell Securities Associate Fund	16.8	6.1	8.0	.....	.....	.....	.....	.....	.....	.....
Cambridge Balanced Fund	-2.4	37.5	10.8	12.7	2.3	8.5	6.9	10.3	29.4	26.7
Canada Life Managed Fund S-35	1.3	15.4	10.9	6.1	-0.7	13.3	3.2	11.4	20.0	27.4
Canada Trust Everest Balanced	-0.5	18.7	9.4	8.3	2.2	18.5	.....	.....	.....	.....
Capstone Investment Trust	3.6	16.2	2.9	10.3	5.5	9.8	-10.6	10.1	24.7	26.9
Cassels Blaikie Canadian Fund	2.6	10.5	12.6	10.8	2.3	12.4	1.8	11.5	14.1	.....
Clean Environment Balanced Fund	9.1	28.4	.....	.....	.....	.....	.....	.....	.....	.....
Common Sense Asset Builder 1	.....	.....	.....	.....	.....	.....	.....	.....	.....	.....
Cornerstone Balanced Fund	-4.2	14.4	5.9	6.5	0.1	9.2	-17.1	7.0	24.5	21.3
CCPE Diversified Growth Fund R	2.8	11.7	8.6	7.6	2.3	14.5	1.0	11.0	.....	.....
CDA Balanced Fund	0.8	12.4	10.2	8.5	2.5	14.2	0.5	13.0	19.2	24.5
CIBC Balanced Inc. and Growth	-2.8	13.1	6.7	8.7	3.2	11.9	.....	.....	.....	.....
CIS Commax Hedge Fund	.....	.....	.....	.....	.....	.....	.....	.....	.....	.....
Dynamic Managed Portfolio Inc.	1.6	38.9	8.3	1.9	1.3	9.2	-2.3	30.0	.....	.....
Dynamic Partners Fund	6.7	40.5	14.4	5.9	4.1	.....	.....	.....	.....	.....
Elliott & Page Balanced Fund	2.4	26.1	9.1	9.0	-0.9	12.4	.....	.....	.....	.....
Empire Balanced Fund	0.1	15.5	8.7	8.1	3.4	.....	.....	.....	.....	.....
Ethical Balanced Fund	0.7	10.4	5.7	11.5	.....	.....	.....	.....	.....	.....
Fidelity Asset Manager Fund	9.3	.....	.....	.....	.....	.....	.....	.....	.....	.....
Fidelity Growth & Income Fund	4.3	16.9	1.6	6.7	0.4	11.0	.....	.....	.....	.....
First Cdn. Asset Allocation	-5.6	12.2	9.3	8.4	-0.6	10.1	.....	.....	.....	.....
Fonds de Professionnels Balanced	0.3	10.6	13.9	14.0	3.6	10.8	4.2	8.7	15.9	21.5
Fonds Desjardins Equilibre	1.0	14.6	8.6	8.5	0.9	12.2	-0.7	.....	.....	.....
Fonds Ficadre Equilibre	2.4	6.3	11.2	5.4	0.9	9.2	-9.5	14.8	23.6	26.5
General Trust of Canada Balanced	-0.5	13.2	9.5	7.6	-1.3	12.0	-0.2	.....	.....	.....
Global Strategy Diversified Growth	5.1	9.1	-5.4	4.2	-0.1	13.0	.....	.....	.....	.....
Global Strategy Income Plus Fund	5.7	18.0	.....	.....	.....	.....	.....	.....	.....	.....
Great-West Life Diversified RS Inv.	-0.8	15.7	9.1	6.0	2.7	10.6	0.4	12.1	14.6	.....
Great-West Life Equity/Bond	-2.9	21.2	11.5	8.8	1.9	10.8	.....	.....	.....	.....
Green Line Balanced Growth	-4.2	10.6	10.0	5.3	-0.3	12.6	.....	.....	.....	.....
Green Line Balanced Income Fund	-0.7	9.3	8.2	6.6	-1.6	14.1	.....	.....	.....	.....
Guardian Balanced Fund	3.5	13.2	12.3	12.2	5.8	9.7	5.9	14.7	11.5	24.4
Guardian International Balanced	.....	15.4	0.1	6.9	8.9	.....	.....	.....	.....	.....
Hongkong Bank Balanced Fund	2.2	20.6	14.7	6.7	2.1	.....	.....	.....	.....	.....
Hyperion Managed Trust	-2.3	12.5	6.7	8.5	6.9	.....	.....	.....	.....	.....
HRL Balanced Fund	2.9	8.0	3.4	9.8	1.5	12.0	1.0	13.3	16.8	21.1
Imperial Growth Diversified Fund	0.8	11.3	10.1	7.4	2.5	.....	.....	.....	.....	.....
Industrial Alliance Ecoflex Fund D	2.3	.....	.....	.....	.....	.....	.....	.....	.....	.....
Industrial Balanced Fund	-0.5	19.7	6.6	.....	.....	.....	.....	.....	.....	.....
Industrial Income Fund	-4.1	16.5	13.3	8.8	-1.4	12.6	13.2	12.3	18.6	38.0
Integra Balanced Fund	1.9	16.7	12.6	9.4	-3.1	8.8	.....	.....	.....	.....
Investors Asset Allocation Fund	.....	.....	.....	.....	.....	.....	.....	.....	.....	.....
Investors Growth Plus Portfolio	8.8	17.1	9.5	5.2	4.9	.....	.....	.....	.....	.....
Investors Income Plus Portfolio	-0.8	8.9	11.8	11.7	3.5	.....	.....	.....	.....	.....

Fund	1994	1993	1992	1991	1990	1989	1988	1987	1986	1985
Investors Retirement Plus Portfolio	3.8	14.1	7.0	6.7	3.4	.....	.....	.....	.....	.....
InvesNat Retirement Balanced	-3.0	13.5	10.1	10.1	-0.9	.....	.....	.....	.....	.....
Jarislowsky Finsco Balanced Fund	1.0	10.0	7.6	6.5	-0.1	6.0	1.1	6.3	8.6	.....
Jones Heward Canadian Balanced	-2.6	24.0	12.9	7.8	-0.3	8.7	-2.3	6.5	22.0	18.4
Laurentian Canadian Balanced	-0.8	9.7	7.6	7.8	2.9	.....	.....	.....	.....	.....
Leith Wheeler Balanced Fund	4.5	13.6	12.0	11.7	-1.2	8.0	.....	.....	.....	.....
London Life Diversified	-0.5	18.9	11.7	5.7	0.8	12.4	.....	.....	.....	.....
Lotus (MKW) Fund	-0.5	24.4	8.2	7.6	0.4	9.0	-6.1	10.4	19.6	25.7
Manulife Vistafund 1 Diversified	-1.7	17.7	9.5	6.4	0.5	10.7	-1.2	18.3	13.1	21.6
Manulife Vistafund 2 Diversified	-2.5	16.8	8.7	5.6	-0.3	9.9	-2.0	17.5	12.3	20.7
Maritime Life Balanced Fund	0.4	12.8	6.4	8.7	0.7	11.2	1.9	.....	.....	.....
Mawer Cdn. Bal. Rtmt Savings	-0.1	14.9	12.4	9.4	2.8	.....	.....	.....	.....	.....
Mawer Cdn. Div. Investment	-0.7	14.2	11.2	10.0	2.5	.....	.....	.....	.....	.....
McLean Budden Balanced Fund	-0.2	15.1	12.5	9.5	2.1	.....	.....	.....	.....	.....
Metlife MVP Balanced Fund	-0.3	10.8	6.1	5.5	2.2	11.0	-4.1	.....	.....	.....
Montreal Tr. Excelsior Total Return	9.0	20.2	15.3	11.4	1.8	.....	.....	.....	.....	.....
Montreal Trust Excelsior Balanced	4.1	14.1	8.2	9.0	8.4	.....	.....	.....	.....	.....
Mutual Diversifund 25	1.0	9.8	9.1	9.0	1.5	11.1	3.0	6.6	15.9	.....
Mutual Diversifund 40	0.1	13.5	7.3	6.3	-2.9	14.1	0.6	6.9	19.7	.....
Mutual Diversifund 55	0.4	14.4	4.6	3.9	-4.2	16.0	-0.9	7.8	20.9	.....
MD Balanced Fund	4.4	.....	.....	.....	.....	.....	.....	.....	.....	.....
National Life Balanced Fund	2.5	18.4	.....	.....	.....	.....	.....	.....	.....	.....
National Trust Balanced Fund	-1.8	15.0	12.2	.....	.....	.....	.....	.....	.....	.....
NAL-Investor Diversified Fund	-3.8	17.1	7.0	7.7	0.4	11.1	1.3	.....	.....	.....
NN Balanced Fund	0.7	15.0	7.4	5.9	0.3	8.1	0.5	.....	.....	.....
Ontario Teachers Group Balanced	1.8	18.5	4.5	7.5	3.2	14.0	2.0	13.2	.....	.....
Optimum Fonds Equilibre	-0.4	14.3	12.6	8.5	0.0	12.3	5.0	8.1	.....	.....
OHA Balanced Fund	-5.4	.....	.....	.....	.....	.....	.....	.....	.....	.....
PH&N Bal Pens Trust	5.0	14.4	11.7	9.5	5.7	.....	.....	.....	.....	.....
PH&N Balanced	4.4	14.3	.....	.....	.....	.....	.....	.....	.....	.....
Protected American Fund	-3.2	37.3	6.4	9.1	8.3	-2.3	7.2	3.1	.....	.....
Prudential Diversified Invest Fund	-4.7	26.8	14.1	9.6	-2.3	13.7	.....	.....	.....	.....
Royal Life Balanced Fund	0.1	13.3	7.9	11.8	.....	.....	.....	.....	.....	.....
Royal Trust Advantage Balanced	2.3	14.2	10.9	8.4	3.2	12.0	0.2	.....	.....	.....
Royal Trust Advantage Growth	-2.9	16.0	8.5	5.8	2.9	10.7	-4.4	.....	.....	.....
Royal Trust Advantage Income	1.7	12.4	12.6	10.3	4.3	11.4	3.1	.....	.....	.....
Royfund Balanced Fund	3.6	19.5	13.0	4.3	3.8	9.8	.....	.....	.....	.....
Saxon Balanced Fund	-1.0	38.6	6.1	3.9	-8.0	3.8	-13.1	4.5	.....	.....
Sceptre Balanced Fund	6.2	13.2	10.2	8.7	0.9	11.8	3.4	13.3	.....	.....
Scotia Stock & Bond Fund	0.5	12.5	4.6	4.3	0.6	12.6	-0.8	.....	.....	.....
Spectrum Diversified Fund	-2.4	13.6	8.8	7.2	-0.1	10.2	1.6	.....	.....	.....
Standard Life Balanced Mutual	-0.9	.....	.....	.....	.....	.....	.....	.....	.....	.....
Standard Life Ideal Balanced Fund	0.9	12.3	14.2	9.9	1.5	8.4	-0.6	.....	.....	.....
Stratafund 40	-1.8	13.6	12.8	10.2	-0.5	.....	.....	.....	.....	.....
Stratafund 60	-0.1	14.6	10.6	7.4	-1.9	.....	.....	.....	.....	.....
Talvest Diversified Fund	3.4	12.4	7.6	8.4	3.2	9.1	6.3	13.9	.....	.....
Talvest U.S. Diversified Fund	3.7	16.8	.....	.....	9.5	7.8	-14.3	15.9	.....	.....
Templeton Balanced Fund	7.6	10.9	7.3	.....	-3.7	8.7	-11.4	19.0	23.0	20.9
Trimark Income Growth Fund	6.0	18.4	12.4	7.2	2.6	13.2	.....	.....	.....	.....
Trimark Select Balanced Fund	5.3	17.9	12.2	10.1	.....	.....	.....	.....	.....	.....
Trust Pret & Revenu Retirement	-0.2	13.3	15.3	8.9	3.7	10.0	-1.4	11.1	16.0	17.2
United Cdn Portfolio of Funds	1.6	20.7	11.3	10.4	0.1	.....	.....	.....	.....	.....
United Global Portfolio of Funds	2.6	16.3	12.4	7.8	2.2	.....	.....	.....	.....	.....
Universal World Balanced RRSP	.....	.....	.....	.....	.....	.....	.....	.....	.....	.....
20/20 Am. Tactical Asset Alloc.	4.6	23.4	17.6	4.7	4.2	.....	.....	.....	.....	.....
20/20 Canadian Asset Allocation	4.6	10.6	9.6	8.9	3.1	.....	.....	.....	.....	.....
20/20 European Asset Allocation	.....	.....	.....	.....	.....	.....	.....	.....	.....	.....
20/20 World Fund	25.1	14.9	18.7	-11.6	10.5	4.0	.....	.....	.....	.....
HIGHEST IN GROUP	25.1	40.5	18.7	17.7	10.5	22.5	13.2	30.0	29.4	38.0
AVERAGE IN GROUP	1.8	16.8	9.5	7.7	1.7	10.8	-0.6	11.7	18.5	23.9
LOWEST IN GROUP	-5.6	6.1	-5.4	-11.6	-8.0	-2.3	-17.1	3.1	8.6	17.2

Fund	1994	1993	1992	1991	1990	1989	1988	1987	1986	1985
Canadian Bond Funds										
Admax Canadian Income Fund	0.1	9.4	10.0	9.9	3.3	.....	.....	.....	.....	.....
Altamira Bond Fund	-5.6	19.2	18.3	11.7	3.6	11.8	.....	.....	.....	.....
Altamira Income Fund	-3.1	16.8	21.4	14.9	5.7	13.6	10.4	7.5	11.8	21.8
AGF Canadian Bond Fund	-3.9	14.6	21.7	10.0	1.4	12.2	7.5	5.8	20.4	31.6
AMI Private Capital Income	-1.7	12.1	17.2	13.6	2.5	10.3	.....	.....	.....	.....
Batirente - Section Obligations	-2.2	15.1	20.3	12.8	0.1	13.7	.....	.....	.....	.....
Beutel Goodman Income Fund	-3.4	11.9	18.5	.....	.....	.....	.....	.....	.....	.....
Bissett Bond Fund	0.3	9.9	17.4	14.4	2.6	11.8	8.5	.....	.....	.....
BNP (Canada) Bond Fund	-1.8	11.2	.....	.....	.....	.....	.....	.....	.....	.....
BPI Bond Fund	-3.9	10.9	17.0	12.9	2.3	.....	.....	.....	.....	.....
BPI Canadian Bond Fund	1.4	6.5	15.1	9.3	4.1	7.9	6.6	1.7	.....	.....
BPI RSP Bond Fund	-3.0	11.6	17.9	14.6	2.5	12.0	.....	.....	.....	.....
C.I. Canadian Bond Fund	-1.3	.....	.....	.....	.....	.....	.....	.....	.....	.....
Canada Life Fixed Income S-19	-2.1	11.4	16.6	12.3	3.4	9.6	6.7	6.4	14.8	24.7
Canada Trust Everest Bond Fund	-2.8	11.4	20.0	13.0	3.0	12.9	11.3	.....	.....	.....
Canada Trust Income Investments	-0.9	12.6	14.0	13.8	3.0	11.0	7.8	.....	.....	.....
Canada Trust Inv. Fund-Income	-5.3	12.7	15.5	11.6	2.3	9.2	6.9	.....	.....	.....
Clean Environment Income Fund	.....	.....	.....	.....	.....	.....	.....	.....	.....	.....
Colonia Bond Fund	-0.2	11.2	.....	.....	.....	.....	.....	.....	.....	.....
Concorde Revenu	-2.5	8.1	.....	.....	.....	.....	.....	.....	.....	.....
Confed Fixed Income	-2.5	10.9	17.3	12.1	2.1	11.9	9.6	10.2	14.0	42.3
Confed Life C	-2.2	11.4	18.0	12.7	2.6	12.6	10.2	10.8	14.7	43.1
Cornerstone Bond Fund	-1.8	11.0	16.1	13.1	7.9	10.4	6.5	.....	.....	.....
CCPE Fixed Income Fund	-0.1	13.7	18.0	12.8	3.9	10.6	4.9	4.8	.....	.....
CDA Bond and Mortgage Fund	-0.4	10.9	16.9	14.1	5.4	11.5	8.2	8.1	14.0	21.3
CIBC Canadian Bond Fund	-7.2	12.9	20.1	12.8	2.6	11.3	.....	.....	.....	.....
CIBC Canadian Income Fund	.....	.....	.....	.....	.....	.....	.....	.....	.....	.....
Dynamic Government Income	.....	14.5	33.8	.....	.....	.....	.....	.....	.....	.....
Dynamic Income Fund	8.5	12.6	16.5	11.6	4.8	13.9	6.6	8.2	14.0	30.3
Elliott & Page Bond Fund	-4.9	10.2	16.2	11.7	6.1	11.8	.....	.....	.....	.....
Empire Bond Fund	-2.0	9.4	17.7	14.0	2.6	11.4	3.0	6.5	.....	.....
Equitable Life Canadian Bond Fund	-1.9	.....	.....	.....	.....	.....	.....	.....	.....	.....
Equitable Life Segregated Accum	-1.7	11.8	19.6	15.9	5.2	10.6	8.7	7.5	15.6	27.4
Ethical Income Fund	-2.0	8.6	8.8	12.8	10.0	7.5	6.8	5.2	10.7	25.5
Fidelity Government Bond Fund	0.3	12.5	13.9	6.5	4.6	7.0	.....	.....	.....	.....
First Canadian Bond Fund	-2.9	11.3	19.2	13.6	0.9	10.2	.....	.....	.....	.....
Fonds de Professionnels Bond	-2.0	10.4	16.7	15.5	3.7	10.3	7.3	8.7	15.1	21.0
Fonds Desjardins Obligations	-2.3	11.6	14.8	13.8	1.1	10.7	7.1	5.4	15.7	29.6
Fonds Ficadre Obligations	-3.3	9.0	16.7	14.0	2.3	10.3	.....	.....	.....	.....
General Trust of Canada Bond	-2.8	12.4	18.1	13.6	0.7	11.6	7.3	5.4	17.8	32.9
Global Strategy Bond Fund	.....	.....	.....	.....	.....	.....	.....	.....	.....	.....
Great-West Life Canadian Bond	-3.6	11.2	17.6	13.3	0.0	10.6	7.4	5.9	14.7	26.0
Green Line Canadian Bond Fund	-3.3	12.3	18.1	12.2	2.5	7.4	.....	.....	.....	.....
Green Line Canadian Govt. Bond	-2.4	11.3	14.4	11.4	-0.8	12.8	.....	.....	.....	.....
Green Line Short Term Income	-0.4	6.3	8.3	11.3	12.2	.....	.....	.....	.....	.....
Guardian Canada Bond Fund	0.8	8.5	6.8	11.4	10.8	10.3	8.4	.....	.....	.....
Gyro Bond Fund	-2.1	11.4	20.8	12.5	.....	.....	.....	.....	.....	.....
GBC Canadian Bond Fund	-1.9	13.0	19.4	14.0	1.4	13.1	8.9	7.0	16.1	.....
Hyperion Fixed Income Trust	-7.4	13.2	19.4	12.3	.....	.....	.....	.....	.....	.....
HRL Bond Fund	-3.2	11.3	14.9	9.7	2.8	11.1	2.9	.....	.....	.....
Industrial Alliance Ecoflex Fund B	-3.5	.....	.....	.....	.....	.....	.....	.....	.....	.....
Industrial Bond Fund	-5.2	12.4	18.3	12.6	1.2	.....	.....	.....	.....	.....
Investors Bond Fund	-2.6	10.9	16.6	13.3	3.3	11.5	7.4	6.4	16.3	28.5
Investors Corporate Bond Fund	.....	.....	.....	.....	.....	.....	.....	.....	.....	.....
InvesNat Bond Fund	0.0	9.1	17.3	14.2	2.6	.....	.....	.....	.....	.....
Ivy Growth & Income Fund	-1.0	.....	.....	.....	.....	.....	.....	.....	.....	.....
Jarislowsky Finsco Bond Fund	-1.4	11.4	17.5	11.3	1.6	9.5	7.9	5.0	14.9	.....
Jones Heward Bond Fund	-3.8	11.4	15.8	12.5	2.4	11.5	7.7	.....	.....	.....
Laurentian Government Bond	-0.3	8.0	13.5	13.8	4.7	.....	.....	.....	.....	.....

Fund	1994	1993	1992	1991	1990	1989	1988	1987	1986	1985
Laurentian Income Fund	-2.3	11.0	15.0	13.0	2.4	10.4	7.7	7.2	16.7	31.0
Leith Wheeler Fixed Income Fund	.....	.....	.....	.....	.....	.....	.....	.....	.....	.....
London Life Bond	-3.1	11.2	17.7	5.2	3.1	13.2	5.3	4.2	21.2	41.3
Lotus (MKW) Bond Fund	.....	.....	.....	.....	.....	.....	.....	.....	.....	.....
Mackenzie Sentinel Canada Bond	-5.8	14.9	18.0	12.3	0.6	10.8	7.4	8.4	.....	.....
Manulife Vistafund 1 Bond Fund	-5.9	14.1	18.1	14.2	2.9	11.8	8.5	7.3	14.8	22.9
Manulife Vistafund 2 Bond Fund	-6.6	13.3	17.2	13.4	2.2	11.0	7.7	6.6	14.0	22.0
Maritime Life Bond Fund	-2.5	11.0	17.0	13.4	.....	.....	.....	.....	.....	.....
Mawer Canadian Bond Fund	-2.5	11.2	.....	.....	.....	.....	.....	.....	.....	.....
McLean Budden Fixed Income	-2.4	12.3	17.6	14.3	5.1	.....	.....	.....	.....	.....
Metlife MVP Bond Fund	-3.3	9.2	14.5	12.3	3.8	11.2	2.1	.....	.....	.....
Montreal Trust Excelsior Income	-1.4	12.0	19.3	13.2	0.9	11.7	6.6	7.6	19.3	24.9
Mutual Bond Fund	-2.0	11.1	16.2	.....	.....	.....	.....	.....	.....	.....
Mutual Premier Bond Fund	-2.0	.....	.....	.....	.....	.....	.....	.....	.....	.....
MD Bond Fund	-1.0	12.2	18.2	13.5	3.8	12.3	.....	.....	.....	.....
National Life Fixed Income Fund	0.4	13.6	19.6	16.0	5.0	12.7	9.0	8.2	17.7	29.8
National Trust Canadian Bond	-3.2	11.7	17.0	13.0	0.7	10.7	7.8	7.3	16.3	30.0
NatCan Canadian Bond Fund	-2.6	.....	.....	.....	.....	.....	.....	.....	.....	.....
NAL-Investor Bond Fund	-1.2	10.9	16.7	12.2	1.8	9.6	9.0	.....	.....	.....
NN Bond Fund	-1.8	11.6	15.2	13.4	3.6	9.6	4.7	.....	.....	.....
Optima Strategy Canadian Income	-2.8	10.3	17.2	12.5	0.1	12.9	1.0	4.9	16.9	22.9
Optima Strategy Sht Term Income	1.4	.....	.....	.....	.....	.....	.....	.....	.....	.....
Optimum Fonds d'Obligations	-2.6	14.2	20.7	12.5	0.4	12.8	7.9	7.4	.....	.....
OHA Bond Fund	-4.4	.....	.....	.....	.....	.....	.....	.....	.....	.....
PH&N Bond Fund	-0.5	12.9	19.8	15.2	3.4	13.2	9.4	9.3	18.6	34.0
Prudential Income Fund of Canada	-3.5	12.2	14.5	12.5	1.7	13.2	9.3	7.3	13.4	22.5
Pursuit Income Fund	4.2	10.8	15.3	8.9	0.6	10.4	.....	.....	.....	.....
PH &N Sht Term Bond & Mort.	.....	.....	.....	.....	.....	.....	.....	.....	.....	.....
Royal Life Income Fund	-4.1	12.0	13.1	10.0	.....	.....	.....	.....	.....	.....
Royal Trust Bond Fund	-1.5	11.9	18.4	13.6	1.9	11.0	7.4	6.2	16.4	29.9
Royfund Bond Fund	-1.1	11.0	19.0	13.4	3.0	9.4	7.8	6.9	15.7	23.9
Sceptre Bond Fund	-5.5	11.4	17.2	16.1	5.8	8.4	8.6	7.1	.....	.....
Scotia Defensive Income Fund	0.9	7.9	12.3	12.3	3.7	8.3	.....	.....	.....	.....
Scotia Income Fund	-0.9	9.7	12.3	11.4	4.5	10.0	7.0	.....	.....	.....
Spectrum Government Bond Fund	-5.7	13.8	19.9	10.7	2.3	.....	.....	.....	.....	.....
Spectrum Interest Fund	-4.6	11.7	17.1	12.1	3.7	9.8	6.0	.....	.....	.....
Standard Life Bond Mutual Fund	-2.6	.....	.....	.....	.....	.....	.....	.....	.....	.....
Standard Life Ideal Bond Fund	-2.6	12.3	18.8	13.3	1.8	8.9	8.6	.....	.....	.....
Strata Government Bond Fund	.....	.....	.....	.....	.....	.....	.....	.....	.....	.....
Strata Income Fund	-3.8	11.3	17.5	14.0	2.5	.....	.....	.....	.....	.....
Talvest Bond Fund	-2.4	11.2	17.7	12.9	2.3	11.6	8.0	9.3	15.9	30.2
Talvest Income Fund	-0.2	10.0	13.7	13.5	5.6	9.1	8.3	8.6	10.3	19.1
Templeton Heritage Bond Fund	1.1	9.2	16.4	7.9	.....	.....	.....	.....	.....	.....
Top Fifty T-Bill/Bond Fund	-8.1	9.5	15.3	11.7	10.4	.....	.....	.....	.....	.....
Tradex Bond Fund	-4.9	10.2	12.7	11.3	.....	.....	.....	.....	.....	.....
Trans-Canada Bond Fund	-1.0	6.1	14.8	11.9	3.9	6.2	9.0	.....	.....	.....
Trimark Government Income Fund	.....	.....	.....	.....	.....	.....	.....	.....	.....	.....
Trust Pret & Revenu Bond Fund	-1.9	9.5	20.0	12.6	4.4	8.6	.....	.....	.....	.....
United Canadian Bond Fund	-4.8	13.4	17.0	14.0	8.4	2.7	5.1	8.0	14.2	29.5
Universal Canadian Bond Fund	-5.6	14.3	17.2	12.0	0.8	13.6	12.1	6.9	15.7	36.4
University Avenue Bond Fund	0.4	.....	.....	.....	.....	.....	.....	.....	.....	.....
20/20 Income Fund	-3.9	11.4	16.6	10.3	1.7	8.5	1.7	12.0	.....	.....
HIGHEST IN GROUP	8.5	19.2	33.8	16.1	12.2	13.9	12.1	12.0	21.2	43.1
AVERAGE IN GROUP	-2.3	11.4	16.9	12.6	3.3	10.7	7.3	7.1	15.6	28.5
LOWEST IN GROUP	-8.1	6.1	6.8	5.2	-0.8	2.7	1.0	1.7	10.3	19.1
Canadian Mortgage Funds										
Canada Trust Everest Mortgage	3.4	8.6	11.1	15.4	8.4	9.2	9.1	8.4	10.9	17.0
Colonia Mortgage Fund	1.7	6.7	.....	.....	.....	.....	.....	.....	.....	.....
Concorde Hypotheques	1.0	9.0	12.8	.....	.....	.....	.....	.....	.....	.....
Confed Mortgage Fund	1.3	8.2	10.2	14.5	9.5	9.1	8.7	8.6	10.5	16.5

Fund	1994	1993	1992	1991	1990	1989	1988	1987	1986	1985
CIBC Mortgage Investment Fund	1.2	9.1	14.5	17.1	7.2	9.4	7.6	8.8	10.3	15.3
First Canadian Mortgage Fund	0.9	8.5	13.9	19.1	7.7	8.9	9.1	9.1	11.4	18.2
Fonds Desjardins Hypotheques	2.2	7.8	10.7	14.7	8.5	9.0	9.4	.....	.....	.....
General Trust of Canada Mortgage	8.1	7.3	13.3	15.3	8.0	8.0	7.9	9.2	12.8	21.7
Great-West Life Mort. Investment	-0.6	9.2	15.7	13.3	3.5	10.8	7.8	6.7	12.5	18.8
Green Line Canadian Mortgage	1.0	9.1	12.5	16.2	9.4	9.8	9.7	8.5	10.5	13.7
Green Line Mortgage-Backed	1.1	6.8	11.6	15.0	11.8	.....	.....	.....	.....	.....
Hongkong Bank Mortgage Fund	7.5	.....	.....	.....	.....	.....	.....	.....	.....	.....
Industrial Alliance Ecoflex Fund H	1.0	.....	.....	.....	.....	.....	.....	.....	.....	.....
Industrial Mortgage Securities	-2.3	17.9	14.0	9.6	-1.0	12.9	13.0	12.5	17.6	30.3
Investors Income Portfolio Fund	-1.8	9.2	13.4	14.2	4.6	.....	.....	.....	.....	.....
Investors Mortgage Fund	-0.7	7.8	10.5	15.7	7.1	9.0	8.8	8.4	11.4	18.5
InvesNat Mortgage Fund	3.3	8.0	.....	.....	.....	.....	.....	.....	.....	.....
Ivy Mortgage Fund	.....	.....	.....	.....	.....	.....	.....	.....	.....	.....
London Life Mortgage	1.0	10.6	12.7	15.7	7.3	8.9	8.7	9.3	13.7	22.9
Mandate National Mortgage Corp.	.....	9.1	9.5	11.2	16.9	16.7	14.6	14.1	15.7	17.3
Montreal Trust Excelsior Mortgage	2.9	8.6	10.1	14.5	8.9	8.8	8.8	8.1	10.6	16.4
Mutual Premier Mortgage Fund	1.6	.....	.....	.....	.....	.....	.....	.....	.....	.....
National Trust Mortgage Fund	-0.2	.....	.....	.....	.....	.....	.....	.....	.....	.....
Ont. Teachers Grp Mortgage Inc	3.8	11.4	9.1	10.5	10.3	9.7	9.2	9.0	10.2	15.5
Royal Trust Mortgage Fund	-0.4	7.7	10.9	15.7	8.6	8.5	9.2	8.7	11.2	16.8
Royfund Mortgage Fund	3.4	9.4	.....	.....	.....	.....	.....	.....	.....	.....
Scotia Mortgage Fund	1.4	.....	.....	.....	.....	.....	.....	.....	.....	.....
Trust Pret & Revenu H Fund	0.1	9.1	12.0	15.7	7.6	9.2	8.5	9.6	10.7	17.5
United Canadian Mortgage Fund	-1.4	6.5	9.4	14.9	7.2	9.0	7.8	7.5	8.7	14.9
HIGHEST IN GROUP	8.1	17.9	15.7	19.1	16.9	16.7	14.6	14.1	17.6	30.3
AVERAGE IN GROUP	1.5	8.9	11.9	14.6	8.0	9.8	9.3	9.2	11.8	18.2
LOWEST IN GROUP	-2.3	6.5	9.1	9.6	-1.0	8.0	7.6	6.7	8.7	13.7

U.S. and International Bond Funds

Fund	1994	1993	1992	1991	1990	1989	1988	1987	1986	1985
Altamira Global Bond Fund	.....	.....	.....	.....	.....	.....	.....			
AGF Global Government Bond	7.2	7.4	28.5	4.4	11.2	2.6	1.6	.....		.....
AGF Strategic Income Fund	.....	16.5	14.1	3.5	-6.2	11.1	.....			
AGF U.S. Income Fund	1.4	.....	.....	.....	.....	.....	.....			
Bullock Global Bond 'A'	.....	.....	.....	.....	.....					
Bullock Global Bond 'B'	.....	.....	.....	.....	.....					
Bullock Global Bond 'C'	.....	.....	.....	.....	.....					
C.I. Global Bond RSP Fund	.....	.....	.....	.....						
C.I. World Bond Fund	4.2	.....	.....	.....						
Canada Life Int'l Bond S-36	.....	.....	.....	.....	.....					
Dynamic Global Bond Fund	11.3	11.4	25.3	-0.7	5.4	2.3				
Fidelity Emerging Markets Bond	.....	.....	.....	.....	.....					
Fidelity Global Bond Fund	.....	.....	.....	.....						
Fidelity North American Income	2.6	.....	.....	.....						
First Cdn. International Bond Fund	.....	.....	.....							
Global Strategy Diversified Bond	-3.3	14.6	19.9	.....	.....					
Global Strategy World Bond Fund	-4.3	19.0	20.4	6.9	1.5	6.3	.....			
Green Line Global Gov't Bond	6.6	.....	.....	.....						
Green Line Global RSP Bond Fund	.....	.....	.....	.....	.....		.....			
Guardian International Income	3.1	16.1	17.2	3.9	3.4	2.1	-1.4	.....		
Hercules World Bond Fund	.....	.....	.....	.....	.....					
Investors Global Bond Fund	7.1	.....	.....	.....	.....					
Lotus (MKW) International Bond	.....	.....	.....	.....						
Optima Strat. Global Fixed Income	.....	.....	.....	.....	.....					
Regent World Income Fund	3.2	26.1	.....	.....	.....					
Royal Trust International Bond	6.9	20.6	.....	.....						
Royfund International Income	10.7	.....	.....	.....						
Scotia Canam Income Fund ($US)	-2.0	8.8	.....	.....						
Spectrum International Bond Fund	8.9	.....	.....	.....	.....					
Talvest Foreign Pay Bond Fund	6.3	.....	.....	.....						

Fund	1994	1993	1992	1991	1990	1989	1988	1987	1986	1985
Templeton Global Income Fund	3.3	11.5	16.8	10.0	9.7	.....	.....	.....	.....	.....
20/20 Foreign RSP Bond Fund	.....	.....	.....	.....	.....	.....	.....	.....	.....	.....
20/20 World Bond Fund	0.1	.....	.....	.....	.....	.....	.....	.....	.....	.....
HIGHEST IN GROUP	11.3	26.1	28.5	10.0	11.2	11.1	1.6	.....	.....	.....
AVERAGE IN GROUP	4.1	15.2	20.3	4.7	4.2	4.9	0.1	.....	.....	.....
LOWEST IN GROUP	-4.3	7.4	14.1	-0.7	-6.2	2.1	-1.4	.....	.....	.....

Canadian Money Market Funds

Fund	1994	1993	1992	1991	1990	1989	1988	1987	1986	1985
Admax Cash Performance Fund	3.1	.....	.....	.....	.....	.....	.....	.....	.....	.....
AGF Money Market Account	3.6	5.3	7.3	11.3	12.0	10.4	8.4	7.8	9.3	10.8
AMI Private Capital Money Market	4.4	5.9	7.9	11.4	11.4	9.6	.....	.....	.....	.....
Batirente - Sec. Marche Monetaire	3.7	5.5	8.7	12.8	9.7	9.7	.....	.....	.....	.....
Beutel Goodman Money Market	4.6	6.2	9.0	.....	.....	.....	.....	.....	.....	.....
Bissett Money Market Fund	4.5	5.9	.....	.....	.....	.....	.....	.....	.....	.....
BNP (Canada) Cdn Money Market	3.6	4.9	.....	.....	.....	.....	.....	.....	.....	.....
BPI Money Market Fund	3.1	4.4	6.6	10.5	12.1	8.8	7.6	7.0	.....	.....
BPI Short Term Interest Fund	.....	5.0	6.4	9.5	10.4	.....	.....	.....	.....	.....
BPI T-Bill Fund	.....	5.5	7.5	11.4	12.2	10.6	8.6	8.1	9.3	10.9
C.I. Money Market Fund	4.1	5.7	7.8	.....	.....	.....	.....	.....	.....	.....
C.I. Sector Short-Term	2.4	3.3	4.1	6.8	7.1	5.1	.....	.....	.....	.....
Canada Life Money Market S-29	4.0	5.3	7.2	11.7	11.1	9.9	7.1	6.0	7.7	10.0
Canada Trust Everest Money Mkt	3.6	4.6	7.6	11.9	12.6	11.5	8.1	.....	.....	.....
Capstone Cash Management Fund	3.6	6.0	8.2	11.9	12.3	10.0	.....	.....	.....	.....
Colonia Money Market Fund	3.2	5.0	.....	.....	.....	.....	.....	.....	.....	.....
Concorde Monetaire	4.2	4.8	.....	.....	.....	.....	.....	.....	.....	.....
Cornerstone Gov Money	3.7	5.1	7.3	11.5	.....	.....	.....	.....	.....	.....
CDA Money Market Fund	3.9	5.8	8.0	11.8	12.0	10.8	8.2	7.5	9.6	11.0
CIBC Canadian T-Bill Fund	3.1	4.6	6.7	.....	.....	.....	.....	.....	.....	.....
CIBC Money Market Fund	3.3	4.5	7.2	11.2	12.4	.....	.....	.....	.....	.....
CIBC Premium T-Bill Fund	3.8	5.3	7.3	.....	.....	.....	.....	.....	.....	.....
Dynamic Money Market Fund	3.7	5.1	7.5	12.0	11.7	8.9	8.0	7.2	8.9	10.3
Elliott & Page Money Fund	4.3	5.4	8.5	12.4	12.5	10.8	8.8	8.5	10.1	.....
Elliott & Page T-Bill Fund	.....	.....	.....	.....	.....	.....	.....	.....	.....	.....
Empire Money Market Fund	3.2	4.6	7.5	11.6	10.0	.....	.....	.....	.....	.....
Ethical Money Market Fund	3.6	5.3	7.2	11.4	12.7	10.5	8.6	7.7	9.2	10.8
Fidelity Short Term Asset Fund	3.3	4.9	7.4	.....	.....	.....	.....	.....	.....	.....
Finsco Money Market Fund	3.8	5.1	7.3	11.3	12.2	9.9	8.4	7.9	9.5	.....
Finsco T-Bill Fund	3.4	4.8	6.9	10.8	11.9	9.9	.....	.....	.....	.....
First Canadian Money Market	3.6	5.1	7.5	11.1	11.3	9.1	.....	.....	.....	.....
First Cdn. T-Bill Fund	.....	.....	.....	.....	.....	.....	.....	.....	.....	.....
Fonds de Prof. Short Term	3.9	6.0	9.7	12.8	9.6	9.9	.....	.....	.....	.....
Fonds Desjardins Monetaire	3.7	5.3	7.0	10.8	11.5	.....	.....	.....	.....	.....
Fonds Ficadre Money Market	3.7	5.9	7.5	11.1	.....	.....	.....	.....	.....	.....
General Trust of Cda Money Mkt	3.5	5.4	8.3	12.2	10.7	8.2	11.2	.....	.....	.....
Global Strategy T-Bill Savings Fund	4.1	5.7	7.5	10.2	11.5	9.6	.....	.....	.....	.....
Great-West Life Money Mkt Invest	3.1	4.6	6.9	10.9	12.0	9.9	7.8	7.0	8.9	10.7
Green Line Canadian Money Mkt	4.2	5.5	8.1	11.7	12.7	10.4	.....	.....	.....	.....
Green Line Canadian T-Bill Fund	3.8	4.9	.....	.....	.....	.....	.....	.....	.....	.....
Guardian Canadian Money Mkt	3.9	5.4	7.2	11.8	13.0	10.9	8.7	7.7	9.3	10.7
GBC Money Market Fund	4.0	5.6	7.5	11.6	12.4	.....	.....	.....	.....	.....
Hongkong Bank Money Market	3.5	5.0	6.5	10.7	11.4	.....	.....	.....	.....	.....
HRL Instant $$ Fund	4.2	5.3	7.5	11.6	12.1	10.5	.....	.....	.....	.....
Imperial Growth Money Market	3.0	4.9	6.2	10.8	10.1	.....	.....	.....	.....	.....
Industrial Alliance Ecoflex Fund M	12.9	-4.7	.....	.....	.....	.....	.....	.....	.....	.....
Industrial Cash Management	4.0	5.6	7.5	11.6	12.5	10.9	8.1	7.8	9.4	.....
Industrial Short-Term Fund	3.1	4.3	6.4	.....	.....	.....	.....	.....	.....	.....
Integra Short Term Investment	5.2	.....	.....	.....	.....	.....	.....	.....	.....	.....
Investors Money Market Fund	3.6	5.0	7.0	11.2	11.9	10.1	8.3	7.3	9.0	.....
InvesNat Money Market Fund	3.7	5.3	7.5	.....	.....	.....	.....	.....	.....	.....
Ivy Short-Term Fund	3.1	.....	.....	.....	.....	.....	.....	.....	.....	.....

Fund	1994	1993	1992	1991	1990	1989	1988	1987	1986	1985
Laurentian Money Market Fund	3.5	5.0	7.0	11.1	11.9	10.7	8.4	8.0	9.4	.....
Leith Wheeler Money Market	.....	.....	.....	.....	.....	.....	.....	.....	.....	.....
London Life Money Market	3.4	5.2	10.4	11.6	11.5	.....	.....	.....	.....	.....
Lotus (MKW) Income Fund	4.2	5.3	7.9	12.1	13.2	10.9	.....	.....	.....	.....
Mackenzie Sentinel Cda Money Mkt	4.0	5.5	7.6	11.6	11.8	9.2	8.2	.....	.....	.....
Manulife Vistafund 1 Sht Term Sec	3.1	4.9	7.5	11.6	11.9	10.2	8.0	7.6	8.9	10.4
Manulife Vistafund 2 Sht Term Sec	2.3	4.1	6.7	10.7	11.1	9.4	7.2	6.8	8.1	9.6
Maritime Life Money Market Fund	3.0	4.4	7.9	10.6	11.0	9.3	7.4	7.3	9.2	9.7
Mawer Canadian Money Market	3.7	5.3	7.3	11.2	12.1	9.9	.....	.....	.....	.....
McLean Budden Money Market	3.9	4.9	7.3	11.1	11.9	.....	.....	.....	.....	.....
Metlife MVP Money Market Fund	3.1	4.1	.....	.....	.....	.....	.....	.....	.....	.....
Montreal Trust Exc. Money Mkt	3.8	5.1	7.3	11.3	11.9	10.2	.....	.....	.....	.....
Mutual Money Market	3.8	5.2	6.9	10.7	11.5	9.8	7.7	6.8	8.7	.....
MD Money Fund	4.0	5.4	7.6	11.4	11.6	9.3	7.6	7.1	9.0	10.5
Natcan Treasury Bill Fund	3.8	5.4	7.5	.....	.....	.....	.....	.....	.....	.....
National Life Money Market Fund	4.7	6.2	.....	.....	.....	.....	.....	.....	.....	.....
National Trust Money Market	3.5	5.3	7.0	.....	.....	.....	.....	.....	.....	.....
NAL-Investor Money Market Fund	3.2	5.1	7.3	11.2	12.3	.....	.....	.....	.....	.....
NN Money Market Fund	4.0	5.7	7.8	11.6	.....	.....	.....	.....	.....	°
NN T-Bill Fund	3.1	5.0	7.7	11.0	9.7	8.7	.....	.....	.....	.....
Ont.Teachers Group Fixed Value	4.3	8.6	8.3	11.1	11.1	9.8	8.7	7.6	9.1	10.5
Optimum Fonds d'Épargne	3.9	5.6	9.0	13.2	9.6	10.0	8.3	9.0	.....	.....
OHA Short Term Fund	4.2	.....	.....	.....	.....	.....	.....	.....	.....	.....
Prudential Money Mkt Fd of Can.	4.4	5.7	8.2	11.9	12.2	10.0	8.8	.....	.....	.....
Pursuit Money Market Fund	4.6	6.7	8.0	12.7	11.0	9.5	.....	.....	.....	.....
PH & N Canadian Money Market	4.1	5.8	7.9	11.7	12.7	10.6	8.3	.....	.....	.....
Royal Life Money Market Fund	5.0	.....	.....	.....	.....	.....	.....	.....	.....	.....
Royal Trust Canadian Money Mkt	3.4	4.8	7.4	11.4	11.4	9.7	.....	.....	.....	.....
Royal Trust Cdn T-Bill Money Mkt	2.7	3.9	.....	.....	.....	.....	.....	.....	.....	.....
Royfund Canadian T-Bill Fund	3.7	5.2	7.8	.....	.....	.....	.....	.....	.....	.....
Royfund Money Market Fund	3.4	5.1	7.8	11.4	12.2	10.0	7.8	.....	.....	.....
Sceptre Money Market Fund	3.9	5.7	7.4	11.5	12.1	10.0	.....	.....	.....	.....
Scotia Gov. of Can. Treasury Bill	3.8	4.7	.....	.....	.....	.....	.....	.....	.....	.....
Scotia Money Market Fund	3.7	4.7	7.3	.....	.....	.....	.....	.....	.....	.....
Scotia Premium T-Bill Fund	4.1	.....	.....	.....	.....	.....	.....	.....	.....	.....
Spectrum Cash Reserve Fund	3.7	5.0	7.2	11.2	12.1	10.3	8.0	.....	.....	.....
Spectrum Savings Fund	3.8	4.9	7.4	11.4	12.3	10.6	.....	.....	.....	.....
Standard Life Ideal Money Market	.....	.....	.....	.....	.....	.....	.....	.....	.....	.....
Standard Life Money Market Fund	3.4	.....	.....	.....	.....	.....	.....	.....	.....	.....
Strata Money Market Fund	3.6	5.0	7.0	10.8	11.3	.....	.....	.....	.....	.....
Talvest Money Fund	4.3	5.7	8.1	12.1	12.2	10.8	7.8	2.7	.....	.....
Templeton Treasury Bill Fund	3.9	5.3	7.4	11.4	12.2	10.2	.....	.....	.....	.....
Trans-Canada Money Market	4.5	5.2	7.7	11.2	10.8	.....	.....	.....	.....	.....
Trimark Interest Fund	3.8	5.5	7.3	11.6	12.8	9.6	8.6	.....	.....	.....
Trust Pret & Revenu Money Mkt	4.1	5.3	7.3	11.4	11.1	.....	.....	.....	.....	.....
United Canadian Interest Fund	4.8	6.1	8.5	11.6	12.9	11.6	.....	.....	.....	.....
20/20 Money Market Fund	4.3	5.8	8.0	10.9	.....	.....	.....	.....	.....	.....
HIGHEST IN GROUP	12.9	8.6	10.4	13.2	13.2	11.6	11.2	9.0	10.1	11.0
AVERAGE IN GROUP	3.9	5.1	7.5	11.4	11.6	9.9	8.2	7.3	9.1	10.5
LOWEST IN GROUP	2.3	-4.7	4.1	6.8	7.1	5.1	7.1	2.7	7.7	9.6

U.S. and International Money Market Funds

Fund	1994	1993	1992	1991	1990	1989	1988	1987	1986	1985
Altamira Short Term Global Inc	11.6	8.8	16.2	.....	.....	.....	.....	.....	.....	.....
AGF U.S. Dollar Money Market	2.7	2.8	4.4	6.7	8.7	.....	.....	.....	.....	.....
BNP (Canada) US$ Money Mkt	2.1	1.9	.....	.....	.....	.....	.....	.....	.....	.....
CIBC U.S. Dollar Money Mkt ($US)	2.3	2.3	4.0	.....	.....	.....	.....	.....	.....	.....
Finsco U.S. Money Mkt Fund ($US)	2.5	2.2	3.9	6.5	7.9	7.2	6.3	.....	.....	.....
Global Strategy Diversified Savings	3.5	6.8	13.6	5.9	9.4	5.9	.....	.....	.....	.....
Global Strategy U.S. Savings ($US)	2.8	2.6	4.1	6.1	7.2	7.3	.....	.....	.....	.....
Green Line U.S. Money Mkt ($US)	2.3	2.4	4.2	6.6	7.8	8.1	.....	.....	.....	.....

Fund	1994	1993	1992	1991	1990	1989	1988	1987	1986	1985
Guardian U.S. Money Mkt ($US)	2.7	2.6	4.3	6.7	8.4	8.7	5.9	5.8	.....	.....
Hercules Global Short-Term Fund	.....	.....	.....	.....	.....	.....	.....	.....	.....	.....
InvesNat U.S. Money Mkt $US	2.1	2.1	.....	.....	.....	.....	.....	.....	.....	.....
PH & N $US Money Market	2.9	2.9	4.7	.....	.....	.....	.....	.....	.....	.....
Royal Trust U.S. Money Mkt ($US)	2.2	2.3	4.0	.....	.....	.....	.....	.....	.....	.....
Royfund U.S. Dollar Money ($US)	2.3	2.2	4.0	.....	.....	.....	.....	.....	.....	.....
United U.S. Dollar Money Market	2.9	2.7	2.5	4.7	7.4	9.4	.....	.....	.....	.....
HIGHEST IN GROUP	11.6	8.8	16.2	6.7	9.4	9.4	6.3	5.8	.....	.....
AVERAGE IN GROUP	3.2	3.2	5.8	6.2	8.1	7.8	6.1	5.8	.....	.....
LOWEST IN GROUP	2.1	1.9	2.5	4.7	7.2	5.9	5.9	5.8	.....	.....

Dividend Funds

Fund	1994	1993	1992	1991	1990	1989	1988	1987	1986	1985
AGF High Income Fund	3.6	6.6	14.9	7.9	6.7	7.4	3.6	7.6	10.2	15.1
Bissett Dividend Income Fund	3.5	.....	5.3	2.9	-0.1	7.9	.....	.....	.....	.....
BPI Income Fund	1.6	6.2	3.9	9.8	0.1	9.2	3.1	9.7	7.6	13.4
Corporate Investors Ltd.	6.8	14.5	10.5	1.7	-2.6	10.3	-2.0	22.3	2.4	27.7
CIBC Equity Income Fund	-1.4	18.1	.....	.....	.....	.....	.....	.....	.....	.....
Dynamic Dividend Fund	3.0	14.6	9.6	7.2	2.0	10.1	5.8	11.1	.....	.....
Dynamic Dividend Growth Fund	5.2	13.5	9.7	-2.6	0.8	12.6	0.5	5.5	.....	.....
Fonds Desjardins Dividendes	.....	.....	.....	.....	.....	.....	.....	.....	.....	.....
Green Line Dividend Fund	1.4	13.8	11.7	13.4	0.1	13.3	.....	.....	.....	.....
Guardian Preferred Dividend Fund	1.0	12.5	10.1	5.7	1.6	8.4	4.0	9.1	.....	.....
Industrial Dividend Fund Ltd.	7.1	40.0	-8.3	-8.7	-5.8	2.7	6.1	27.4	16.5	33.2
Investors Dividend Fund	0.6	11.3	12.0	10.6	1.5	12.9	3.6	9.9	9.8	24.2
Investors Mutual of Canada Ltd.	4.3	21.5	6.4	5.8	-0.6	11.6	-1.9	18.4	12.7	21.6
Laurentian Dividend Fund Ltd.	1.0	11.0	8.0	6.2	1.8	14.0	3.6	11.6	15.2	23.5
Mawer Canadian Income Fund	-1.0	.....	.....	.....	.....	.....	.....	.....	.....	.....
Montreal Trust Excelsior Dividend	2.6	13.2	6.0	9.3	1.4	10.0	-0.2	.....	.....	.....
MD Dividend Fund	2.7	.....	.....	.....	.....	.....	.....	.....	.....	.....
National Trust Dividend Fund	4.1	.....	.....	.....	.....	.....	.....	.....	.....	.....
NatCan Dividend Fund	2.4	.....	.....	.....	.....	.....	.....	.....	.....	.....
PH&N Div. Income	5.4	14.7	5.7	5.3	3.5	14.7	2.0	18.8	10.2	20.3
Prudential Dividend Fund of Cda	9.2	34.8	6.1	5.5	-11.8	8.0	6.3	.....	.....	.....
Royal Trust Growth and Income	0.2	10.8	4.7	5.5	-0.6	8.2	0.7	7.2	.....	.....
Royfund Dividend Fund	2.2	.....	.....	.....	.....	.....	.....	.....	.....	.....
Spectrum Dividend Fund	2.5	9.7	4.9	8.9	1.9	12.7	3.4	.....	.....	.....
Trans-Canada Income Fund	6.5	5.0	-7.0	5.0	-2.0	10.9	3.7	17.1	30.3	32.4
20/20 Dividend Fund	3.6	14.5	7.4	6.4	2.9	14.0	1.0	14.3	.....	.....
HIGHEST IN GROUP	9.2	40.0	14.9	13.4	6.7	14.7	6.3	27.4	30.3	33.2
AVERAGE IN GROUP	3.1	15.1	6.4	5.6	0.0	10.5	2.5	13.6	12.8	23.5
LOWEST IN GROUP	-1.4	5.0	-8.3	-8.7	-11.8	2.7	-2.0	5.5	2.4	13.4

Benchmarks

Fund	1994	1993	1992	1991	1990	1989	1988	1987	1986	1985
91-Day Canada T-Bill	4.8	6.5	7.3	10.9	12.8	11.1	8.7	8.0	9.3	10.7
Consumer Price Index	0.0	1.8	1.3	6.1	4.5	4.9	4.1	4.6	4.1	4.0
ScotiaMcLeod Universe Bond Index	-0.8	13.2	20.1	15.3	2.8	12.3	8.7	8.4	18.2	31.9
Standard & Poor's 500 Index(Cdn$)	9.3	21.5	15.2	0.3	11.9	18.9	-15.2	20.6	38.2	34.9
TSE Total Return Index	3.9	20.8	1.1	1.9	-2.4	13.5	-5.2	24.6	17.4	26.7

Survey of Fund Volatility and Compound Performance

(for periods ending June 30, 1994)

This survey provides the total return for the year ended June 30, 1994 and the average annual compound return over three, five and ten years. The star-rating used by the *Financial Times of Canada* ranks funds on their average monthly performance over the past 36 months. The top 10% in a category earn five stars. The bottom 10% earn one star. The variation in a fund's monthly rate of return, the standard deviation, is used to rank the volatility of funds in a category from HIGH to LOW. Under the column labelled RRSP: "R" = 100% eligible for an RRSP or RRIF, "F" = eligible as foreign content, "N" = not eligible at all. Under the column labelled Fees: N = no sales fees, F = front-end load, D = deferred load, O = option, B = both, usually a front-end and back-end fee but can be a redemption fee and a deferred load. MER represents the management expense ratio. An "m" indicates the ratio represents the management fee only. An * indicates additional fees might be charged directly to the investor.

Return	Vol.	Fund	RRSP	Fees	MER	1yr	3yr	5yr	10yr
Canadian Equity Funds									
★★	AV-	20/20 Canadian Growth Fund	R	O	2.50*	7.9	6.8	6.0	NA
NA	NA	20/20 RSP Aggressive Equity	R	O	2.50*	NA	NA	NA	NA
★★★★★	HIGH	ABC Fundamental Value Fund	R	N	2.00	38.2	32.4	25.7	NA
★★	AV-	Admax Cdn Performance Fund	R	O	2.46*	-2.5	6.1	NA	NA
★★	AV-	AGF Canadian Equity Fund	R	O	2.38*	1.2	6.7	1.8	7.9
★★★★	AV+	AGF Growth Equity Fund Ltd.	R	O	2.38*	3.0	23.2	12.9	12.0
★★★★	AV+	AIC Advantage Fund	R	D	2.73*	10.1	18.8	12.1	NA
★★★	AV-	All-Canadian CapitalFund	R	F	2.00*	7.8	9.8	7.0	8.0
★★★	AV-	All-Canadian Compound	R	N	0.00*	8.1	9.7	7.0	8.0
NA	NA	All-Canadian ConsumerFund	R	F	1.97*	5.7	NA	NA	NA
★★★★	AV+	Altafund Investment Corp.	R	N	2.28*	2.3	23.1	NA	NA
★★★★	AV	Altamira Capital Growth Fund	R	N	2.03*	6.6	15.5	11.0	10.4
★★★★★	AV+	Altamira Equity Fund	R	N	2.37*	0.4	29.8	24.0	NA
NA	NA	Altamira N. American Recovery	R	N	2.37*	NA	NA	NA	NA
★★★★	AV+	Altamira Special Growth Fund	R	N	1.81*	-9.8	23.2	17.4	NA
★★	AV-	AMI Private Capital Equity	R	N	1.75*	4.3	6.5	2.4	NA
★	LOW	Associate Investors Ltd.	R	N	2.06	0.2	5.6	3.3	8.6
★	LOW	Batirente - Section Actions	R	N	1.61	-0.8	2.2	0.1	NA
★	AV	Beutel Goodman Cdn Equity	R	N	2.50*	8.3	4.7	NA	NA
★★★	LOW	Bissett Canadian Equity Fund	R	N	1.41	0.2	11.5	8.3	10.9
NA	NA	Bissett Small Cap Fund	R	N	1.5.0	6.7	NA	NA	NA
NA	NA	BNP (Canada) Equity Fund	R	N	2.45	-2.8	NA	NA	NA
★★	AV+	BPI Canadian Equity Fund	R	O	2.81*	-3.5	7.9	3.6	NA
★★★	LOW	BPI Cdn Equity Value Fund	R	O	2.45*	-3.7	9.7	7.2	NA
★★★★	AV	BPI Canadian Small Cap Fund	R	O	2.60*	-1.6	17.1	10.0	NA

Return	Vol.	Fund	RRSP	Fees	MER	1yr	3yr	5yr	10yr
★★★★	AV	Bullock Growth Fund	R	O	2.25	2.4	15.1	8.1	8.2
NA	NA	C.I. Canadian Growth Fund	R	O	2.45	7.3	NA	NA	NA
★★★	AV+	C.I. Sector Canadian Fund	F	O	2.45	6.4	9.2	2.4	NA
★	AV-	CAMAF	R	N	1.31*	-1.8	3.4	2.5	8.6
★★★★	AV+	Cambridge Growth Fund	R	O	2.66*	-4.4	14.2	10.6	15.8
★★★	HIGH	Cambridge Special Equity	R	O	2.66*	-14.8	8.5	0.2	NA
★★	AV-	Canada Life Cdn Equity S-9	R	R	2.00	0.9	7.8	3.6	10.0
★★★★	AV+	Canada Trust Everest Spec. Eqty	R	N	2.09	-5.3	13.9	8.7	NA
★★★	AV-	Canada Trust Everest Stock	R	N	1.94	0.8	11.3	7.2	NA
★★★	AV-	Canada Trust Investment -Eqty	R	N	1.25	-0.1	8.4	5.4	NA
★	LOW	Canadian Investment Fund	R	O	2.25	-0.1	2.3	1.2	6.3
★★★	LOW	Canadian Protected Fund	R	R	2.10	-5.1	8.8	7.9	NA
★	LOW	CCPE Growth Fund R	R	N	1.31	4.8	4.4	2.8	NA
NA	NA	CDA Aggressive Equity Fund	R	N	1.00	NA	NA	NA	NA
★★★	AV-	CDA Common Stock Fund	R	N	0.87	3.2	9.6	6.2	11.8
★	AV-	Chou RRSP Fund	R	F	2.44*	3.1	5.8	2.2	NA
★	AV	CIBC Canadian Equity Fund	R	N	2.25*	-4.7	1.9	2.0	NA
NA	NA	CIBC Capital Appreciation	R	N	2.50*	-6.2	NA	NA	NA
NA	NA	Clean Environment Equity	R	O	2.98*	5.0	NA	NA	NA
NA	NA	Colonia Equity Fund	R	D	2.00	-3.3	NA	NA	NA
NA	NA	Colonia Special Growth Fund	R	D	2.00	NA	NA	NA	NA
NA	NA	Concorde Croissance	R	O	2.10	1.5	NA	NA	NA
★★	AV-	Confed Equity Fund	R	N	2.00	3.3	7.8	2.9	8.8
★★	LOW	Confed Growth Fund	R	F	2.00	4.8	8.2	3.3	9.7
★★★	AV-	Confed Life B	R	F	0.96	4.0	8.8	4.0	10.0
★★★	AV-	Cornerstone Cdn Growth	R	N	2.13*	-3.9	8.8	4.0	NA
★★★★	AV+	Corporate Investors Stock Fund	R	F	2.45*	-1.5	15.3	8.2	6.6
★★	AV	Cundill Security Fund	R	F	2.16*	17.9	7.4	3.0	8.1
★★★★★	HIGH	Dynamic Cdn Growth Fund	R	O	2.75*	1.7	30.8	19.9	NA
★★★★	AV+	Dynamic Fund of Canada	R	O	2.56*	-6.9	14.4	9.2	11.8
★★★★	AV+	Elliott & Page Equity Fund	R	O	1.75*	-2.0	12.3	7.6	NA
★★★	LOW	Empire Elite Equity Fund 5	R	D	2.59	-1.7	9.5	5.4	10.0
★★★	AV	Empire Equity Growth Fund 3	R	F	1.30	3.5	9.9	6.2	12.2
★★★	LOW	Empire Premier Equity Fund 1	R	F	1.56	1.6	8.9	5.5	11.4
NA	NA	Equitable Life Cdn Stock Fund	R	D	2.25	4.0	NA	NA	NA
★★	LOW	Equitable Life Seg. Common Stk	R	F	1.04m*	6.9	7.6	3.6	8.4
★	LOW	Ethical Growth Fund	R	O	2.39*	-1.7	5.1	5.3	NA
★★	AV	Fidelity Capital Builder Fund	R	O	2.21*	-2.9	6.3	6.8	NA
★★	AV	First Canadian Equity Index	R	N	1.44*	2.4	6.4	2.9	NA
NA	NA	First Cdn. Growth Fund	R	N	2.20*	NA	NA	NA	NA
NA	NA	First Cdn. Special Growth Fund	R	N	2.24*	NA	NA	NA	NA
★	LOW	Fonds de Prof. Cdn. Equity	R	N	0.75	-1.7	3.9	2.4	NA
★	AV	Fonds Desjardins Actions	R	N	1.98	-3.1	5.0	2.6	NA
NA	NA	Fonds Desjardins Croissance	R	N	1.80m	NA	NA	NA	NA
★	AV+	Fonds Desjardins Environnement	R	N	1.98	0.2	4.1	NA	NA
★	AV	Fonds Ficadre Actions	R	R	2.75	3.0	5.8	-0.4	NA
★★★★	AV+	GBC Canadian Growth Fund	R	N	1.96	-4.1	18.7	16.3	NA
★	AV-	General Trust of Canada Cdn Equity	R	N	1.50	-1.1	2.9	1.0	6.4
★★★★	AV	General Trust of Canada Growth	R	N	1.83	-2.6	18.0	8.6	NA
NA	NA	Global Strategy Cda Growth	R	O	2.89	0.7	NA	NA	NA
★★★	AV-	Great-West Life Cdn Equity	R	N	2.64	-3.0	11.3	7.8	NA
★	AV	Great-West Life Equity Index	R	N	2.64	1.6	5.9	2.7	7.5
★	LOW	Green Line Blue Chip Equity	R	N	2.27	0.1	4.9	3.1	NA
★★	AV	Green Line Cdn Equity Fund	R	N	2.15	1.7	8.0	3.8	NA

Return	Vol.	Fund	RRSP	Fees	MER	1yr	3yr	5yr	10yr
★★	AV	Green Line Canadian Index	R	N	1.06	2.7	6.9	3.4	NA
NA	NA	Green Line Value Fund	R	N	2.14	NA	NA	NA	NA
★	LOW	Guardian Canadian Equity	R	O	2.64*	-2.4	5.1	1.7	7.4
★★	LOW	Guardian Enterprise Fund	R	O	2.60*	-0.2	7.4	5.9	8.5
★★★★	LOW	Guardian Growth Equity Fund	R	O	2.54*	1.2	15.3	11.2	NA
★★★	AV	Gyro Equity Fund	R	N	0.90*	-2.0	9.1	4.5	NA
★★★★	AV+	Hongkong Bank Equity Fund	R	N	1.53*	4.7	14.1	8.4	NA
★	AV	HRL Canadian Fund	R	N	1.75	1.6	3.8	3.4	NA
NA	NA	Hyperion Aurora Trust	R	F	2.50	NA	NA	NA	NA
★★★	LOW	Imperial Growth Cdn Equity	R	F	2.10	1.5	8.5	4.4	14.4
NA	NA	Industrial Alliance Ecoflex A	R	R	2.00*	6.1	NA	NA	NA
★★★★★	AV+	Industrial Equity Fund Ltd.	R	O	2.63*	3.6	25.7	8.6	10.2
★★★	AV+	Industrial Future Fund	R	O	2.55*	5.3	11.1	5.8	NA
★★	AV+	Industrial Growth Fund	R	O	2.48*	4.2	8.0	3.9	10.0
★★	AV	Industrial Horizon Fund	R	O	2.48*	6.2	8.0	4.5	NA
★★★	AV+	Industrial Pension Fund	R	O	2.59*	11.4	9.2	1.6	8.6
NA	NA	Industrial Strat. Cap Protection	R	O	2.00m*	3.5	NA	NA	NA
★★	AV-	InvesNat Equity Fund	R	N	2.18*	-2.1	7.4	5.3	NA
★★★★	LOW	Investors Canadian Equity	R	B	2.08	5.3	12.3	8.8	10.7
★★★	LOW	Investors Rtmt Gth. Portfolio	R	B	0.18	6.3	8.7	5.9	NA
★★	LOW	Investors Rtmt Mutual Fund	R	B	2.08	5.3	7.2	4.1	9.6
★★	LOW	Investors Summa Fund Ltd.	R	B	2.09	3.2	7.6	4.2	NA
NA	NA	Ivy Canadian Fund	R	O	2.00m*	3.8	NA	NA	NA
NA	NA	Ivy Capital Protection 1994	R	O	2.00m*	NA	NA	NA	NA
NA	NA	Ivy Capital Protection Fund	R	O	2.00m*	-0.7	NA	NA	NA
★	LOW	Jarislowsky Finsco Cdn Equity	R	F	2.41*	1.9	2.4	2.0	NA
★★★★	AV+	Jones Heward Fund Ltd.	R	O	2.50	-5.1	13.5	6.7	10.8
★	AV-	Laurentian Cdn Equity Fund	R	O	2.70*	-0.5	5.6	1.2	7.4
★★★	AV-	Laurentian Special Equity Fund	R	O	2.70*	11.7	12.3	NA	NA
NA	NA	Leith Wheeler Cdn Equity Fund	R	N	1.40m*	NA	NA	NA	NA
★★★	AV	London Life Canadian Equity	R	R	1.50*	-1.5	9.8	4.2	10.1
NA	NA	Lotus Canadian Equity Fund	R	N	2.00*	NA	NA	NA	NA
★★	AV+	Mackenzie Equity Fund	R	O	2.00*	9.9	8.2	1.5	8.7
★★★★	AV+	Mackenzie Sentinel Cda Equity	R	O	2.36*	13.3	15.2	6.5	NA
★★★★	AV	Manulife Vista 1 Cap. Gains Gth	R	F	1.63*	-2.7	12.6	7.9	10.7
★★★	AV	Manulife Vista 1 Equity Fund	R	F	1.63*	-0.5	8.3	5.3	8.0
★★★	AV	Manulife Vista 2 Cap. Gains Gth	R	R	2.38*	-3.4	11.7	7.1	9.8
★★	AV	Manulife Vista 2 Equity Fund	R	R	2.38*	-1.2	7.5	4.5	7.2
★★★★★	HIGH	Marathon Equity Fund	R	N	2.50	11.3	42.7	20.4	NA
★★	AV	Maritime Life Growth Fund	R	N	2.01*	-2.6	6.8	3.0	8.5
NA	NA	Mawer Canadian Equity Fund	R	N	1.64	-2.7	NA	NA	NA
★★★★	AV-	Mawer New Canada Fund	R	N	1.59	16.2	22.5	17.1	NA
★★★	AV-	McLean Budden Eqty Growth	R	N	1.75	1.0	8.6	4.6	NA
★★★	AV-	MD Equity Fund	R	N	1.00	11.0	12.2	7.2	12.5
NA	NA	MD Select Fund	R	N	1.00	NA	NA	NA	NA
★	AV-	Metlife MVP Equity Fund	R	R	2.00m	1.1	3.5	1.7	NA
NA	NA	Metlife MVP Growth Fund	R	R	2.00m	10.6	NA	NA	NA
★★★★	HIGH	Middlefield Growth Fund	R	O	3.14	-10.2	14.0	NA	NA
★★	AV	Montreal Trust Excelsior Equity	R	N	2.08	5.9	7.5	5.2	8.8
★★★★★	HIGH	Multiple Opportunities Fund	R	F	2.73*	47.0	33.8	24.0	NA
★	AV	Mutual Canadian Indexfund	R	F	1.95	3.5	3.9	2.4	NA
★	AV-	Mutual Equifund	R	F	1.80	0.8	4.4	0.5	NA
NA	NA	Mutual Premier Blue Chip	R	N	2.31	1.0	NA	NA	NA
NA	NA	Mutual Premier Growth Fund	R	N	2.29	2.6	NA	NA	NA

Return	Vol.	Fund	RRSP	Fees	MER	1yr	3yr	5yr	10yr
★	AV	NAL-Investor Equity Fund	R	B	1.75	-4.5	4.5	3.3	NA
NA	NA	NatCan Canadian Equity Fund	R	N	1.53*	-1.9	NA	NA	NA
★★★	AV	National Life Equities Fund	R	D	2.00m	6.0	10.6	7.4	12.0
★	AV	National Trust Cdn Eqty Fund	R	N	1.70	-4.3	6.0	5.1	9.2
NA	NA	National Trust Special Eqty	R	N	2.70	-0.9	NA	NA	NA
★	AV	NN Canadian 35 Index	R	R	2.00*	3.2	3.5	2.1	NA
★	AV-	NN Canadian Growth	R	R	2.25*	0.5	5.5	2.8	6.9
NA	NA	OHA Canadian Equity Fund	R	N	0.50*	-15.1	NA	NA	NA
★	AV-	Ont. Teachers Grp Diversified	R	N	0.90	1.4	4.8	2.5	9.3
★	LOW	Ont. Teachers Group Growth	R	N	0.90	1.7	4.6	2.8	10.0
★★	LOW	Optima Strategy Cdn Equity	R	O	0.39*	7.6	6.1	3.3	8.0
NA	NA	Optimum Fonds d'Actions	R	N	1.50m*	NA	NA	NA	NA
★★	LOW	PH&N RSP/RIF Eqt.	R	N	1.24	6.4	7.7	5.8	11.0
★★	AV-	PH&N Cdn. Equity	R	N	1.16	5.7	6.6	5.0	11.0
★★★	LOW	PH&N Vintage	R	F	1.79	4.9	11.8	11.8	NA
★	LOW	Polymetric Performance Fund	R	O	2.45*	-1.1	1.7	NA	NA
★★★★	AV+	Prudential Growth Canada Ltd.	R	F	1.75*	-7.9	14.6	7.5	10.6
★★★	AV-	Pursuit Canadian Equity Fund	R	F	2.00*	-3.1	10.4	6.2	NA
NA	NA	Resolute Growth Fund	R	F	1.00	NA	NA	NA	NA
★★	LOW	Royal Life Equity Fund	R	D	2.37	5.0	7.2	NA	NA
NA	NA	Royal Trust Cdn Special Grth	R	N	2.05*	0.9	NA	NA	NA
★★	LOW	Royal Trust Canadian Stock	R	N	1.93*	2.5	7.1	3.8	7.9
★★★	AV-	Royfund Equity Ltd.	R	N	2.03	5.0	9.7	4.4	9.8
NA	NA	Royfund Growth Fund	R	N	2.19	0.7	NA	NA	NA
★★★★	AV	Saxon Small Cap	R	N	1.75	6.8	16.1	5.9	NA
★★★★	AV+	Saxon Stock Fund	R	N	1.75	-2.0	14.1	7.4	NA
★★★	AV	Sceptre Equity Fund	R	N	2.00*	22.7	11.3	7.3	NA
★★	AV-	Scotia Canadian Equity Growth	R	N	2.15	-3.0	6.9	5.1	NA
★	LOW	Spectrum Canadian Equity	R	O	1.99	3.9	5.5	2.9	NA
NA	NA	Standard Life Equity Mutual	R	N	2.00	4.5	NA	NA	NA
★★	LOW	Standard Life Ideal Equity Fund	R	D	2.00	4.0	7.4	5.6	NA
NA	NA	Strata Canadian Fund	R	N	2.48*	NA	NA	NA	NA
★★	AV	Strata Growth Fund	R	F	1.53	0.7	7.6	4.0	NA
★	AV-	Talvest Growth Fund Inc.	R	O	2.40*	1.3	4.7	4.6	9.6
NA	NA	Talvest New Economy	R	O	2.50*	NA	NA	NA	NA
★★	AV	Templeton Heritage Rtmt Fund	R	O	2.98	10.4	6.7	3.1	NA
★	AV-	Top Fifty Equity Fund	R	F	2.35*	-2.4	2.9	1.0	NA
★★	LOW	Tradex Equity Fund Ltd.	R	N	1.35*	5.8	7.3	4.6	9.6
★	AV+	Trans-Canada Equity Fund	R	O	2.66*	-0.4	5.9	3.6	12.6
★★	HIGH	Trans-Canada Pension Fund	R	O	2.66*	2.6	8.1	6.4	9.7
★★★★	AV-	Trimark Canadian Fund	R	F	1.56*	10.7	13.7	9.7	13.4
★★★	LOW	Trimark RSP Equity Fund	R	D	2.00*	8.8	10.9	8.3	NA
NA	NA	Trimark Select Cdn Growth	R	O	2.60*	9.2	NA	NA	NA
★★★	AV	Trust Pret & Revenu Cdn Fund	R	N	1.80*	-0.8	9.5	5.5	6.3
★★★★	AV-	United Canadian Equity Fund	R	O	2.21*	5.5	14.0	9.2	12.5
★★★★	AV+	United Canadian Growth Fund	R	O	2.29*	4.6	18.5	8.7	11.6
★★★	AV+	Universal Cdn Equity Fund Ltd.	R	O	2.70*	10.5	11.4	3.7	10.6
★★★★★	AV+	University Avenue Cdn Fund	R	N	2.72	-4.1	23.9	NA	NA
NA	NA	Working Opportunity Fund	R	N		1.6	NA	NA	NA
★	LOW	Working Ventures Cdn Fund	R	R	2.23*	1.2	3.0	NA	NA
		HIGHEST IN GROUP				47.0	42.7	25.7	15.8
		AVERAGE IN GROUP				2.4	10.2	6.0	9.7
		LOWEST IN GROUP				-15.1	1.7	-0.4	6.3

Return	Vol.	Fund	RRSP	Fees	MER	1yr	3yr	5yr	10yr
Special Equity Funds									
★★★	AV	AGF Canadian Resources Fund	R	O	2.52*	-9.2	24.2	14.4	8.0
★★	AV+	All-Canadian Resources Corp	R	F	1.94*	11.3	16.9	4.2	3.8
★★★★★	AV-	Altamira Resource Fund	R	N	2.36*	-5.7	42.5	NA	NA
★★★	AV-	BPI Canadian Resource Fund	R	O	2.50*	-9.4	26.3	16.8	10.2
NA	NA	BPI Global Real Estate Sec	F	O	2.00m	NA	NA	NA	NA
★★★	HIGH	Cambridge Resource Fund	R	O	2.66*	-19.9	26.1	11.1	9.8
NA	NA	CIS Global Telecommunications	R	F	2.40*	NA	NA	NA	NA
★★★★	AV+	Dominion Equity Resource	R	R	1.80	-17.6	30.3	16.2	NA
★★★★	AV+	Dynamic Precious Metals Fund	R	O	2.86*	23.1	28.3	16.0	NA
NA	NA	First Cdn. Resource Fund	R	N	2.26*	NA	NA	NA	NA
★★	AV-	First Heritage Fund	R	F	6.25*	-3.8	13.4	4.2	NA
NA	NA	Global Strategy Div. Gold Plus	R	O	2.59	NA	NA	NA	NA
★★★	AV+	Goldfund Ltd.	F	F	3.38	34.6	27.1	16.0	7.8
★★	AV	Goldtrust	R	F	2.48	22.0	24.2	13.8	7.8
NA	NA	Green Line Resource Fund	R	N	2.20	NA	NA	NA	NA
NA	NA	Green Line Science & Tech.	F	N	2.56	NA	NA	NA	NA
★	LOW	Investors Real Property Fund	R	B	2.13	-0.3	-0.1	2.4	6.2
★★	AV-	MD Realty Fund A Units	R	N	1.50m	-4.6	-12.4	-5.2	2.8
★	AV-	MD Realty Fund B Units	F	N	1.50m	-1.1	-12.0	-5.0	2.5
★★★★	AV	Prudential Natural Resource	R	F	1.77*	-7.8	33.4	20.5	NA
★★★	AV	Prudential Precious Metals	R	F	1.83*	15.4	24.5	12.8	NA
★	LOW	Royal Lepage Comm. Real Estate	R	N	3.24	-0.4	-1.8	2.0	NA
★★★	AV	Royal Trust Energy Fund	R	N	2.17*	-7.7	27.3	15.9	9.6
★★	LOW	Royal Trust Precious Metals	R	N	2.70*	1.0	12.7	5.1	NA
★	LOW	Roycom-Summit Realty Fund	F	D	3.70	10.0	5.5	7.2	NA
★	LOW	Roycom-Summit TDF Fund	R	D	3.29*	3.9	5.1	6.4	NA
NA	NA	Scotia CanAm Growth Fund	R	N	1.25m	NA	NA	NA	NA
NA	NA	Scotia Precious Metals Fund	R	N	1.99	NA	NA	NA	NA
★★★★	AV	Universal Canadian Resource	R	O	2.77*	-0.1	35.8	15.7	9.7
NA	NA	Universal Wld Precious Metals	F	O	2.00m*	NA	NA	NA	NA
		HIGHEST IN GROUP				34.6	42.5	20.5	10.2
		AVERAGE IN GROUP				1.6	18.0	9.5	7.1
		LOWEST IN GROUP				-19.9	-12.4	-5.2	2.5
U.S. Equity Funds									
NA	NA	20/20 Aggressive Growth	F	O	2.50*	8.7	NA	NA	NA
★★★	LOW	20/20 U.S. Growth Fund	F	O	2.48*	15.4	14.1	11.4	NA
★	AV+	Admax American Performance	F	O	2.49	2.0	5.2	NA	NA
★★★	AV	AGF American Growth Fund	F	O	2.29*	9.7	13.8	8.5	11.0
★★★	AV+	AGF Special Fund Ltd.	F	O	2.32*	7.8	13.3	10.5	12.1
★★★★	AV+	AIC Value Fund	F	D	2.81*	9.1	17.4	NA	NA
★★★★★	AV+	Altamira Select American Fund	F	N	2.35*	17.2	26.9	NA	NA
NA	NA	Altamira U.S. Larger Company	F	N	2.40*	NA	NA	NA	NA
★★★★	LOW	Beutel Goodman Am. Equity	F	N	4.50	11.3	16.0	NA	NA
★★	AV-	Bissett American Equity Fund	F	N	1.50	7.6	11.1	8.8	NA
★★★★★	AV	BPI American Equity Growth	F	O	3.10*	17.2	23.4	17.8	NA
★★	LOW	BPI American Equity Value	F	O	2.48*	7.3	11.3	9.6	NA
★★★	HIGH	Bullock American Fund	F	O	2.25	-1.4	13.4	18.7	16.9
NA	NA	Bullock Optimax U.S.A.'A'	F	F	2.21	NA	NA	NA	NA
NA	NA	Bullock Optimax U.S.A. 'B'	F	R	2.53	NA	NA	NA	NA
NA	NA	Bullock Optimax U.S.A. 'C'	F	N	2.77	NA	NA	NA	NA
NA	NA	C.I. American Fund	F	O	2.55	16.5	NA	NA	NA

Return	Vol.	Fund	RRSP	Fees	MER	1yr	3yr	5yr	10yr
NA	NA	C.I. Sector North American	F	O	2.55	16.0	NA	NA	NA
NA	NA	Cambridge American Growth	N	O	2.66*	1.4	NA	NA	NA
NA	NA	Cda Trust Everest AmeriGrowth	R	N	1.38	0.4	NA	NA	NA
★★	AV	Canada Trust Everest U.S. Eqty	F	N	2.11	0.6	8.6	NA	NA
★	AV	Cassels Blaikie American Fund	F	F	1.16	-5.9	2.5	7.2	13.3
★	LOW	Century DJ Fund	F	F	1.80	2.8	5.6	7.5	NA
★★★	AV-	Chou Associates Fund	F	F	2.06*	4.8	15.0	8.9	NA
★★★	AV-	CIBC U.S. Equity Fund	F	N	2.50*	3.6	12.2	NA	NA
★★	AV	Cornerstone U.S. Fund	F	N	2.20*	7.8	10.8	9.5	7.0
★★	AV	Dynamic American Fund	F	O	2.56*	4.3	10.5	6.8	11.3
★★	AV	Elliott & Page Am. Growth	F	O	1.73*	8.6	10.8	9.1	8.9
★	LOW	Ethical North American Equity	F	O	2.55*	3.6	7.9	4.6	8.2
★★★★	AV	Fidelity Growth America Fund	F	O	2.18*	8.6	19.8	NA	NA
NA	NA	Fidelity Small Cap America	F	O	2.33*	NA	NA	NA	NA
NA	NA	First American	R	R	2.30	-7.4	NA	NA	NA
NA	NA	First Cdn. U.S. Growth Fund	F	N	2.20*	NA	NA	NA	NA
★★★★	AV+	GBC North American Growth	F	N	1.84	4.6	21.3	10.6	12.2
★★★★	HIGH	General Trust of Canada U.S. Eqty	F	N	1.62	2.8	18.6	13.0	14.0
★	LOW	Global Strategy Div. Americas	R	O	2.91	-3.0	4.1	4.1	NA
NA	NA	Global Strategy U.S. Growth	F	O	2.84	-3.2	NA	NA	NA
★	LOW	Green Line US Index ($US)	N	N	0.55	0.6	7.7	8.4	NA
★★★★	AV+	Guardian American Equity	F	O	2.99*	11.8	16.8	13.1	10.6
★★★★	AV+	Guardian North American	F		2.61*	11.9	17.0	11.2	8.0
★★★	AV	Guardian Vantage U.S. Equity	F		2.79*	9.4	14.3	12.3	NA
★★★	AV+	Hyperion Value Line Eqty Trust	F	O	3.00	-3.3	15.3	NA	NA
★★★	AV-	Imperial Growth Nth Am. Eqt.	F	F	1.62	11.8	13.6	4.0	9.6
★★★	AV	Industrial American Fund	F	O	2.48*	11.0	13.5	9.3	11.9
NA	NA	InvesNat American Eqty (US$)	F	N	2.66*	-4.3	NA	NA	NA
★★★★	LOW	Investors U.S. Growth Fund	F	B	2.03	15.9	18.7	14.3	13.8
★	AV-	Jarislowsky Finsco American	F	F	2.41	1.9	8.2	8.0	NA
★★★	AV	Jones Heward American Fund	F	O	2.50	2.6	12.3	9.1	11.4
★★	AV	Laurentian American Equity	F	O	2.70	8.5	11.7	6.3	11.6
NA	NA	Leith Wheeler U.S. Equity Fund	F	N	1.25m*	NA	NA	NA	NA
★★★	AV-	London Life U.S. Equity	F	R	1.50*	4.9	12.4	5.0	NA
★★★	AV-	Mackenzie Sentinel Am. Eqty	F		2.48*	9.1	12.2	8.4	NA
★	LOW	Margin of Safety Fund	N	N	1.91	7.6	8.5	9.3	NA
NA	NA	Mawer U.S. Equity Fund	F	N	2.07	4.7	NA	NA	NA
★★	AV	McLean Budden Am. Growth	F	N	1.75	6.2	9.9	12.4	NA
NA	NA	MD U.S. Equity Fund	F	N	1.00	9.6	NA	NA	NA
NA	NA	Metlife MVP U.S. Equity Fund	N	R	2.00m	7.2	NA	NA	NA
★★	AV	Mutual Amerifund	F	F	2.06	9.2	10.8	6.5	NA
NA	NA	Mutual Premier American Fund	N	N	2.35	9.0	NA	NA	NA
NA	NA	NAL-Investor U.S. Equity Fund	F	B	2.25	NA	NA	NA	NA
NA	NA	NatCan American Eqty ($US)	F	N	1.82*	0.3	NA	NA	NA
NA	NA	National Trust Am. Eqty Fund	F	N	2.48	4.9	NA	NA	NA
NA	NA	NN Can-Am Fund	R	R	2.25*	-0.5	NA	NA	NA
NA	NA	Optima Strategy U.S. Equity	F	O	0.18*	NA	NA	NA	NA
★★★	AV	PH&N U.S. Equity	F	N	1.13	12.4	16.0	15.1	14.2
NA	NA	Prosperity Am. Performance	F	O	2.50	NA	NA	NA	NA
★	AV	Pursuit American Fund ($US)	F	F	2.00*	-7.3	-0.3	7.3	NA
★★★	AV	Royal Trust American Stock	F	N	1.87*	8.7	13.7	12.1	12.5
NA	NA	Royal Trust Zweig Strat. Grth	F	N	2.50*	13.1	NA	NA	NA
NA	NA	Royfund U.S. Equity Fund	F	N	2.29	11.1	NA	NA	NA
★★★	LOW	Scotia American Equity Grth	F	N	2.30	11.3	12.0	10.8	NA
★★★	AV	Talvest U.S. Growth Fund Ltd.	F	O	2.25*	4.8	12.0	13.0	11.8

Return	Vol.	Fund	RRSP	Fees	MER	1yr	3yr	5yr	10yr
NA	NA	Top Fifty U.S. Equity Fund	F	F	2.54	-3.1	NA	NA	NA
★★	AV-	Trust Pret & Revenu American	F	N	2.40*	4.6	10.7	9.7	10.3
NA	NA	U.S. Polymetric Performance	F	O	2.40	3.1	NA	NA	NA
★★★	AV-	United American Growth	F	O	2.18*	7.3	14.2	11.4	12.0
NA	NA	Universal U.S. Emerging Grth	F	O	3.03*	3.6	NA	NA	NA
★	AV-	University Avenue Growth	F	N	2.83	-0.5	-4.3	-2.1	NA
		HIGHEST IN GROUP				17.2	26.9	18.7	16.9
		AVERAGE IN GROUP				5.9	12.3	9.5	11.5
		LOWEST IN GROUP				-7.4	-4.3	-2.1	7.0

International Equity Funds

Return	Vol.	Fund	RRSP	Fees	MER	1yr	3yr	5yr	10yr
NA	NA	20/20 Asia Pacific Fund	F	O	2.50*	29.5	NA	NA	NA
NA	NA	20/20 Latin America	F	O	3.50	NA	NA	NA	NA
NA	NA	20/20 Multimanager Em. Mkts	F	O	2.50m*	NA	NA	NA	NA
NA	NA	20/20 RSP Int'l Equity Alloc.	R	O	2.50*	NA	NA	NA	NA
NA	NA	Admax Global Health Sciences	F	O	2.49	16.2	NA	NA	NA
NA	NA	AGF Asian Growth Fund	F	O	2.65*	38.7	NA	NA	NA
NA	NA	AGF China Focus Fund Ltd. 'A'	F	F	2.00m*	NA	NA	NA	NA
NA	NA	AGF China Focus 'B & C'	F	D	2.50m*	NA	NA	NA	NA
NA	NA	AGF European Growth 'B & C'	F	D	2.50m*	NA	NA	NA	NA
NA	NA	AGF European Growth 'A'	F	F	2.00m*	NA	NA	NA	NA
★★	AV+	AGF Japan Fund Ltd.	F	O	2.53*	21.8	12.1	6.5	14.7
NA	NA	AIC World Fund	F	D	2.75m	NA	NA	NA	NA
NA	NA	Altamira Asia Pacific Fund	F	N	2.38*	31.4	NA	NA	NA
★★	AV-	Altamira Diversified Fund	F	N	2.00*	17.9	12.4	3.0	NA
NA	NA	Altamira European Equity Fund	F	N	2.35*	NA	NA	NA	NA
NA	NA	Beutel Goodman Intrn'l Equity	F	N	3.30	37.5	NA	NA	NA
★★★	LOW	BPI Global Equity Fund	F	O	3.40*	23.1	15.4	12.0	NA
NA	NA	BPI Global Small Companies	F	O	2.17*	43.1	NA	NA	NA
★★★	LOW	BPI International Equity Fund	F	O	2.46*	19.6	15.1	12.2	NA
NA	NA	Bullock Asian Dynasty 'A'	F	F	2.12	NA	NA	NA	NA
NA	NA	Bullock Asian Dynasty 'B'	F	R	2.42	NA	NA	NA	NA
NA	NA	Bullock Asian Dynasty 'C'	F	N	2.72	NA	NA	NA	NA
NA	NA	Bullock Emerging Markets 'A'	F	F	2.10	NA	NA	NA	NA
NA	NA	Bullock Emerging Markets 'B'	F	R	2.42	NA	NA	NA	NA
NA	NA	Bullock Emerging Markets 'C'	F	N	2.68	NA	NA	NA	NA
NA	NA	C.I. Emerging Asian Fund	F	O	2.85	NA	NA	NA	NA
NA	NA	C.I. Emerging Markets Fund	F	O	2.85	30.5	NA	NA	NA
NA	NA	C.I. European Fund	F	O	2.55	13.7	NA	NA	NA
NA	NA	C.I. Global Equity RSP Fund	R	O	2.60	NA	NA	NA	NA
★★★★	AV	C.I. Global Fund	F	O	2.60	19.6	19.5	14.1	NA
NA	NA	C.I. Latin American Fund	F	O	2.85	NA	NA	NA	NA
★★★★	AV+	C.I. Pacific Fund	F	O	2.60	36.3	25.1	17.2	20.7
NA	NA	C.I. Sector Emerging Markets	F	O	2.85	29.9	NA	NA	NA
NA	NA	C.I. Sector European Fund	F	O	2.55	13.3	NA	NA	NA
★★★★	AV-	C.I. Sector Global Fund	F	O	2.60	19.5	19.2	13.8	NA
★★★★	AV+	C.I. Sector Pacific Fund	F	O	2.60	35.7	24.8	16.9	NA
NA	NA	Caldwell Securities Intern'l	F	D	3.20	19.9	NA	NA	NA
★	AV+	Cambridge Americas Fund	N	O	2.66*	-1.6	10.3	8.1	NA
★★	AV+	Cambridge Global Fund	N	O	2.66*	8.5	11.9	4.9	11.5
★	AV+	Cambridge Pacific Fund	N	O	2.66*	14.3	10.8	10.3	NA
★★★	LOW	Canada Life U.S.&Int. Eqty S-34	F	R	2.00	18.9	19.1	14.6	15.1
NA	NA	Cda Trust Everest AsiaGrowth	R	N	1.30	NA	NA	NA	NA
NA	NA	Cda Trust Everest EuroGrowth	R	N	1.30	NA	NA	NA	NA
★★	LOW	Cda Trust Everest International	F	N	2.67	25.0	12.9	11.4	NA
★	LOW	Cda Trust Everest N. American	F	N	2.14	-1.0	10.5	6.3	9.3

Return	Vol.	Fund	RRSP	Fees	MER	1yr	3yr	5yr	10yr
★★★	AV-	Capstone Int. Investment Trust	F	N	2.00*	13.0	15.0	12.7	NA
★	AV	Cassels Blaikie International	N	F	1.88	18.2	9.4	4.3	NA
NA	NA	CIBC Far East Prosperity Fund	F	N	2.75	NA	NA	NA	NA
★★★	LOW	CIBC Global Equity Fund	F	N	2.50*	14.7	15.7	9.4	NA
NA	NA	Clean Environment Int'l Equity	F	O	2.00m*	NA	NA	NA	NA
★★	AV	Cornerstone Global Fund	F	N	2.54*	20.5	14.8	12.2	NA
★★★★	LOW	Cundill Value Fund Ltd.	F	F	2.04	23.4	19.2	10.2	12.4
★	AV	Dynamic Europe 1992 Fund	F	O	3.10*	21.2	9.0	NA	NA
NA	NA	Dynamic Far East Fund	N	O	2.60*	NA	NA	NA	NA
★	AV	Dynamic Global Green Fund	F	O	3.41*	-8.3	4.5	3.3	NA
NA	NA	Dynamic Global Partners Fund	F	O	2.60*	NA	NA	NA	NA
★★★	AV	Dynamic International Fund	F	O	2.75*	8.5	15.1	8.8	NA
★★★	LOW	Empire International Fund	F	O	2.59	15.7	16.6	13.1	NA
NA	NA	Fidelity European Growth Fund	F	O	2.63*	22.7	NA	NA	NA
NA	NA	Fidelity Far East Fund	F	O	2.54*	24.7	NA	NA	NA
★★★	AV-	Fidelity International Portfolio	F	O	2.57*	19.7	17.6	13.1	NA
NA	NA	Fidelity Japanese Growth Fund	F	O	2.69*	NA	NA	NA	NA
NA	NA	Fidelity Latin Am. Growth	F	O	3.13*	NA	NA	NA	NA
★★★	AV	Finsco Global Fund	F	F	1.66	25.9	18.9	NA	NA
NA	NA	First Canadian Int'l Growth	F	N	1.88*	26.2	NA	NA	NA
NA	NA	Fonds de Prof. Int'l Equity	N	N	0.75	NA	NA	NA	NA
★★★	AV	Fonds Desjardins International	F	N	2.22	24.9	18.8	13.7	NA
★	AV+	GBC International Growth	F	N	1.31	13.6	9.0	NA	NA
★★★	AV-	General Trust of Canada Intl.	F	N	1.80	27.4	17.3	12.0	NA
NA	NA	Global Strategy Asia Fund	F	O	2.15	NA	NA	NA	NA
NA	NA	Global Strategy Div. Japan Plus	R	O	2.00m	NA	NA	NA	NA
NA	NA	Global Strategy Diversified Asia	R	O	1.25m	NA	NA	NA	NA
NA	NA	Global Strategy Div. Europe	R	O	2.84	6.0	NA	NA	NA
NA	NA	Global Strategy Div. Latin	R	O	2.25m	NA	NA	NA	NA
★	AV-	Global Strategy Europe	F	O	2.72	4.5	7.7	4.5	NA
★	AV	Global Strategy Fund	F	O	2.50	6.7	8.5	5.8	NA
★★	AV+	Global Strategy Japan Plus	F	O	2.90	20.1	11.4	8.3	NA
NA	NA	Global Strategy Latin Fund	F	O	2.25m	NA	NA	NA	NA
★	AV	Global Strategy Real Estate	F	D	2.91	1.4	1.6	NA	NA
NA	NA	Green Line Asian Growth Fund	F	N	2.46	NA	NA	NA	NA
NA	NA	Green Line Emerging Markets	F	N	2.97	27.8	NA	NA	NA
NA	NA	Green Line Global Select Fund	F	N	2.37	NA	NA	NA	NA
NA	NA	Green Line International Equity	F	N	2.37	27.5	NA	NA	NA
NA	NA	Green Line North Am. Growth	F	N	2.32	NA	NA	NA	NA
★	AV	Guardian Global Equity (EAFE)	F	O	2.52*	26.2	10.6	5.5	9.8
★★★	AV	Guardian Pacific Rim Corp.	F		2.80*	24.8	16.0	8.4	NA
NA	NA	Hercules European Value Fund	F	N	2.00m	NA	NA	NA	NA
NA	NA	Hercules Latin American Value	F	N	2.00m	NA	NA	NA	NA
NA	NA	Hercules N. Amer. Grth & Inc.	F	N	2.00m	NA	NA	NA	NA
NA	NA	Hercules Pacific Basin Value	F	N	2.00m	NA	NA	NA	NA
NA	NA	Hongkong Bank Asian Growth	F	N	2.32*	NA	NA	NA	NA
NA	NA	HRL Overseas Growth Fund	N	N	1.75m	24.7	NA	NA	NA
★★★★★	HIGH	Hyperion Asian Trust	F	O	3.25	42.0	27.0	NA	NA
★★★	AV	Hyperion European Trust	F	O	3.00	17.5	15.2	NA	NA
NA	NA	InvesNat Eur. Equity Fund	F	N	2.88*	27.6	NA	NA	NA
★★	AV	Investors Eur. Growth Fund	F	B	2.16	18.6	13.1	NA	NA
★★★	AV-	Investors Global Fund Ltd.	F	B	2.07	23.4	15.2	11.5	NA
★★★	AV-	Investors Growth Portfolio	F	B	0.18	17.7	16.2	10.7	NA
★★★	HIGH	Investors Japanese Growth	F	B	2.08	30.4	18.8	8.3	14.9
★★	LOW	Investors North Am. Growth	F	B	2.05	5.7	14.2	11.5	13.7

Return	Vol.	Fund	RRSP	Fees	MER	1yr	3yr	5yr	10yr
★★★★★	AV+	Investors Pacific International	F	B	2.24	43.6	28.6	NA	NA
★★★	AV	Investors Special Fund Ltd.	F	B	2.07	-0.6	14.9	13.2	12.7
NA	NA	Investors World Grth Portfolio	F	B	0.40	18.5	NA	NA	NA
NA	NA	Ivy Foreign Equity Fund	F	O	2.00m*	10.2	NA	NA	NA
★★	LOW	Laurentian Commonwealth	F	O	2.70	14.0	13.6	9.0	12.8
★	LOW	Laurentian Global Balanced	F	O	2.70	8.8	10.5	NA	NA
★★	AV-	Laurentian International Fund	F	O	2.70	18.0	14.5	9.4	11.2
★★	AV	Mackenzie Sentinel Global	F		2.55*	27.0	14.7	7.0	NA
★★★	AV-	Mawer World Investment	F	N	1.44	26.6	18.5	13.0	NA
★★★★	AV	MD Growth Investments Ltd.	F	N	1.00	28.4	21.5	12.3	15.8
★★★	AV	Montreal Trust Excelsior Intl	F	N	2.11	19.5	16.3	11.8	13.4
NA	NA	Mutual Premier International	N	N	2.33	23.5	NA	NA	NA
NA	NA	NAL-Investor Global Equity	F	B	2.50	29.6	NA	NA	NA
NA	NA	National Life Global Equities	F	D	2.40m	NA	NA	NA	NA
NA	NA	NN Can-Asian Fund	R	R	2.25*	NA	NA	NA	NA
NA	NA	OHA Foreign Equity Fund	F	N	0.50*	20.9	NA	NA	NA
★	LOW	Ontario Teachers Group Global	F	N	1.00	7.6	10.2	NA	NA
NA	NA	Optima Strategy Int'l Equity	F	O	0.18*	NA	NA	NA	NA
★★	LOW	Orbit World Fund	F	F	2.98	18.6	12.9	9.9	NA
NA	NA	PH&N North American Equity	F	N	1.27	7.3	NA	NA	NA
NA	NA	Regent Dragon 888 Fund	F	O	2.75	NA	NA	NA	NA
NA	NA	Regent Europa Performance	F	O	2.90	3.0	NA	NA	NA
★★★★	AV+	Regent International Fund	F	O	2.25	36.1	21.9	13.0	NA
NA	NA	Regent Korea Fund	F	O	3.75	32.7	NA	NA	NA
NA	NA	Regent Nippon Fund	F	O	3.50	11.2	NA	NA	NA
★★★★	AV	Regent Tiger Fund	F	O	3.39	38.1	22.1	NA	NA
NA	NA	Royal Trust Asian Growth Fund	F	N	2.29	NA	NA	NA	NA
★★★	AV+	Royal Trust European Growth	F	N	2.98	24.5	16.1	6.7	NA
★★	HIGH	Royal Trust Japanese Stock	F	N	3.10	32.4	13.5	5.0	NA
NA	NA	Royfund International Equity	F	N	2.47	24.6	NA	NA	NA
★★★	AV	Saxon World Growth	F	N	1.75	16.0	18.8	8.6	NA
NA	NA	Sceptre Asian Growth Fund	F	N	2.42*	50.3	NA	NA	NA
★★★★★	AV	Sceptre International Fund	F	N	2.00*	29.5	26.8	18.3	NA
NA	NA	Scotia Global Growth Fund	F	N	2.48	NA	NA	NA	NA
★	AV-	Special Opportunities Fund	F	F	2.13	6.7	6.0	NA	NA
★★★	AV	Spectrum International Equity	F	O	2.25	17.2	15.2	10.1	NA
★★★	AV-	Talvest Global Diversified Fund	F	O	2.75*	19.7	16.1	10.6	NA
NA	NA	Talvest Global Growth Fund	F	O	2.50*	19.1	NA	NA	NA
NA	NA	Templeton Emerging Markets	F	O	3.14	29.5	NA	NA	NA
★★★	AV-	Templeton Global Smaller Comp.	F	O	2.59	18.1	17.2	11.5	NA
★★★★	LOW	Templeton Growth Fund Ltd.	F	O	1.89*	23.9	22.6	14.5	15.1
★★★★	AV+	Templeton International Stock	F	O	2.54	32.8	25.6	15.0	NA
★★	AV	Total Return Fund Inc.	F	N	2.88	1.5	11.8	6.8	NA
NA	NA	Trimark - The Americas Fund	F	O	2.85*	11.7	NA	NA	NA
★★★★	AV	Trimark Fund	F	F	1.54*	23.2	23.9	15.8	16.6
★★★★	AV	Trimark Select Growth Fund	F	O	2.41*	19.2	21.7	15.0	NA
★	LOW	United American Equity Fund	F	O	2.50*	2.0	7.5	6.9	11.5
★★	AV-	United Global Equity Fund	F	O	2.60*	12.5	13.2	NA	NA
★★★	AV-	United Global Growth Fund	F	O	2.30*	21.0	18.6	6.8	8.1
NA	NA	United Global Telecomm.	F	O	0.03	NA	NA	NA	NA
★★★	AV	Universal Americas Fund	F	O	2.72*	12.1	15.8	11.2	12.8
NA	NA	Universal Far East Fund	F	O	2.00m*	NA	NA	NA	NA
NA	NA	Universal Japan Fund	F	O	2.00m*	NA	NA	NA	NA
NA	NA	Universal World Asset Alloc.	F	O	2.00m*	NA	NA	NA	NA
NA	NA	Universal World Emerging Grth	F	O	2.00m*	NA	NA	NA	NA

Return	Vol.	Fund	RRSP	Fees	MER	1yr	3yr	5yr	10yr
★★★	AV	Universal World Equity Fund	F	O	2.55*	29.0	15.9	7.8	NA
NA	NA	Vision Europe Fund	F	R	3.82	16.4	NA	NA	NA
		HIGHEST IN GROUP				50.3	28.6	18.3	20.7
		AVERAGE IN GROUP				20.4	15.6	10.3	13.3
		LOWEST IN GROUP				-8.3	1.6	3.0	8.1

Balanced Funds

Return	Vol.	Fund	RRSP	Fees	MER	1yr	3yr	5yr	10yr
★★★★	AV+	20/20 Am. Tactical Asset Alloc.	F	O	2.61*	4.6	14.9	10.6	NA
★★★	AV	20/20 Canadian Asset Alloc.	R	O	2.42*	4.6	8.2	7.3	NA
NA	NA	20/20 European Asset Alloc.	F	O	2.50*	NA	NA	NA	NA
★★★★★	HIGH	20/20 World Fund	F	O	2.57*	25.1	19.5	10.8	NA
★★★★★	HIGH	ABC Fully-Managed Fund	R	N	2.00	20.2	18.0	15.3	NA
NA	NA	Admax Asset Allocation Fund	R	O	2.45*	5.6	NA	NA	NA
★★★★	AV+	Altamira Balanced Fund	R	N	2.00*	-4.4	11.6	5.5	NA
★★★★	AV+	Altamira Growth & Income	R	N	1.41*	8.9	15.1	11.8	NA
★★	AV	AMI Private Capital Optimix	R	N	1.75*	2.0	7.9	6.0	NA
★★★	AV	Batirente - Section Diversifiee	R	N	1.61	-1.1	8.2	6.7	NA
★★★	AV	Beutel Goodman Balanced	R	N	2.20*	5.2	8.3	NA	NA
NA	NA	Bissett Retirement Fund	R	N	0.50	1.9	NA	NA	NA
★★★	AV-	BPI Balanced Fund	R	O	2.39*	-2.4	9.7	6.9	NA
★★★★★	AV	BPI Global Balanced Fund	R	O	3.28*	10.2	16.5	9.8	NA
NA	NA	BPI North American TAA RSP	R	O	2.57*	-2.8	NA	NA	NA
★★	AV+	BPI One Decision Balanced	R	O	3.29*	-2.1	8.0	5.8	NA
NA	NA	BPI World TAA RSP Fund	R	O	2.49*	5.3	NA	NA	NA
NA	NA	Bullock Asset Strategy Fund	R	O	2.25	1.6	NA	NA	NA
NA	NA	C.I. Canadian Balanced	R	O	2.30	8.4	NA	NA	NA
★★★	HIGH	Caldwell Securities Associate	R	D	2.34	16.8	10.2	NA	NA
★★★★	HIGH	Cambridge Balanced Fund	R	O	2.66*	-2.4	14.1	11.4	13.7
★★★	AV	Canada Life Mgd Fund S-35	R	R	2.00	1.3	9.0	6.4	10.5
★★★	AV	Canada Trust Everest Balanced	R	N	2.10	-0.5	8.9	7.4	NA
★★	AV-	Capstone Investment Trust	R	N	2.00*	3.6	7.4	7.6	9.4
★★★	LOW	Cassels Blaikie Canadian Fund	R	F	1.21	2.6	8.4	7.7	NA
★★	LOW	CCPE Div. Growth Fund R	R	N	1.31	2.8	7.6	6.5	NA
★★	AV-	CDA Balanced Fund	R	N	0.92	0.8	7.7	6.8	10.3
★	AV	CIBC Balanced Inc. & Growth	R	N	2.25*	-2.8	5.5	5.6	NA
NA	NA	CIS Commax Hedge Fund	R	F	2.40*	NA	NA	NA	NA
NA	NA	Clean Environment Balanced	R	O	2.97*	9.1	NA	NA	NA
NA	NA	Common Sense Asset Builder 1	R	D	2.10m*	NA	NA	NA	NA
★	AV	Cornerstone Balanced Fund	R	N	2.07*	-4.2	5.1	4.4	6.1
★★★★	AV+	Dynamic Managed Portfolio	R	O	1.04*	1.6	15.2	9.5	NA
★★★★★	AV	Dynamic Partners Fund	R	R	2.67*	6.7	19.7	13.6	NA
★★★★	AV+	Elliott & Page Balanced Fund	R	O	1.78*	2.4	12.1	8.8	NA
★★	LOW	Empire Balanced Fund	R	O	2.20	0.1	7.9	7.0	NA
★	LOW	Ethical Balanced Fund	R	O	2.30*	0.7	5.5	NA	NA
NA	NA	Fidelity Asset Manager Fund	F	O	2.76*	9.3	NA	NA	NA
★★	AV+	Fidelity Growth & Income	R	O	2.41*	4.3	7.4	5.8	NA
★	AV+	First Cdn. Asset Allocation	R	N	1.86*	-5.6	5.0	4.5	NA
★★★	LOW	Fonds de Prof. Balanced	R	N	0.75	0.3	8.1	8.3	10.2
★★	AV-	Fonds Desjardins Equilibre	R	N	1.98	1.0	7.9	6.6	NA
★	AV-	Fonds Ficadre Equilibre	R	R	2.37	2.4	6.6	5.2	8.6
★★	LOW	General Trust of Canada Bal.	R	N	1.66	-0.5	7.3	5.5	NA
★	AV+	Global Strategy Div. Grth	R	O	2.91	5.1	2.7	2.5	NA
NA	NA	Global Strategy Income Plus	R	O	1.99	5.7	NA	NA	NA
★★	AV-	Great-West Life Diversified RS	R	N	2.64	-0.8	7.8	6.4	NA

Return	Vol.	Fund	RRSP	Fees	MER	1yr	3yr	5yr	10yr
★★★	AV	Great-West Life Equity/Bond	R	N	2.64	-2.9	9.5	7.8	NA
★	AV	Green Line Balanced Growth	R	N	2.39	-4.2	5.2	4.1	NA
★	AV-	Green Line Balanced Income	R	N	2.39	-0.7	5.5	4.3	NA
★★★	LOW	Guardian Balanced Fund	R	O	1.88*	3.5	9.5	9.3	11.2
NA	NA	Guardian International Bal.	R	O	2.58*	NA	NA	NA	NA
★★★★	AV	Hongkong Bank Balanced	R	N	2.04*	2.2	12.2	9.0	NA
★	AV	HRL Balanced Fund	R	N	1.75	2.9	4.8	5.1	8.8
★	AV+	Hyperion Managed Trust	R	O	2.20	-2.3	5.5	6.4	NA
★★	LOW	Imperial Growth Diversified	R	F	2.00	0.8	7.3	6.3	NA
NA	NA	Industrial Alliance Ecoflex D	R	R	2.00*	2.3	NA	NA	NA
★★★	AV	Industrial Balanced Fund	R	O	2.55*	-0.5	8.2	NA	NA
★★★	AV	Industrial Income Fund	R	O	2.01*	-4.1	8.2	6.3	12.3
★★★	AV-	Integra Balanced Fund	R	N	2.15	1.9	10.2	7.3	NA
★★	LOW	InvesNat Retirement Balanced	R	N	2.97*	-3.0	6.6	5.7	NA
NA	NA	Investors Asset Allocation Fund	R	B	2.30	NA	NA	NA	NA
★★★★	LOW	Investors Growth Plus Portfolio	F	B	0.17	8.8	11.7	9.0	NA
★	LOW	Investors Income Plus Portfolio	R	B	0.17	-0.8	6.5	6.9	NA
★★★	LOW	Investors Rtmt Plus Portfolio	R	B	0.17	3.8	8.2	6.9	NA
★	LOW	Jarislowsky Finsco Balanced	R	F	1.82*	1.0	6.1	4.9	NA
★★★	AV	Jones Heward Canadian Bal'd	R	O	2.40	-2.6	10.9	8.0	9.1
★	LOW	Laurentian Canadian Balanced	R	O	2.70*	-0.8	5.4	5.3	NA
★★★	AV	Leith Wheeler Balanced Fund	R	N	1.10	4.5	10.0	8.0	NA
★★★	AV-	London Life Diversified	R	R	1.50*	-0.5	9.7	7.1	NA
★★★	AV	Lotus Fund	R	N	2.10*	-0.5	10.3	7.7	9.4
★★★	AV	Manulife Vista 1 Diversified	R	F	1.63*	-1.7	8.2	6.2	9.2
★★	AV	Manulife Vista 2 Diversified	R	R	2.38*	-2.5	7.4	5.4	8.4
★	AV-	Maritime Life Balanced Fund	R	N	2.03*	0.4	6.4	5.7	NA
★★★	AV-	Mawer Cdn. Bal. Rtmt Savings	R	N	0.94	-0.1	8.9	7.7	NA
★★	LOW	Mawer Cdn. Div'd Investment	F	N	1.02	-0.7	8.0	7.3	NA
★★★	AV	McLean Budden Balanced	R	N	1.75	-0.2	8.9	7.6	NA
NA	NA	MD Balanced Fund	R	N	1.00	4.4	NA	NA	NA
★	AV-	Metlife MVP Balanced Fund	R	R	2.00m	-0.3	5.4	4.8	NA
★★★★	AV+	Montreal Tr. Exc. Ttl Return	R	N	2.32	9.0	14.8	11.4	NA
★★★	AV-	Montreal Trust Exc. Balanced	R	N	2.33	4.1	8.7	8.7	NA
★	LOW	Mutual Diversifund 25	R	F	1.93	1.0	6.6	6.0	NA
★★	AV-	Mutual Diversifund 40	R	F	1.78	0.1	6.8	4.7	NA
★	AV	Mutual Diversifund 55	R	F	1.80	0.4	6.3	3.6	NA
★	AV	NAL-Investor Diversified Fund	R	B	1.75	-3.8	6.4	5.4	NA
NA	NA	National Life Balanced Fund	R	D	2.00m	2.5	NA	NA	NA
★★★	AV	National Trust Balanced Fund	R	N	2.09	-1.8	8.2	NA	NA
★★	AV-	NN Balanced Fund	R	R	2.25*	0.7	7.6	5.7	NA
NA	NA	OHA Balanced Fund	R	N	0.50*	-5.4	NA	NA	NA
★★★	AV-	Ontario Teachers Grp Balanced	R	N	0.90	1.8	8.0	6.9	NA
★★★	AV	Optimum Fonds Equilibre	R	N	1.50m*	-0.4	8.6	6.8	NA
★★★	LOW	PH&N Bal Pens Trust	R	N		5.0	10.3	9.2	NA
NA	NA	PH&N Balanced	R	N		4.4	NA	NA	NA
★★★★	AV	Protected American Fund	R	R	2.10	-3.2	12.2	10.8	NA
★★★★	AV+	Prudential Diversified Invest	R	F	1.51*	-4.7	11.3	8.1	NA
★★	AV	Royal Life Balanced Fund	R	D	2.34	0.1	6.9	NA	NA
★★★	LOW	Royal Trust Adv. Balanced	R	N	1.68*	2.3	9.0	7.7	NA
★★	AV	Royal Trust Adv. Growth	R	N	1.97*	-2.9	6.9	5.9	NA
★★★	LOW	Royal Trust Adv. Income Fund	R	N	1.69*	1.7	8.8	8.1	NA
★★★★	AV-	Royfund Balanced Fund	R	N	2.25	3.6	11.9	8.7	NA

Return	Vol.	Fund	RRSP	Fees	MER	1yr	3yr	5yr	10yr
★★★★	AV+	Saxon Balanced Fund	R	N	1.75	-1.0	13.4	6.8	NA
★★★	AV-	Sceptre Balanced Fund	R	N	1.62*	6.2	9.8	7.8	NA
★	LOW	Scotia Stock & Bond Fund	R	N	2.09	0.5	5.8	4.4	NA
★	AV	Spectrum Diversified Fund	R	O	2.25	-2.4	6.4	5.3	NA
NA	NA	Standard Life Balanced Mutual	R	N	2.00	-0.9	NA	NA	NA
★★★	AV-	Standard Life Ideal Balanced	R	D	2.00	0.9	9.0	7.6	NA
NA	NA	Strata Tactical Fund	R	N	2.45*	NA	NA	NA	NA
★★	AV+	Stratafund 40	R	F	1.54	-1.8	8.0	6.6	NA
★★★	AV+	Stratafund 60	R	F	1.54	-0.1	8.2	5.9	NA
★★	AV	Talvest Diversified Fund	R	O	2.42*	3.4	7.7	6.9	NA
NA	NA	Talvest U.S. Diversified Fund	F	O	2.25*	3.7	NA	NA	NA
★★★	AV+	Templeton Balanced Fund	R	F	2.57	7.6	8.6	NA	NA
★★★★	AV	Trimark Income Growth Fund	R	F	1.75*	6.0	12.1	9.2	NA
★★★★	AV	Trimark Select Balanced Fund	R	O	2.39*	5.3	11.7	NA	NA
★★★	AV	Trust Pret & Revenu Rtmt	R	N	1.70*	-0.2	9.3	8.1	9.2
★★★★	AV	United Cdn Portfolio of Funds	R	O	0.94*	1.6	10.9	8.5	NA
★★★	AV-	United Global Portf. of Funds	F	O	0.70*	2.6	10.3	8.1	NA
NA	NA	Universal World Bal'd RRSP	R	O	2.00m*	NA	NA	NA	NA
		HIGHEST IN GROUP				25.1	19.7	15.3	13.7
		AVERAGE IN GROUP				1.8	9.0	7.2	9.8
		LOWEST IN GROUP				-5.6	2.7	2.5	6.1

Canadian Bond Funds

Return	Vol.	Fund	RRSP	Fees	MER	1yr	3yr	5yr	10yr
★	LOW	Admax Canadian Income Fund	R	O	2.05*	0.1	6.4	6.5	NA
★★★★	AV+	AGF Canadian Bond Fund	R	O	1.37*	-3.9	10.3	8.4	11.7
★★★★	HIGH	Altamira Bond Fund	R	N	1.33*	-5.6	10.0	9.0	NA
★★★★★	AV+	Altamira Income Fund	R	N	1.00*	-3.1	11.2	10.8	11.9
★★★	AV	AMI Private Capital Income	R	N	1.25*	-1.7	8.9	8.5	NA
★★★★★	AV+	Batirente - Section Obligations	R	N	1.61	-2.2	10.6	8.8	NA
★★★	AV	Beutel Goodman Income Fund	R	N	1.40*	-3.4	8.6	NA	NA
★★★★	AV-	Bissett Bond Fund	R	N	0.75	0.3	8.9	8.7	NA
NA	NA	BNP (Canada) Bond Fund	R	N	1.68	-1.8	NA	NA	NA
★★	AV	BPI Bond Fund	R	O	2.25*	-3.9	7.6	7.6	NA
★★	LOW	BPI Canadian Bond Fund	R	O	3.00*	1.4	7.5	7.2	NA
★★★	AV	BPI RSP Bond Fund	R	F	1.50*	-3.0	8.5	8.4	NA
NA	NA	C.I. Canadian Bond Fund	R	O	1.70	-1.3	NA	NA	NA
★★★	AV	Canada Life Fixed Income S-19	R	R	2.00	-2.1	8.3	8.1	10.2
★★★★	AV	Canada Trust Everest Bond	R	N	1.32	-2.8	9.1	8.6	NA
★★★	AV-	Canada Trust Inc. Investments	R		1.08	-0.9	8.4	8.3	NA
★	HIGH	Canada Trust Inv. Fund-Inc.	R	N	1.25	-5.3	7.2	7.1	NA
★★★★	LOW	CCPE Fixed Income Fund	R	N	1.31	-0.1	10.3	9.5	NA
★★★	LOW	CDA Bond and Mortgage Fund	R	N	0.86	-0.4	8.9	9.2	10.8
★★	AV+	CIBC Canadian Bond Fund	R	N	1.50*	-7.2	8.0	7.8	NA
NA	NA	CIBC Canadian Income Fund	R	N	0.85*	NA	NA	NA	NA
NA	NA	Clean Environment Income	R	O	2.39*	NA	NA	NA	NA
NA	NA	Colonia Bond Fund	R	D	1.50	-0.2	NA	NA	NA
NA	NA	Concorde Revenu	R	O	2.35	-2.5	NA	NA	NA
★★★	AV-	Confed Fixed Income	R	N	2.00	-2.5	8.2	7.7	12.3
★★★	AV-	Confed Life C	R	F	1.44	-2.2	8.7	8.2	12.8
★★★	AV	Cornerstone Bond Fund	R	N	1.36*	-1.8	8.2	9.1	NA
NA	NA	Dynamic Government Income	R	F	0.85*	NA	NA	NA	NA
★★★★★	LOW	Dynamic Income Fund	R	O	1.68*	8.5	12.5	10.7	12.5
★	AV-	Elliott & Page Bond Fund	R	O	1.53*	-4.9	6.8	7.6	NA

Return	Vol.	Fund	RRSP	Fees	MER	1yr	3yr	5yr	10yr
★★	AV-	Empire Bond Fund	R	O	2.20	-2.0	8.1	8.1	NA
NA	NA	Equitable Life Canadian Bond	R	D	2.00	-1.9	NA	NA	NA
★★★★	AV-	Equitable Life Seg. Accum Inc	R	F		-1.7	9.5	9.9	11.8
★	LOW	Ethical Income Fund	R	O	1.70*	-2.0	5.0	7.5	9.2
★★★	AV-	Fidelity Government Bond	R	O	2.06*	0.3	8.7	7.4	NA
★★★	AV+	First Canadian Bond Fund	R	N	1.41*	-2.9	8.8	8.1	NA
★★	LOW	Fonds de Professionnels Bond	R	N	0.75	-2.0	8.1	8.6	10.5
★★	AV-	Fonds Desjardins Obligations	R	N	1.66	-2.3	7.8	7.6	10.5
★	AV-	Fonds Ficadre Obligations	R	R	1.82	-3.3	7.2	7.5	NA
★★★★	AV	GBC Canadian Bond Fund	R	N	1.14	-1.9	9.8	8.9	NA
★★★	AV-	General Trust of Canada Bond	R	N	1.30	-2.8	8.9	8.1	11.3
NA	NA	Global Strategy Bond Fund	R	O	0.63m	NA	NA	NA	NA
★★	AV	Great-West Life Cdn Bond	R	N	2.40	-3.6	8.0	7.4	10.0
★★★	AV	Green Line Canadian Bond	R	N	0.91	-3.3	8.6	8.1	NA
★★	AV	Green Line Cdn Govt. Bond	R	N	2.07	-2.4	7.5	6.5	NA
★	LOW	Green Line Short Term Income	R	N	1.18	-0.4	4.7	7.4	NA
★	LOW	Guardian Canada Bond Fund	R	O	0.01	0.8	5.3	7.6	NA
★★★★	AV	Gyro Bond Fund	R	N	1.30*	-2.1	9.6	NA	NA
★	AV-	HRL Bond Fund	R	N	1.50	-3.2	7.4	6.9	NA
★★	AV+	Hyperion Fixed Income Trust	R	O	2.10	-7.4	7.8	NA	NA
NA	NA	Industrial Alliance Ecoflex B	R	R	2.00*	-3.5	NA	NA	NA
★★	AV+	Industrial Bond Fund	R	O	2.22*	-5.2	8.0	7.5	NA
★★★	LOW	InvesNat Bond Fund	R	N	1.40*	0.0	8.6	8.5	NA
★★	AV-	Investors Bond Fund	R	R	1.82	-2.6	8.0	8.1	10.9
NA	NA	Investors Corporate Bond Fund	R	R	1.80	NA	NA	NA	NA
NA	NA	Ivy Growth & Income Fund	R	O	1.75m*	-1.0	NA	NA	NA
★★★	LOW	Jarislowsky Finsco Bond Fund	R	F	1.92*	-1.4	8.9	7.9	NA
★	AV	Jones Heward Bond Fund	R	O	1.75	-3.8	7.5	7.4	NA
★	LOW	Laurentian Government Bond	R	O	2.20*	-0.3	7.0	7.8	NA
★★	LOW	Laurentian Income Fund	R	O	2.20*	-2.3	7.7	7.6	10.9
NA	NA	Leith Wheeler Fixed Income	R	N	0.75m*	NA	NA	NA	NA
★★★	AV	London Life Bond	R	R	1.50*	-3.1	8.3	6.6	11.3
NA	NA	Lotus Bond Fund	R	N	1.25m*	NA	NA	NA	NA
★★★	AV+	Mackenzie Sentinel Cda Bond	R	O	1.78*	-5.8	8.5	7.6	NA
★★★	AV+	Manulife Vistafund 1 Bond	R	F	1.63*	-5.9	8.2	8.3	10.6
★	AV+	Manulife Vistafund 2 Bond	R	R	2.38*	-6.6	7.4	7.5	9.8
★★★	AV	Maritime Life Bond Fund	R	N	1.98*	-2.5	8.2	NA	NA
NA	NA	Mawer Canadian Bond Fund	R	N	0.96	-2.5	NA	NA	NA
★★★	AV	McLean Budden Fixed Income	R	N	1.30	-2.4	8.8	9.1	NA
★★★★	AV-	MD Bond Fund	R	N	1.00	-1.0	9.5	9.1	NA
★	AV-	Metlife MVP Bond Fund	R	R	2.00m	-3.3	6.6	7.1	NA
★★★★	AV-	Montreal Trust Exc. Income	R	N	1.57	-1.4	9.6	8.5	11.1
★★★	AV	Mutual Bond Fund	R	F	1.87	-2.0	8.2	NA	NA
NA	NA	Mutual Premier Bond Fund	R	N	1.90	-2.0	NA	NA	NA
★★★	AV-	NAL-Investor Bond Fund	R	B	1.75	-1.2	8.5	7.9	NA
NA	NA	NatCan Canadian Bond Fund	R	N	1.24*	-2.6	NA	NA	NA
★★★★★	AV+	National Life Fixed Income	R	D	2.00m	0.4	10.9	10.7	12.9
★★★	AV	National Trust Canadian Bond	R	N	1.41	-3.2	8.2	7.6	10.8
★★	AV-	NN Bond Fund	R	R	2.00*	-1.8	8.1	8.2	NA
NA	NA	OHA Bond Fund	R	N	0.50*	-4.4	NA	NA	NA
★★	AV+	Optima Strategy Cdn Income	R	O	0.43*	-2.8	7.9	7.2	9.3
NA	NA	Optima Strategy Sht Term Inc.	R	O	0.29*	1.4	NA	NA	NA
★★★★	AV	Optimum Fonds d'Obligations	R	N	1.25m*	-2.6	10.3	8.7	NA
NA	NA	PH&N Sht Term Bond & Mortg	R	N	0.50m	NA	NA	NA	NA

Return	Vol.	Fund	RRSP	Fees	MER	1yr	3yr	5yr	10yr
★★★★	AV	PH&N Bond Fund	R	N	0.60	-0.5	10.4	9.9	13.2
★	AV+	Prudential Income Fund of Cda	R	F	1.51*	-3.5	7.5	7.3	10.1
★★★★	AV-	Pursuit Income Fund	R	F	1.00*	4.2	10.0	7.8	NA
★	LOW	Royal Life Income Fund	R	D	1.88	-4.1	6.7	NA	NA
★★★★	AV	Royal Trust Bond Fund	R	N	1.38*	-1.5	9.3	8.6	11.2
★★★★	AV	Royfund Bond Fund	R	N	1.50	-1.1	9.3	8.8	10.7
★	AV	Sceptre Bond Fund	R	N	1.22*	-5.5	7.2	8.7	NA
★	LOW	Scotia Defensive Income Fund	R	N	1.41	0.9	6.9	7.3	NA
★	LOW	Scotia Income Fund	R	N	1.41	-0.9	6.9	7.3	NA
★★★	HIGH	Spectrum Government Bond	R	O	1.70	-5.7	8.8	7.8	NA
★★	AV+	Spectrum Interest Fund	R	O	1.60	-4.6	7.7	7.7	NA
NA	NA	Standard Life Bond Mutual	R	N	1.50	-2.6	NA	NA	NA
★★★★	AV	Standard Life Ideal Bond Fund	R	D	2.00	-2.6	9.1	8.4	NA
NA	NA	Strata Government Bond Fund	R	N	2.15*	NA	NA	NA	NA
★★	AV	Strata Income Fund	R	F	1.53	-3.8	8.0	8.0	NA
★★★	AV	Talvest Bond Fund	R	O	1.99*	-2.4	8.5	8.1	11.4
★★	LOW	Talvest Income Fund	R	O	1.50*	-0.2	7.7	8.4	9.7
★★★	LOW	Templeton Heritage Bond	R	O	2.99	1.1	8.7	NA	NA
★	AV-	Top Fifty T-Bill/Bond Fund	R	F	2.08*	-8.1	5.1	7.4	NA
★	LOW	Tradex Bond Fund	R	N	1.36*	-4.9	5.7	NA	NA
★	LOW	Trans-Canada Bond Fund	R	O	2.66*	-1.0	6.4	7.0	NA
NA	NA	Trimark Government Income	R	O	0.00*	NA	NA	NA	NA
★★★	AV	Trust Pret & Revenu Bond	R	N	1.50*	-1.9	8.8	8.7	NA
★★	HIGH	United Canadian Bond Fund	R	O	1.80*	-4.8	8.1	9.3	10.4
★★	AV+	Universal Canadian Bond Fund	R	O	1.81*	-5.6	8.1	7.4	11.9
NA	NA	University Avenue Bond Fund	R	N	2.19	0.4	NA	NA	NA
★★	AV+	20/20 Income Fund	R	O	1.93*	-3.9	7.7	7.0	NA
		HIGHEST IN GROUP				8.5	12.5	10.8	13.2
		AVERAGE IN GROUP				-2.3	8.3	8.1	11.1
		LOWEST IN GROUP				-8.1	4.7	6.5	9.2

Canadian Mortgage Funds

Return	Vol.	Fund	RRSP	Fees	MER	1yr	3yr	5yr	10yr
★★★	AV-	Canada Trust Everest Mortg	R	N	1.57	3.4	7.7	9.3	10.1
★★★★	AV+	CIBC Mortgage Investment	R	N	1.50*	1.2	8.1	9.7	10.0
NA	NA	Colonia Mortgage Fund	R	D	1.75	1.7	NA	NA	NA
★★★	AV	Concorde Hypotheques	R	O	1.90*	1.0	7.5	NA	NA
★★	LOW	Confed Mortgage Fund	R	F	1.75	1.3	6.5	8.7	9.7
★★★	AV+	First Canadian Mortgage Fund	R	N	1.02*	0.9	7.6	9.9	10.6
★★	AV-	Fonds Desjardins Hypotheques	R	N	1.66	2.2	6.8	8.7	NA
★★★★★	AV-	General Trust of Canada Mort	R	N	1.48	8.1	9.5	10.3	11.1
★★★	AV+	Great-West Life Mortgage Inv.	R	N	2.40	-0.6	7.9	8.1	9.6
★★★	AV	Green Line Cdn Mortgage	R	N	1.50	1.0	7.4	9.5	10.0
★	AV-	Green Line Mortgage-Backed	R	N	1.65	1.1	6.4	9.1	NA
NA	NA	Hongkong Bank Mortgage	R	N	1.65*	7.5	NA	NA	NA
NA	NA	Industrial Alliance Ecoflex H	R	R	2.00*	1.0	NA	NA	NA
★★★★	HIGH	Industrial Mortgage Securities	R	O	1.98*	-2.3	9.5	7.4	12.1
NA	NA	InvesNat Mortgage Fund	R	N	1.33*	3.3	NA	NA	NA
★★	AV+	Investors Income Portfolio	R	R	0.17	-1.8	6.7	7.7	NA
★	AV-	Investors Mortgage Fund	R	R	1.82	-0.7	5.8	7.9	9.5
NA	NA	Ivy Mortgage Fund	R	O	1.50m*	NA	NA	NA	NA
★★★★	LOW	London Life Mortgage	R	R	1.50*	1.0	8.0	9.4	11.0
NA	NA	Mandate National Mortgage	R	N		NA	NA	NA	NA
★★	AV	Montreal Trust Exc. Mortgage	R	N	1.56	2.9	7.2	8.9	9.7

Return	Vol.	Fund	RRSP	Fees	MER	1yr	3yr	5yr	10yr
NA	NA	Mutual Premier Mortgage	R	N	1.63	1.6	NA	NA	NA
NA	NA	National Trust Mortgage Fund	R	N	1.63	-0.2	NA	NA	NA
****	LOW	Ontario Teachers Grp Mortg	R	N	0.65	3.8	8.1	9.0	9.8
*	LOW	Royal Trust Mortgage Fund	R	N	1.94*	-0.4	5.9	8.4	9.6
NA	NA	Royfund Mortgage Fund	R	N	1.73	3.4	NA	NA	NA
NA	NA	Scotia Mortgage Fund	R	N	1.46	1.4	NA	NA	NA
**	AV	Trust Pret & Revenu H Fund	R	N	1.60*	0.1	7.0	8.8	9.9
*	AV	United Canadian Mortgage	R	O	1.95*	-1.4	4.7	7.2	8.4
		HIGHEST IN GROUP				8.1	9.5	10.3	12.1
		AVERAGE IN GROUP				1.5	7.3	8.8	10.1
		LOWEST IN GROUP				-2.3	4.7	7.2	8.4

U.S. and International Bond Funds

Return	Vol.	Fund	RRSP	Fees	MER	1yr	3yr	5yr	10yr
NA	NA	20/20 Foreign RSP Bond Fund	R	O	2.00*	NA	NA	NA	NA
NA	NA	20/20 World Bond Fund	F	O	2.00*	0.1	NA	NA	NA
****	AV+	AGF Global Government Bond	F	O	1.26*	7.2	13.9	11.4	NA
NA	NA	AGF Strategic Income Fund	R	O	2.10*	NA	NA	NA	NA
NA	NA	AGF U.S. Income Fund	F	O	1.54*	1.4	NA	NA	NA
NA	NA	Altamira Global Bond Fund	R	N	1.84*	NA	NA	NA	NA
NA	NA	Bullock Global Bond 'A'	F	F	1.79	NA	NA	NA	NA
NA	NA	Bullock Global Bond 'B'	F	R	2.15	NA	NA	NA	NA
NA	NA	Bullock Global Bond 'C'	F	N	2.27	NA	NA	NA	NA
NA	NA	C.I. Global Bond RSP Fund	R	O	2.00	NA	NA	NA	NA
NA	NA	C.I. World Bond Fund	F	O	2.00	4.2	NA	NA	NA
NA	NA	Canada Life Int'l Bond S-36	R	R	2.00	NA	NA	NA	NA
*****	HIGH	Dynamic Global Bond Fund	R	O	2.18*	11.3	15.8	10.2	NA
NA	NA	Fidelity Emerging Mkts Bond	F	O	2.44*	NA	NA	NA	NA
NA	NA	Fidelity Global Bond Fund	R	O	2.22*	NA	NA	NA	NA
NA	NA	Fidelity Nth Am. Income Fund	F	O	1.75*	2.6	NA	NA	NA
NA	NA	First Cdn. International Bond	F	N	1.81*	NA	NA	NA	NA
***	AV+	Global Strategy Div. Bond	R	O	2.10	-3.3	9.9	NA	NA
****	AV+	Global Strategy World Bond	F	O	2.09	-4.3	11.1	8.2	NA
NA	NA	Green Line Global Gov't Bond	F	N	2.15	6.6	NA	NA	NA
NA	NA	Green Line Global RSP Bond	R	N	1.95	NA	NA	NA	NA
****	AV+	Guardian International Income	R	O	1.68*	3.1	12.0	8.5	NA
NA	NA	Hercules World Bond Fund	R	N	1.50m*	NA	NA	NA	NA
NA	NA	Investors Global Bond Fund	F	R	2.15	7.1	NA	NA	NA
NA	NA	Lotus International Bond Fund	R	N	1.50m*	NA	NA	NA	NA
NA	NA	Optima Strategy Glbl Fixd Inc.	F	O	0.13*	NA	NA	NA	NA
NA	NA	Regent World Income Fund	R	O	2.00*	3.2	NA	NA	NA
NA	NA	Royal Trust International Bond	R	N	1.79*	6.9	NA	NA	NA
NA	NA	Royfund International Income	R	N	1.92	10.7	NA	NA	NA
NA	NA	Scotia Canam Income ($US)	R	N	1.60	-2.0	NA	NA	NA
NA	NA	Spectrum International Bond	R	O	1.90	8.9	NA	NA	NA
NA	NA	Talvest Foreign Pay Bond Fund	R	O	2.15*	6.3	NA	NA	NA
****	AV	Templeton Global Income	F	O	2.25	3.3	10.4	10.2	NA
		HIGHEST IN GROUP				11.3	15.8	11.4	NA
		AVERAGE IN GROUP				4.1	12.2	9.7	NA
		LOWEST IN GROUP				-4.3	9.9	8.2	NA

Canadian Money Market Funds

Return	Vol.	Fund	RRSP	Fees	MER	1yr	3yr	5yr	10yr
****	AV-	20/20 Money Market Fund	R	O	1.04*	4.3	6.0	NA	NA
NA	NA	Admax Cash Performance	R	O	1.20*	3.1	NA	NA	NA
***	AV	AGF Money Market Account	R	O	0.83*	3.6	5.4	7.9	8.6
****	AV-	AMI Private Capital Money Mkt	R	N	0.75*	4.4	6.1	8.1	NA

Return	Vol.	Fund	RRSP	Fees	MER	1yr	3yr	5yr	10yr
★★★★	AV+	Batirente - Sec. Marche Mntr.	R	N	1.61	3.7	6.0	8.0	NA
★★★★★	AV	Beutel Goodman Money Mkt	R	N	0.60*	4.6	6.6	NA	NA
NA	NA	Bissett Money Market Fund	R	N	0.50	4.5	NA	NA	NA
NA	NA	BNP (Cda) Cdn Money Mkt	R	N	1.43	3.6	NA	NA	NA
★	AV	BPI Money Market Fund	R	D	1.48*	3.1	4.7	7.3	NA
NA	NA	BPI Short Term Interest Fund	R	D	1.00*	NA	NA	NA	NA
NA	NA	BPI T-Bill Fund	R	F	0.65*	NA	NA	NA	NA
★★★	LOW	C.I. Money Market Fund	R	O	0.59	4.1	5.8	NA	NA
★	AV	C.I. Sector Short-Term	F	O	0.59	2.4	3.3	4.7	NA
★★★	AV+	Canada Life Money Mkt S-29	R	R	1.25	4.0	5.5	7.8	8.0
★★	AV	Cda Trust Everest Money Mkt	R	N	0.75	3.6	5.2	8.0	NA
★★★★	AV+	Capstone Cash Management	R	N	0.60*	3.6	5.9	8.4	NA
★★★	AV+	CDA Money Market Fund	R	N	0.55	3.9	5.9	8.2	8.8
★	AV-	CIBC Canadian T-Bill Fund	R	N	1.20*	3.1	4.8	NA	NA
★	AV	CIBC Money Market Fund	R	N	1.20*	3.3	5.0	7.7	NA
★★★	AV-	CIBC Premium T-Bill Fund	R	N	0.55*	3.8	5.4	NA	NA
NA	NA	Colonia Money Market Fund	R	N	1.00	3.2	NA	NA	NA
NA	NA	Concorde Monetaire	R	O	1.50	4.2	NA	NA	NA
★★	AV	Cornerstone Gov Money	R	N	1.14*	3.7	5.4	NA	NA
★★★	AV	Dynamic Money Market Fund	R	O	0.80*	3.7	5.4	7.9	8.3
★★★★	AV+	Elliott & Page Money Fund	R	F	0.56*	4.3	6.1	8.6	NA
NA	NA	Elliott & Page T-Bill Fund	R	D	1.77*	NA	NA	NA	NA
★	AV+	Empire Money Market Fund	R	N	1.56	3.2	5.1	7.4	NA
★★	AV-	Ethical Money Market Fund	R	O	1.26*	3.6	5.4	8.0	8.7
★	AV	Fidelity Short Term Asset Fund	R	O	1.00*	3.3	5.2	NA	NA
★★	AV-	Finsco Money Market Fund	R	F	1.07*	3.8	5.4	7.9	NA
★	LOW	Finsco T-Bill Fund	R	F	1.29*	3.4	5.0	7.5	NA
★★★	AV	First Canadian Money Market	R	N	0.95*	3.6	5.4	7.7	NA
NA	NA	First Cdn. T-Bill Fund	R	N	1.02*	NA	NA	NA	NA
★★★★★	AV+	Fonds de Prof. Short Term	R	N	0.40	3.9	6.5	8.4	NA
★★	HIGH	Fonds Desjardins Monetaire	R	N	1.10	3.7	5.3	7.6	NA
★★★	AV+	Fonds Ficadre Money Market	R	R	1.21	3.7	5.7	NA	NA
★★★	AV-	GBC Money Market Fund	R	N	0.50	4.0	5.7	8.2	NA
★★★	AV+	Gen'l Trust of Cda Money Mkt	R	N	0.83	3.5	5.7	8.0	NA
★★★	AV-	Global Strategy T-Bill Savings	R	D	0.45	4.1	5.8	7.8	NA
★	AV	Great-West Life Money Mkt	R	N	1.74	3.1	4.9	7.4	8.1
★★★★	AV	Green Line Cdn Money Mkt	R	N	0.66	4.2	5.9	8.4	NA
NA	NA	Green Line Cdn T-Bill Fund	R	N	0.68	3.8	NA	NA	NA
★★★	AV	Guardian Cdn Money Market	R	O	0.72*	3.9	5.5	8.2	8.8
★	LOW	Hongkong Bank Money Mkt	R	N	1.08*	3.5	5.0	7.4	NA
★★★	LOW	HRL Instant $$ Fund	R	N	0.50	4.2	5.7	8.1	NA
★	AV	Imperial Growth Money Mkt	R	F	1.50	3.0	4.7	7.0	NA
NA	NA	Industrial Alliance Ecoflex M	R	R	1.50*	12.9	NA	NA	NA
★★★	LOW	Industrial Cash Management	R	F	0.50*	4.0	5.7	8.2	NA
★	LOW	Industrial Short-Term Fund	R	R	1.54*	3.1	4.6	NA	NA
NA	NA	Integra Short Term Investment	R	N	1.00*	5.2	NA	NA	NA
★★★	AV-	InvesNat Money Market Fund	R	N	1.09*	3.7	5.5	NA	NA
★★	LOW	Investors Money Market Fund	R	R	1.08*	3.6	5.2	7.7	NA
NA	NA	Ivy Short-Term Fund	R	O	1.00*	3.1	NA	NA	NA
★	LOW	Laurentian Money Market	R	N	1.20*	3.5	5.1	7.6	NA
NA	NA	Leith Wheeler Money Market	R	N	0.60m*	NA	NA	NA	NA
★★★★	AV+	London Life Money Market	R	R	1.30*	3.4	6.3	8.4	NA
★★★	AV	Lotus Income Fund	R	N	0.75*	4.2	5.8	8.4	NA
★★★	AV-	Mackenzie Sentinel Cda M. Mkt	R	N	0.96*	4.0	5.7	8.1	NA

Return	Vol.	Fund	RRSP	Fees	MER	1yr	3yr	5yr	10yr
★	HIGH	Manulife Vista 1 Sht Term Sec	R	F	1.63*	3.1	5.2	7.7	8.4
★	AV+	Manulife Vista2 Sht Term Sec	R	R	2.38*	2.3	4.4	6.9	7.6
★	AV	Maritime Life Money Market	R	N	1.75*	3.0	5.1	7.4	8.0
★★★	AV	Mawer Canadian Money Mkt	R	N	0.69	3.7	5.4	7.9	NA
★★★	AV-	McLean Budden Money Mkt	R	N	0.75	3.9	5.4	7.8	NA
★★★	AV	MD Money Fund	R	N	0.50	4.0	5.6	7.9	8.3
NA	NA	Metlife MVP Money Market	R	R	1.50m	3.1	NA	NA	NA
★★★	HIGH	Mont'l Trust Exc. Money Mkt	R	N	1.07	3.8	5.4	7.8	NA
★★	LOW	Mutual Money Market	R	N	1.03	3.8	5.3	7.6	NA
★★	AV	NAL-Investor Money Market	R	B	1.25	3.2	5.2	7.8	NA
★★★	AV-	Natcan Treasury Bill Fund	R	N	0.87*	3.8	5.6	NA	NA
NA	NA	National Life Money Market	R	D	1.60m	4.7	NA	NA	NA
★★	LOW	National Trust Money Market	R	N	1.16	3.5	5.3	NA	NA
★★★	AV-	NN Money Market Fund	R	N	0.75*	4.0	5.8	NA	NA
★★	AV	NN T-Bill Fund	R	R	1.75*	3.1	5.2	7.3	NA
NA	NA	OHA Short Term Fund	R	N	0.50*	4.2	NA	NA	NA
★★★★★	AV	Ont. Teachers Grp Fixed Value	R	N	0.50	4.3	7.0	8.7	8.9
★★★★	AV+	Optimum Fonds d'Epargne	R	N	0.60m*	3.9	6.2	8.2	NA
★★★	AV	PH&N Canadian Money Mkt	R	N	0.52	4.1	5.9	8.4	NA
★★★★	AV	Prudential Money Mkt Fd of Cda	R	N	0.66*	4.4	6.1	8.4	NA
★★★★	AV	Pursuit Money Market Fund	R	N	0.50*	4.6	6.4	8.6	NA
NA	NA	Royal Life Money Market Fund	R	D	1.00	5.0	NA	NA	NA
★★	AV	Royal Trust Cdn Money Mkt	R	N	1.16*	3.4	5.2	7.6	NA
NA	NA	Royal Trust Cdn T-Bill Mon. Mkt	R	N	1.71*	2.7	NA	NA	NA
★★★	AV	Royfund Canadian T-Bill Fund	R	N	0.84	3.7	5.5	NA	NA
★★★	AV	Royfund Money Market Fund	R	N	1.18	3.4	5.4	7.9	NA
★★★	AV	Sceptre Money Market Fund	R	N	0.83*	3.9	5.7	8.1	NA
NA	NA	Scotia Gov. of Can. T-Bill	R	N	0.80	3.8	NA	NA	NA
★★	LOW	Scotia Money Market Fund	R	N	1.00	3.7	5.2	NA	NA
NA	NA	Scotia Premium T-Bill Fund	R	N	0.55	4.1	NA	NA	NA
★★	LOW	Spectrum Cash Reserve Fund	R	O	1.10	3.7	5.3	7.8	NA
★★	AV-	Spectrum Savings Fund	R	N	1.00	3.8	5.4	7.9	NA
NA	NA	Standard Life Ideal Money Mkt	R	D	1.40	NA	NA	NA	NA
NA	NA	Standard Life Money Market	R	N	0.90	3.4	NA	NA	NA
★★	LOW	Strata Money Market Fund	R	N	1.27	3.6	5.2	7.5	NA
★★★★	AV	Talvest Money Fund	R	F	0.75*	4.3	6.0	8.4	NA
★★★	LOW	Templeton Treasury Bill Fund	R	N	0.75	3.9	5.5	8.0	NA
★★★	AV	Trans-Canada Money Market	R	O	0.66*	4.5	5.8	7.8	NA
★★★	AV-	Trimark Interest Fund	R	F	0.75*	3.8	5.5	8.1	NA
★★★	LOW	Trust Pret & Revenu Mny Mkt	R	N	1.20*	4.1	5.5	7.8	NA
★★★★	AV	United Canadian Interest Fund	R	O	1.31*	4.8	6.4	8.7	NA
		HIGHEST IN GROUP				12.9	7.0	8.7	8.9
		AVERAGE IN GROUP				3.9	5.5	7.9	8.4
		LOWEST IN GROUP				2.3	3.3	4.7	7.6

U.S. and International Money Market Funds

Return	Vol.	Fund	RRSP	Fees	MER	1yr	3yr	5yr	10yr
★★★★	AV	AGF U.S. Dollar Money Mkt	F	F	0.36*	2.7	3.3	5.0	NA
★★★★★	HIGH	Altamira Short Term Global Inc	R	N	1.28*	11.6	12.2	NA	NA
NA	NA	BNP (Canada)US$ Money Mkt	R	N	1.46	2.1	NA	NA	NA
★★★	AV	CIBC U.S. Dollar Money Mkt	F	N	0.95*	2.3	2.9	NA	NA
★★★	AV	Finsco U.S. Money Mkt ($US)	F	F	1.05	2.5	2.9	4.6	NA
★★★★	AV+	Global Strategy Div. Savings	R	O	1.50	3.5	7.9	7.8	NA
★★★	AV-	Global Strat. U.S. Savings ($US)	R	D	0.45	2.8	3.2	4.6	NA

Return	Vol.	Fund	RRSP	Fees	MER	1yr	3yr	5yr	10yr
★★★	AV+	Green Line U.S. M. Mkt ($US)	R	N	0.96	2.3	2.9	4.6	NA
★★★★	AV	Guardian U.S. M. Mkt ($US)	R	O	0.54*	2.7	3.2	4.9	NA
NA	NA	Hercules Global Short-Term	F	N	0.75m	NA	NA	NA	NA
NA	NA	InvesNat U.S. Money Mkt $US	F	N	1.19*	2.1	NA	NA	NA
★★★★	AV+	PH&N $US Money Market	R	N	0.53	2.9	3.5	NA	NA
★★★	AV-	Royal Trust U.S. M. Mkt ($US)	F	N	1.20	2.2	2.8	NA	NA
★★	AV	Royfund U.S. Dollar Money	R	N	1.09	2.3	2.8	NA	NA
★★	AV+	United U.S. Dollar Money Mkt	F	O	0.60*	2.9	2.7	4.0	NA
		HIGHEST IN GROUP				11.6	12.2	7.8	NA
		AVERAGE IN GROUP				3.2	4.2	5.1	NA
		LOWEST IN GROUP				2.1	2.7	4.0	NA

Dividend Funds

Return	Vol.	Fund	RRSP	Fees	MER	1yr	3yr	5yr	10yr
★★★	AV+	20/20 Dividend Fund	R	O	2.08*	3.6	8.4	6.9	NA
★★★	LOW	AGF High Income Fund	R	O	1.42*	3.6	8.3	7.9	8.3
NA	NA	Bissett Dividend Income Fund	F	N	1.50	3.5	NA	NA	NA
★	AV-	BPI Income Fund	R	F	1.15*	1.6	3.9	4.3	6.4
NA	NA	CIBC Equity Income Fund	R	N	2.00*	-1.4	NA	NA	NA
★★★★	AV	Corporate Investors Ltd.	R	F	1.35*	6.8	10.6	6.0	8.8
★★★	LOW	Dynamic Dividend Fund	R	O	1.80*	3.0	9.0	7.2	NA
★★★★	AV-	Dynamic Dividend Growth	R	O	1.80*	5.2	9.5	5.2	NA
NA	NA	Fonds Desjardins Dividendes	R	N	1.80m	NA	NA	NA	NA
★★★	AV	Green Line Dividend Fund	R	N	2.20	1.4	8.8	7.9	NA
★★	LOW	Guardian Preferred Dividend	R	O	1.24*	1.0	7.8	6.1	NA
★★★★	HIGH	Industrial Dividend Fund Ltd.	R	O	2.52*	7.1	11.2	3.4	9.8
★★	AV	Investors Dividend Fund	F	B	2.01	0.6	7.8	7.1	9.5
★★★★	AV	Investors Mutual of Canada	F	B	2.03	4.3	10.5	7.2	9.7
★★	AV-	Laurentian Dividend Fund Ltd.	R	O	2.70*	1.0	6.6	5.5	9.4
NA	NA	Mawer Canadian Income Fund	F	N	1.08	-1.0	NA	NA	NA
NA	NA	MD Dividend Fund	R	N	1.00	2.7	NA	NA	NA
★★	AV-	Montreal Trust Exc. Dividend	R	N	1.08	2.6	7.2	6.4	NA
NA	NA	NatCan Dividend Fund	R	N	1.63*	2.4	NA	NA	NA
NA	NA	National Trust Dividend Fund	R	N	2.20	4.1	NA	NA	NA
★★★	AV+	PH&N Div. Income	N	N	1.23	5.4	8.5	6.9	9.9
★★★★★	AV+	Prudential Div. Fund of Cda	R	F	1.53*	9.2	16.0	7.8	NA
★	AV-	Royal Trust Growth & Income	R	N	2.80*	0.2	5.1	4.0	NA
NA	NA	Royfund Dividend Fund	R	N	1.78	2.2	NA	NA	NA
★★	AV	Spectrum Dividend Fund	R	O	1.55	2.5	5.7	5.5	NA
★	AV+	Trans-Canada Income Fund	R	O	2.66*	6.5	1.3	1.4	9.5
		HIGHEST IN GROUP				9.2	16.0	7.9	9.9
		AVERAGE IN GROUP				3.1	8.1	5.9	9.0
		LOWEST IN GROUP				-1.4	1.3	1.4	6.4

Benchmarks

						1yr	3yr	5yr	10yr
		91-Day Canada T-Bills				4.8	6.5	8.9	9.4
		Consumer Price Index				0.0	0.9	2.6	3.5
		ScotiaMcLeod Universe Bond Index				-0.8	10.5	9.8	12.7
		Standard & Poor's 500 Index (U.S.$)				1.4	9.3	10.4	15.2
		TSE Total Return Index				3.9	8.3	4.8	9.7
		Morgan Stanley The World Index				19.5	18.2	10.1	16.9
		Morgan Stanley Europe (14)				25.4	19.3	13.5	19.0
		Morgan Stanley Japan				24.5	18.2	3.5	19.4
		Morgan Stanley EAFE				26.5	19.5	8.4	19.2

Index